SAY YES
to
LIFE

SAY YES
to
LIFE

Feeling Well, Doing Well,
Staying Well

CLIVE WOOD

MSc, DPhil
Linacre College, Oxford

J. M. Dent and Sons Ltd
London

ISBN 0 460 86018 6 Cased
ISBN 0 460 86032 1 Paperback

Printed in Great Britain at The Bath Press, Avon

Contents

Acknowledgements

A book like this is never written by one person in isolation. It resulted from many stimulating exchanges that I have been fortunate enough to have with workers in the many different fields that the book describes. There are too many to mention by name, so let me acknowledge them in groups. They can all, no doubt, recognize themselves.

My most profound thanks are due to my friends and colleagues in the Departments of Biological Anthropology, Psychiatry, and Experimental Psychology and at Linacre College, Oxford; and to those specialists whom I have met at the British Association of Behavioural Psychotherapy, The British Holistic Medical Association, The Society for Behavioral Medicine and the American Psychological Association. Whilst all of these people have provided me with ideas, none of them should be shouldered with any responsibility for the views that I have expressed.

And of course it is pleasure to acknowledge the essential help that I have received from those volunteers who have taken part in my various research projects, and particularly the most recent – the Oxford Energy Project.

Finally, my thanks are also due to the following for permission to reproduce existing material:

To Professor Hans Eynsenck and Maurice Temple Smith Ltd for material from H. Eynsenck, G. Wilson, *Know Your Own Personality*. (London: Temple Smith, 1975), reproduced in Boxes 2, 3 and 6; to Dr David Wilson and the Editors of Psychological Bulletin for D. Wilson and A. Tellegen, *Psychological Bulletin*

1988; 98: 219–35, Figure 1, reproduced in Box 6; to Dr Michael Scheier and the Editors of *Health Psychology* for M.F.Scheier and S.C.Carver, *Health Psychology* 1985; 4: 219–47, Table 1, reproduced in Box 7; to Professor Aaron Beck and the Editors of Archives of General Psychiatry for material from A.T.Beck *et al. Archives of General Psychiatry* 1964; 4: 561–71, reproduced in Box 8; to Dr Michael Fordyce for material reproduced in Box 9; to Dr Richard Rahe and the Editors of the Journal of Psychosomatic Research for material from T.H.Holmes and R.H.Rahe. *Journal of Psychosomatic Research* 1967; 11: 213–18, reproduced in Box 13; to Dr Susan Folkman and the Editors of the Journal of Personality and Social Psychology for material from S. Folkman *et al. Journal of Personality and Social Psychology* 1986; 50: 992–1003, reproduced in Box 14; to Dr B.D.Cox and the Health Promotion Research Trust for permission to reproduce material from the *Health and Lifestyle Survey*, London: Health Promotion Research Trust, 1987, reproduced in Boxes 15 and 16 and to Dr Tom Borkovec and Research Press for permission to reproduce extracts from D.A.Bernstein and T.D.Borkovec *Progressive Relaxation Training: A manual for the helping professions.* Champaign, Illinois: Research Press, 1973, found in Chapter 12.

CLIVE WOOD

New Years Eve 1989

CHAPTER 1

Crisis and Opportunity: A Sort of Preface

THIS is a book about mental and physical health and about the links that run between them. It is about energy, vigour and vitality; about thinking and feeling; about seeing the world more clearly and dealing with it more effectively; about living in ways that are life-affirming. In short, it is a book about *saying yes to life*.

A couple of years ago it might have gone on the bookstore shelf in the section on Psychology. But times are changing fast. Today's bookshops have shelves for a new subject known as 'mind–body-health'. And there are whole organizations set up to study it. For example, the Institute for the Advancement of Health in New York now produces the *Mind–Body-Health Digest*.[1] Mind–body connections are on public display. Whether the links between them are strong or weak, the subject has a label, which means it must exist. So although I didn't know it when I started, this is a book about mind–body-health. And for anyone who isn't comfortable with the idea of 'mind' simply read 'brain'. I'll try to persuade you that we are talking about the same thing.

I wrote it for those of you who are tired of seeing books about stress and how to avoid it, or even worse, how to make it work for you. You can't avoid stress and it doesn't ever work on your behalf. But you can come to terms with it and try to defuse its harmful effects. You can certainly ride on the challenge that it throws out to you. But that's not stress; that's opportunity.

The Chinese know this well enough. The Chinese symbol *Ji* actually means 'opportunity', but it also means 'threat' or even 'crisis'. The Chinese understand that many events happen without our being able to control them. But we can control the way that we respond to them, and turn a threat into a challenge (see Box 1).

The way that we let ourselves feel about the crisis (or the opportunity) is often all-important in deciding the effect it has on us. For most events that feeling is something you can largely control for yourself. Much of this book is about the way that people struggle to get some control over their lives, about the vulnerabilities that lay them open and the resources that protect them.

It is about those qualities that we all have – qualities that we can describe as 'life-affirming' – it is a book about saying yes to life.

Our first line of defence to any challenge should be to meet it squarely, though often we try to avoid doing so, because it hurts. You simply have to learn how. But if confronting it doesn't work, then most of us are expert at finding ways to comfort our emotions and even to fall back on a set of illusions that protect our image of ourselves and our world. All of these approaches may be needed to reduce the pain and keep us functioning in the here and now. And all of them have a single, vital purpose. They stop us from feeling hopeless.

There would be no book to write if I didn't think that we all have qualities that can protect us against mental or physical breakdown, and that these qualities can be developed and expanded by 'ordinary' people.

But health depends on a whole mixture of factors, and the mix is different from one person to the next. Our mental and physical well-being both depend on our physical world and our reactions to it – on our lifestyle, health habits and social contacts. So whilst our health is related to our psychology and our social interactions as well, the physical pressures that influence it are very strong. We certainly know a lot more about biological effects on health than we do about the influence of thinking and feeling. And this is why many experts still play down the effects of the mind. Its influence on your physical well-being may be 'swamped' under a mass of other pressures that result from your age, the fat in your diet or what your parents died from.

In other words, we mustn't expect too much from *mind–body-health*, certainly not as much as the magazines would have us believe. But the affirmation of life is a fact all the same. It works in surprisingly simple ways to maintain both our mental and physi-

Box 1.   *The Chinese symbol Ji denotes some event that happens to you 'out of the blue' – what insurance agents call 'an Act of God'. It gives you an opportunity for benefit, but at the same time it has a threatening side. Things might go wrong. In the West we see 'crisis' and 'opportunity' as being different things. In China they are simply two consequences of the same event. Which one develops often depends largely on how we view the event and what we decide to do about it.*

cal well-being. And just as important, it sustains our sense of 'subjective well-being', the technical term that psychologists use when they really mean happiness.

Now, there is more than one way to look at this whole mind–body area. So perhaps I should say what the book *isn't* about, just to avoid any misunderstanding. I've said already that it isn't primarily about stress, though of course we look at stress when we come to consider how to stay well.

Nor is it really a book about 'alternative' approaches to health. There isn't going to be much here about the 'cosmic energy' which, according to my more 'alternative' colleagues, flows through the universe and controls our well-being. That's not necessarily because I reject the whole 'energetic' package. It's because when I try to look at cosmic energy at a practical level, I'm struck by the fact that we can't do very much with it.

The new window

Maybe that situation will change.

'Everyone is rushing to see what can be seen through the new window,' said David Cohen of Massachusetts Institute of Technology in an interview some years ago. A world expert in biomagnetic research, he was referring to a new window into the human body, opened up by the discovery that the body itself creates an extremely weak electromagnetic field. But although it is so weak, it can be detected using ultra-sensitive measuring equipment.

Its discovery was a tremendous boost for those practitioners of alternative medicine whose approach depends on manipulating the 'subtle energies' of the body, the 'aura' or energy field that they believe gets out of balance long before ill health shows itself at a bodily level. Acupuncture and homoeopathy, dowsing and radionics are only a few of the approaches that depend on plugging in to this subtle energy that they believe to flow through the body and through the world.[2]

And it has now become a subject for scientific study as well. In Great Britain, Julian Kenyon has begun a major research programme using the latest in electromagnetic equipment to investigate this type of energy. Kenyon, a vigorous, charismatic figure whose looks belie his age, started as an orthodox doctor and acquired all the 'right' medical qualifications before he set up the Centre for the Study of Alternative Therapies in Southampton. With their extensive contacts in the field of energy medicine his group are as well placed as anyone to throw light on the question of whether the aura is a rarefied electromagnetic field, and if so how we can use it to stay healthy.

Personally I doubt whether subtle energies and the types of energy that physicists measure will turn out to be the same. Of course, many scientists still need convincing that subtle energies exist at all.[3] In the same way, talking with specialists in Chinese medicine always leads us to the combined conclusion that the Chinese and Western systems simply can't be combined together. The whole set of concepts that underpin each of them is so totally different.

But at a more practical level, acupuncturists will simply tell you that their treatments often work, and recent research suggests that acupuncture may release mood-altering chemicals from the brain. Their patients usually agree that it works as well, and anyone who has lain there with the needles stuck into his meridians can have little doubt that *something* is happening. But until we know more there isn't much I want to say about it in a book like this.

There are other types of mind–body connection that I have little to say about either. One is the possibility of directly inducing changes to occur in our immune system by visualizing our white blood cells (lymphocytes) going into combat against invading cells. This procedure is written up in a host of books and magazine articles and the possibilities are fascinating. But no one has yet shown that the effects occur consistently, let alone that they increase the survival or even the health of sufferers from, say, cancer or AIDS. Like subtle energy, visualization is intriguing. But until it shows some practical results, until people's physical well-being is shown to improve as a consequence (and I mean dozens of people, studied in detail, not just one or two who tell you that they are feeling better), then I can't say much about it, except to wish its practitioners luck, and early results.

A senior physician was once asked by the parents of a child who seemed beyond help from orthodox medicine whether he would mind if they took her to Lourdes, in the hope of achieving a miracle. 'Not at all,' he said, 'we need all the help we can get.' In this book you will find a lot of speculation about where that help might come from. And we will stray beyond the 'established' facts. But I don't propose to lead you into areas where there are no reliable data at all.

And let me say one other thing about data, while we're on the subject. You will find plenty of it here – dates, facts and figures. That's because I don't just want you to take my word about it, to accept my conclusions. I also want you to know for yourself what they are based on. And if you should want to follow them further there is a brief selection of references at the back – enough to get you started.

I hope to give you enough facts to enable you to recognize yourself as well – where you stand on this personality feature or that health practice. So although I originally set out just to report the facts – to tell you where mind–body-health had got to by the end of the 1980s – a little bit of how-to has inevitably crept in.

Yes, but does it work?

A famous professor of psychology (now retired but still very active) used to have a plaque outside his office. On it was written, 'Everything that exists in nature, exists in some quantity and can therefore be measured.' The quote is from E. L. Thorndyke, one of the founders of modern psychology in the United States, and you will see that it certainly reflects my own view. But it's a view that I try not to force on others. Indeed, I've often been the one to tell unorthodox practitioners that they don't need to prove what they are doing in scientific terms. If they and their patients are convinced, and if the clients keep voting with their fees, then who needs a scientific explanation of what they are about?

Ironically enough, the pressure usually comes from the practitioners themselves. They seem to want to establish their credentials to orthodox medicine, and to try to gain some respectability, or at least acceptance, before the single European legislation of 1992 throws a hostile spotlight on everything that they believe in.

But if they do want scientific recognition, they can only do it by buying into science, by using the same techniques that scientists use to prove (at least to their satisfaction) that something works. Unfortunately, few practitioners outside the orthodox camp have the expertise or the sheer financial backing to do so. We should welcome the emergence of bodies like the Research Council for Complementary Medicine in London which, in its modest way, is trying to provide both. On the other side of the Atlantic, bodies like the American Holistic Medical Association have also encouraged the efforts of alternative practitioners.

Perhaps most important, however, has been the Institute for the Advancement of Health (IAH), an organization which I will mention several times and one with which I have had the pleasure of collaborating over the years. Set up in New York in the early 1980s, its aim was to promote the study of all forms of mind–body connections. The IAH certainly has a 'mainstream' orientation, promoting a lot of orthodox research. However, the Institute and its journal *Advances* have never been afraid to consider subjects like homoeopathy and acupuncture and to look at the question of whether they are effective, even though they are not based on established scientific principles.

And this issue is a major stumbling block to the acceptance of alternative therapies in both Britain and America.

The climate is not helped by bodies like the British Medical Association producing a report in 1986 telling us that 'many alternative approaches to medicine do not base their rationale on theories which are consistent with natural laws as we understand them'.[4] In other words, alternative approaches are unscientific. When I responded to the report I suggested that, whilst that might be true, it was completely missing the point. The public are not concerned with whether alternative approaches are scientific. What they want to know is 'Do they work?'

Obviously many people do believe that complementary therapists have something to offer. How else do we account for their growing clientele? My guess is that they never will be 'consistent with natural laws as we [doctors] understand them', any more than Chinese and Western medicine are consistent with each other. In the meantime, thousands of people will take their homoeopathic potencies, have their necks realigned and get on with their aromatherapy, convinced that it works for them.

It is for others to write books about how it works (and God knows there is no shortage of paperbacks on alternative approaches to health). It is my task to look at mind–body links in the context of what we (more or less) understand.

But let me warn you once again. Don't expect too much from mind–body-health. If the links were that obvious they would have been realized long ago and there wouldn't be any argument left today. But argument is what we constantly find – argument about how much of cancer or heart disease or glandular fever is due to your personality; about whether optimism and being in love (to say nothing of fast walking and selenium) increase your life-span; about why fat, cantankerous chain-smokers sometimes out-live thin, easygoing exercisers.

So let's start with the realization that saying yes to life doesn't mean living for ever. But it does mean living better and living more happily. Let's acknowledge from the outset that the health gains that come from straight thinking and from feeling 'in the flow' are often small, sometimes even marginal. But what the health experts don't tell you is that the gains that come from reducing your cholesterol, controlling your blood pressure and getting on your bike are marginal as well. Health results from combining a cluster of marginal benefits. Mind–body links provide some of them.

And as the physician said, 'We need all the help we can get.'

CHAPTER 2

The Well-Oiled Machine

WHEN I feel physically ill, my psychology slips out of balance. I lose my sense of well-being. My self-esteem starts to go and I find myself wondering why I can't do the things that I can get through quite easily when I'm healthy. On other days, when I'm feeling well, I also feel optimistic about myself. I'm confident about how much I can do and about how I am going to enjoy doing it.

So illness is a feeling – a state of mind. That doesn't mean that I dream it up. It is really there – anchored in my body, triggered by the physical complaint that's troubling me. Illness is what I feel; pathology is what I've got. I may be half delirious and shivering with flu. Or I may be lying still so as not to increase the pain from my recent surgery. Either way, the feeling (illness) springs from the condition (disease or pathology).

Of course, that's not the only scenario. I may feel ill – perhaps desperately ill – when no doctor can find any pathology. Two out of three of the thousands of patients who complain to their GP about feeling exhausted ('I'm tired all the time, doctor') come away again without him finding any physical cause. Does that mean that there isn't one? Maybe yes. Does it mean that they are over-sensitive to the messages that their body is sending them? Again maybe yes. It seems hard to believe that they are all suffering from post-viral syndrome.

But there is quite another aspect to feeling ill. It's not the result of my body mounting an immune response to a virus, or of two rows of stitches in my groin. Instead it relates to how I feel about myself.

Let's assume that I see myself as someone who can cope reasonably well with life; not superman, but a competent individual who generally gets most things done. Then suddenly, my body lets me down. Because I'm ill I can't think straight. I certainly can't work and I may not be able even to move very fast. In short, I lose my capacity to be independent, useful and productive. No wonder that my emotional well-being slips away and I start to feel depressed. No wonder either that my sense of self-esteem starts to dive.

As a species, we have developed many different strategies to keep these feelings of helplessness and hopelessness at bay. We have a tremendous capacity to maintain our optimism, even when there is little 'real' reason for us to do so. And this is as it should be, because 'giving up' seems to be one of the very few mental attitudes that can lead to an early death.

Redefining health

But if losing the ability to function is a crucial feature of illness, then the capacity to get things done is surely one of the fundamental features of health. So much so that a recent trend has been to redefine our whole notion of health in exactly these terms.

Peter Drucker, one of the doyens of American business management, tells us that 'Health now means wellness: the capacity to function well.' He adds that 'I'm not sure the definition of health is yet understood by hospitals. We are seeing one of those major shifts in awareness that creates an entirely new market, a community of demands. It has to do with nothing less than the individual's desire for efficient use of his or her capacities, physical and mental.'[1] Note the interest in health as a market-place.

In an interview with T. George Harris, the seemingly unstoppable driving force behind the immensely successful magazine *American Health* and more recently the editor-in-chief of *Psychology Today*, Drucker describes the new health movement as 'part of people being entrepreneurs of the self ... *doing*, not just surviving'.

Harris himself also insists that, in the USA at least, 'health has become the new individualism', and again 'health has to do with performance – to be at your best, to be doing what you do best'.[2] He is another one who sees the health movement as entrepreneurship of the self – 'pushing yourself to the limit'. That is why he describes *American Health*, perhaps the principal magazine to chart these trends, as 'life worshipping'.

These ideas are not just a clever strategy to increase the (already huge) market for vitamins and running shoes. They result from following what is actually happening out there in the world. A telephone survey that the magazine conducted in collaboration with the Gallup Organization contacted about 1,000 respondents in 1986. Claiming results to be accurate within 4 per cent, it reported that nine out of ten Americans agreed that 'If I take the right actions, I can stay healthy.' A quarter of those questioned *strongly* agreed with the suggestion that they could control their own health. These people, who were christened the *health confidents*, contrasted with the 50 per cent of *health uncertains* who were much less sure about their ability to keep themselves healthy.

The *confidents* were most likely to exert direct actions over their health by exercise and diet. The sense of guiding their own health that they gained as a result related to satisfaction in all areas of their lives, more strongly indeed than any other factor, even earning an adequate salary. Four out of ten of the *confidents* agreed that they were 'very satisfied with the way my life is right now', whilst the national average was only half as many. For the *uncertains* the figure was far lower – only 10 per cent were very satisfied with their lives. A third of the *health confidents* also considered themselves to be in excellent health, again twice the national average.

More than half of the 1,000 survey respondents were exercisers. Two-thirds of those who exercised felt that they had more energy, and a third thought that they were more creative at work as a result. They were 'lured onward by the belief that exercise transforms their lives and helps them to become the best humans they can be'.[3] George Gallup himself apparently said that this switch to physical activity (which we will look at later) was the most fundamental social change that his Organization had ever studied. And Harris is convinced that such trends represent a redefining of health as 'a cultural reach towards individual excellence', an 'urgent sense of being fully myself, at my best'.

If we follow this line of thinking then health becomes a question of gaining control, of taking charge of your life, of becoming 'empowered'. *Empowerment* is one of the new buzz-words, like *holism* or *spirituality*. And it is not the creation of account executives and magazine editors, people with a major interest in the economics of health. More utopian organizations like the New World Foundation have also suggested that self-responsibility in health may be one of the few areas in which Americans can maintain a sense of self-control and some feeling of power over their lives.[4] It is no coincidence that this trend has arisen in a society where both patients and their doctors have become over-dependent on high-tech medicine.

And it is now becoming true in Great Britain. The UK lags five to ten years behind the USA in social and medical innovation. Some see this as a good thing. The time difference means that the more outrageous notions created in the US appear, develop, explode and vanish without ever crossing the Atlantic. 'I have seen the future and it (sometimes) works.'

But the trend to 'self-empowerment' through health has come to the attention of market researchers in Britain as well. One recent projection of social change in the UK predicted that by the late 1980s nearly 40 per cent of the population would belong to the group they called *inner-directed*. They have much in common with the American *health confidents* – people who set their own standards for behaviour and who are propelled by their own notions of success. They contrast sharply with the *outer-directed* groups, those who are motivated by more Yuppie ideals of gaining esteem and status, and with the *sustenance-driven* group, whose major drive is the need for security.

Inner-directed people, like the *confidents*, can be identified by their strong disagreement with statements like 'There is little I can do to prevent disease.' They are the ones who are most prepared to change their lifestyle for the sake of their health and who are most likely to seek out alternative therapies like acupuncture and homoeopathy when they see that 'orthodox' doctors can do nothing for them.[5]

The details of those marketing projections may be wrong. The growth of the inner-directed sector may not be as fast as predicted. But changing patterns of health care, and particularly the trend to self-care, are a reality that is already creating a major financial turnover in the UK. It has passed the acid test of credibility: it is a trend that manufacturers are prepared to invest in. And if you doubt it, look at the boom in the sales of selenium or vitamin E, or take home a low-fat spread to put on your low-calorie biscuits after your dance class.

The need to compromise

What are we to make of this redefinition of health – health is being my functional best? Certainly, it captures one aspect of what it means to be healthy. Research studies, my own among them, are showing how much importance people attach to ideas like energy, vigour and vitality – to being able to get things done. But it also contains the seeds of disappointment. What about those days (probably most days) when you are not at your best, doing what you do best? Does that label you as being unhealthy for most of your life?

We all know that total freedom from disease is rare. So there aren't going to be many occasions when I can function at my best in what matters to me. However fit I am, my life is a constant process of accommodating to my body, a continual compromise to achieve what I can, fully aware that it is much less than I would like. Maybe that accounts for the difference in transatlantic perceptions. The British are much more likely to compromise than their North American cousins.

Then too, the idea of 'an urgent sense of being fully myself, at my best' smacks of the frantic activity that we see in people who are driven by perfectionism or insecurity so that they simply can't stop. They have a quality that specialists in Chinese medicine call 'empty heat'. It is productive, but it leads to exhaustion and perhaps to a premature heart attack. And if you ask such people how they actually feel, their answers rarely describe a sense of healthy well-being. Quite the reverse.

To love and to work

So the main problem with this idea of health-as-productivity is that it is simply too restricted. Not only does it relate to the purely physical, but it captures only one physical aspect at that.

Can we do better?

People have been arguing about definitions of health at least since Pericles in the fifth century BC described it as 'That state of moral, mental and physical well-being which enables men to face any crisis in life with the utmost facility and grace'. For him, it was the ability to withstand change, to bend in the wind, that characterizes the healthy person. And it seems that, with human nature, little changes over the centuries. A more recent specialist, commenting on a long-term survey of healthy students, remarked that 'The luckiest of lives ... had its full share of diffi- culty and private despair ... pathology is always with us and soundness is a way of reacting to problems, not an absence of them'.[6]

The definition of health that everyone knows was produced by the World Health Organization. As long ago as 1946 the WHO defined health as 'A state of complete physical, mental and social well-being and not merely the absence of disease or infirmity'. Many doctors have since regretted that they chose a definition that you can't do very much with. One famous cynic (now deceased) said that the only patients he had ever seen who matched that description were either manic or about to have a heart attack.

But the WHO definition does recognize that health is more than simply not being diseased. We can feel ill without having any pathology. And it also takes us beyond the realms of the purely physical. It tries to integrate our mental and social well- being too. In that, it echoes Sigmund Freud's idea of health as the capacity to love and to work. And as John Horder, a past President of the Royal College of General Practitioners, has pointed out, that opens up the whole concept, so that health comes to include ideas like having a purpose, and finding a meaning in life.

This search for meaning is another topic we will explore. Indeed as the book develops we will look at many facets in this kaleido- scopic view of health. We will see Aaron Antonovsky suggesting that it is how we manage inevitable tensions that determines whether we get ill or not; W.F.Lefcourt describing vitality as 'an active grappling with events that we regard as being person- ally important'; and Salvatore Maddi talking about the 'special motivational edge' that keeps some people more healthy than others.

But the experts are not the only ones to listen to. They only become experts on health and what it means by talking to ordinary people and listening to what they have to say.

Asking the people

A now famous survey carried out in France in the 1960s was one of the first to come to grips with what individuals themselves mean by the idea of being healthy. Not surprisingly, it means different things to different people.[7]

At the simplest, some of them really did regard health as just the absence of illness. 'Health is not something positive ... it is simply not being ill.' But many respondents went further than this. For them, health had to do with physical robustness and strength, and the ability to fight off illness and fatigue. It seemed to be something that was inbuilt ('I've always had a sturdy constitution'), something you inherit ('I was born with excellent health'). So for these people two aspects were uppermost in their minds: health as not being ill and health as the capacity to resist disease.

But surely there must be more to it than that?

Indeed there is, and other respondents gave more all-embracing replies. Listen to some of them: 'When I am enjoying good health I feel well. There's a sense of equilibrium when I feel that everything is going well and difficulties appear insignificant.' Another said, 'Real health [is] when the body functions like a well-oiled machine, without having to be looked after.' Then again 'It is optimism ... a kind of continuous dynamism.' Alternatively, health is the state 'when in the morning you wake up fresh and in good shape, when you have your mind on your job, when everything looks rosy, when work is no bother.' Or finally, good health 'is to be able to act so as to do what you want to do, to live how you want to live ... to be completely free.'

Which takes us back to health as the capacity to function.

The vision of health in this French survey has many facets. It has to do with physical well-being, with being able to avoid fatigue and with having sufficient physical resources to do what you want to do. But notice too how it relates to psychological well-being, to a feeling that things are going as they should go. People recognize having a healthy constitution and the capacity to resist disease. They also recognize the sense of well-being that goes with that confidence in your ability to stay healthy and do the things you want to do.

Three forms of wellness

It is time to put all of these comments about health into some sort of framework, to zip them together. It is a framework of my own, and it is extremely simple, but I hope it takes in most of the key features.

It is a framework that came from two sources. Firstly, and naturally enough, it came from my own listening to what people had to say, in much the same way as the French findings did. Secondly, it came out of my trying to decide what was meant by yet another buzz-word. This time the word was *positive health*.

There are literally hundreds of clinics and health clubs on both sides of the Atlantic devoted to the ideal of 'positive health'. It is what we all aspire to. And it is what their treatments promise us. But looking at what was on offer at many of these centres – sometimes basic medical screening, sometimes rather un-inspired circuit training – made me wonder what their claims could be based on. Before we can start to enquire how positive health can be achieved – how empowerment translates into well-being – we have to know how to recognize it.

So let me ask you a naive question. How do you recognize a healthy person? What are *your* criteria? Certainly we do it by assessing their vitality, their energy and their zest. But there is more to health than stamina and drive. Positive health must have other aspects too.

Let me suggest that there are three of them.

First, and most obviously, is a feeling of well-being within the person herself. It is that positive perception of the well-oiled machine that we can describe most simply as 'feeling well'.

But there is more than just a subjective feeling. One of the cardinal attributes of health is productivity – the ability to do what you want to do, without your body restricting your freedom or your options. So the idea of positive health must include the capacity for working well, or managing well, or simply 'doing well'.

Thirdly, people who enjoy positive health are rarely sick. They succeed in staying healthy most of the time. Their bodies seem to be able to withstand the unhealthy influences that we expose them to, from impossible deadlines to viral infection. The healthy person is less likely than others to have his physical balance disturbed. In other words, he has the capacity for 'staying well'.

So a body that is positively healthy is one that feels that way to its owner. It allows her to do what she wants to do. And it is a body that stays in tune even when it is exposed to hazards. In short, positive health is feeling well, doing well and staying well.

And that's the foundation on which I propose to build the rest of this book.

But, of course, having a healthy body is only half of the story. The other question that we have to ask is: what does it mean to have a healthy mind?

CHAPTER 3

People Who Say Yes to Life

A psychology of health

THERE is now emerging over the horizon a new conception of human sickness and of human health, a psychology that I find so thrilling and so full of wonderful possibilities that I yield to the temptation to present it publicly even before it is checked and confirmed, and before it can be called reliable scientific knowledge.

It is more than thirty years since Abraham Maslow, a world-renowned psychologist then at Brandeis University, delivered these resounding words to an audience in New York. Maslow was a cult figure in the 1950s. His 'new conception' was the foundation for a whole movement called *humanistic psychology*. He intended to provide a new 'third force' in psychology. The movement was seen as an alternative both to psychoanalysis, with its emphasis on subconscious conflict, and to behaviourism, with its belief that all human behaviour occurs through our developing the appropriate sets of conditioned reflexes.

Published in 1956 with the inspirational title *Towards a Psychology of Health*,[1] Maslow's lecture presented the humanistic manifesto. It was based on the view that we all have 'an essentially biologically based inner nature ... if it is permitted to guide our life, we grow healthy, fruitful and happy'. However, when it is denied or suppressed, we get sick. But even when denied, it still persists and presses for 'actualization'. This is the key concept

in much of Maslow's thinking. It means something like self-realization, coming into being, or blossoming.

In part, at least, self-actualization results from deprivation and
frustration, pain and tragedy:

> these experiences have something to do with a sense of
> achievement and ego strength and therefore the sense of
> healthy self-esteem and self-confidence. The person who hasn't
> conquered, withstood and overcome, continues to feel doubtful
> that he *could*. This is true not only for external dangers; it
> holds also for the ability to control and delay one's own
> impulses and therefore to be unafraid of them.

The ideas of humanistic psychology are what many people want
to hear. They tell us that we have the capacity to grow and
develop. They represent a psychology of hope and optimism. They
suggest that the move towards self-actualization, though it may
proceed through pain, will make us healthier, mentally and perhaps even physically.

And this is where it came unstuck. Maslow was eager to share
the good news with his audience 'even before it can be called
reliable scientific knowledge'. But, unfortunately, it never got
that far. In the three decades since he made the declaration, there
has been little scientific research linking self-actualization with
mental health. Even less have humanistic psychologists tried to
discover whether self-actualizing people are physically healthier
than those who show no such urge to grow and develop.

In fairness, I have to say that doing this type of research is
more difficult than it seems. For example, consider the most
routine way of measuring people's attitudes. We put together
a questionnaire aimed to reflect what they feel about a particular
issue. They fill it in, and their replies tell the researchers something about their perceptions, say of vigour and fatigue. But producing reliable questionnaires to measure how people differ in
their self-actualizing has been full of problems. Few psychologists
have been convinced enough by Maslow's ideas even to explore
their health-related possibilities. And his own writings say
nothing tangible about physical health at all.

One attempt to put some of these humanistic ideas on to a
firmer basis was a conference organized in the mid-1980s by the
Institute for the Advancement of Health, the New York-based
organization devoted to research in the mind–body-health area.
Maslow's great interest in the 1950s was with positive experi-

ences, what he called 'peak experiences', and with positive ways of dealing with negative experiences. But between the mid-1950s and the mid-1980s the whole language of psychology had changed. Few professionals can talk comfortably about peak experiences or self-actualization today. But they can talk about 'positive emotions' without embarrassment. So this conference addressed itself to the simpler question of how might positive emotions affect physical health.

On balance, it concluded that our patterns of thinking and feeling do affect our bodies. They do so in ways that might be either damaging or beneficial to our health. But there are no simple labels that can be used to distinguish positive (health-promoting) from negative (health-damaging) emotional states. We can't say that joy and contentment will make everyone live longer or that sadness and frustration will always make people ill. The truth is much more varied, and much more difficult to get hold of. And that is simply because people are varied too.

Life-affirmers – life-deniers

The most valuable result of this conference for me was in helping to crystallize an idea that I had been turning over for some years. It's the distinction between those people who can be called *life-affirming* and those who are *life-denying*.

At first glance, this is as vague as self-actualization itself. But the distinction between life-affirmers and -deniers is a real one. It's something that many people recognize. I know because I've asked them. I suspect that it means something to you as well.

What do the life-affirmers have in common? As one of the conference delegates put it, 'They are people who say yes to life.' By contrast, you can recognize the life-deniers long before you can say just what it is about them that makes them so negative. Naomi Remen of the Saybrook Institute in San Francisco came perhaps closest when she said that they are people who 'don't live as well as they know how to'. They contrast with the life-affirmers – we might even call them *life-enhancers* – who make a conscious effort to live up to their full potential.

Now, just like the humanistic manifesto, these are also inspiring ideas. Most of us want to live up to our full potential, just as most of us would like to become self-actualized. But before I allowed myself to get carried away, I wanted to know what these ideas actually meant. Just how do you recognize someone who is living in a life-affirming way; what exactly is she doing?

Finding the answers represents part of an ongoing research project that I'm involved in. At the risk of 'presenting it publicly before it is checked and confirmed', it does seem that the notion of life-enhancement is real; you can recognize the people who have it; it has different facets that can be measured; possessing them does seem to go with increased mental and even physical health (to say nothing of happiness) and most of them can be developed by anyone who is prepared to make the effort. But it will certainly take an effort to unlearn the fundamentally life-denying outlook that some of us have taken on board since childhood.

So where was I to start in my search to know what it means to say yes to life?

I soon discovered that there was nothing in any scientific index listed under 'life-enhancement', as there was for diet or exercise or meditation. Life-affirmation, at least under that name, wasn't in the scientific literature at all. So I would have to ask people what they thought it was and what its components were. Armed with their answers I could go back to what had been written by psychologists and clinicians about the individual parts of the pattern. I could then try to put the two sets of ideas together and see whether anything was known about the effect that life-affirmation might have on mental or physical health.

Do you mind if I ask you a question?

In our search for life-affirmation the first question that we asked (and we are still asking it) is the following:

> When we look around we sometimes see people whom we would describe as life-affirming or life-enhancing, people who 'say yes to life'.
> We also see people whom we think of as life-negating or life-diminishing, people who seem to deny life instead of affirming it.
> Does this difference seem real to you?

If people said the difference was real, and the great majority did, we went on to ask them to list three characteristics that life-affirmers had that allowed you to recognize them and, by contrast, three features by which you could recognize life-denying people. These features could relate to what they did or said or the way they looked. We emphasized that there were no right or wrong answers and that we simply wanted to know what they thought.

Before we go any further, perhaps you would like to try answering the question for yourself. If the very idea of saying yes to life makes no sense to you, then don't reach for a pencil. But if it does, then write down three characteristics that come into your head that life-affirmers and life-deniers might show. Don't think too hard about it. An initial impression is more valuable than something you have to dredge up from the back of your mind.

In our early studies we asked the question of three groups of people. First were fifty-odd students at the local Polytechnic. Then there were a similar number of aerobic teachers who were attending an exercise convention. Finally came a comparable group of bus drivers and mechanics (mostly men) whom Allison, my young, attractive and very determined research assistant, waylaid in the bus depot during their work breaks.

We chose these three groups to represent a range of age and social class. We had no idea how different people might respond to the question of life-affirmation, but we knew that each would filter it through the lens of their own previous experience. This phase of the study was never meant to be more than a pointer to give us some clue to what we were looking for. We knew that it would have to be repeated on far more people. This is happening now.

But this early phase fulfilled our initial purpose. Potential volunteers were stopped by Allison or myself and asked, 'Could you please spare five minutes to help us with a research project on well-being, by filling out the attached form? Your reply will be treated in confidence. Anyway, it will be anonymous: you don't need to sign it.' If they agreed, they completed the question on page 1, about whether the distinction between affirmers and deniers was real for them. Over 85 per cent said that it was. They then turned over and filled in the three positive and negative characteristics. Finally, they indicated their sex and age within a fifteen-year age range.

Then we sat down to analyse their replies.

Individual responses were very varied. For example, life-affirmers might be 'enthusiastic' or 'prepared to have a go'; life-deniers might be 'predictable' or 'worried what people will think about them'. We grouped the nearly 1,000 individual replies on the basis of which features seemed to hang together. This gave us about fifty categories, for example 'attractive' and 'well respected' in contrast to 'untidy' or 'little education'. These groups were then lumped together to form seven major clusters of characteristics by which (according to our respondents) life-affirmers or life-deniers could be recognized.

We didn't make any attempt to do proper statistics on such a small sample. The groupings were made simply by eye. They were intended to reflect those features which seemed to go together on commonsense grounds. We will use more detailed statistics on any larger-scale investigation.

The major categories that we ended up with were those that had been mentioned by more than 10 per cent of our volunteers. Each of them was itself made up of perhaps five or ten characteristics.

For life-affirmers, the main features were:

Drive, defined by qualities like a high degree of enthusiasm, high levels of ambition, achievement, involvement and a ready capacity to accept change.

Sociability, which included unselfishness, good manners, tolerance and the capacity to be affectionate.

Happiness, including being contented, satisfied and enjoying life.

Optimism, which contained such features as having a positive attitude and being open-minded.

Vigour, which included notions like having a high level of energy and good physical health.

The major features that distinguish the life-deniers were:

Unsociability, including being selfish, hostile and introverted.

Poor coping, which included being emotionally unstable, depressed, having a poor sense of humour and little personal control over events.

Pessimism, which took account of being cynical, close-minded and having a set of negative attitudes.

Lack of drive, which related to having low levels of enthusiasm, ambition, achievement or involvement, having little capacity to adapt to change and having uncertain goals or no goals at all.

Unhappiness, which included being discontented, dissatisfied and miserable.

How did you do? Were any of these characteristics on your list? I'd be surprised if none of them were, but if you have a different set it simply reflects your different experience. Or you may have chosen some others that I will describe in a minute.

When we rated the replies in their order of frequency, we found that, of the affirming features, drive was the most common, endorsed by 20 per cent of our respondents. Next came sociability, happiness and optimism, each mentioned by 15 per cent, and vigour at roughly 10 per cent. If we take the first and the last together, it is clear that features relating to energy and the capacity to do things – 'doing well' – were recognized as life-affirming by nearly a third of all those who replied. This was what we might have predicted, knowing a little about public perceptions of positive health.

Of the life-negating features, unsociability and poor coping were endorsed by some 20 per cent, pessimism and lack of drive by about 15 per cent each, and unhappiness was mentioned by little over 10 per cent. So it is clear, even from these very sketchy results, that the notion of saying yes (or no) to life does have a meaning. It represents a set of characteristics that you can actually see. However, as we suspected, there were differences in the order that our respondents rated them.

The major life-affirming feature listed overall was drive, which is a measure of high enthusiasm, ambition and achievement motivation. This was mentioned most frequently by the students and the exercisers. For bus drivers it was only rated third, behind sociability and happiness. This probably reflects the greater investment that the two younger groups make in the future.

Sociability was higher in the students than the exercisers. Its number-one place among the bus drivers may reflect their doing a job that is made easier by smooth, cheerful contact with the public, rather than constantly having to be on the defensive. The drivers gave second place to happiness (with its elements of satisfaction, contentment and enjoyment of life). This was ranked third by the students and fourth by the exercisers. This older group of drivers preferred to have their satisfaction now, rather than striving for gains in the future.

The life-negating characteristics are interesting because they are not simply the list of life-affirming features in reverse. For example, poor coping, which contains the ideas of emotional instability and the sense of not being able to exercise much control over your life, was the most frequently mentioned negative feature among both students and exercisers. But good coping, the positive 'mirror image' of poor coping, was mentioned by less than 10 per cent of the sample overall, and so didn't even get included on the list. This is probably because someone who hasn't much influence over their own life often displays an anxious, haunted type of personality that you can hardly miss. But most people think that the ability to cope well and remain emotionally buoyant is simply normal, and not even worth mentioning in a survey like this.

In the paper where we published these findings, we asked whether this set of life-affirming and life-negating attitudes actually has any influence on our physical health.[2] It seems that they do. For example, the concept of drive contains the idea of a high level of enthusiasm for what we are doing (rather than a half-hearted, clock-watching attitude) and the welcoming of change for the opportunities that it may bring (rather than the fear of threats that it may create).

So drive has a lot in common with an attitude to life that we will look at later. It is known as the 'hardy personality'. We pointed out that in long-term stressful situations, possessing this set of hardy attitudes reduces the chance of physical illness.[3] In a similar way, sociability not only increases personal happiness, but is also essential for attracting other people to you, for creating what specialists call 'social support'. The importance to our physical well-being of belonging to a social support network has been found many times. For example, we quoted a Californian study (that I will describe later) showing that the death rate measured over nearly a decade was twice as high in people with low rather than high levels of social involvement.[4]

Finally, we drew attention to the fact that (contrary to what many people believe) there is no direct evidence linking emotional instability (a critical factor in poor coping) to physical illness. However, emotional ups and downs are a powerful predictor of who gets clinically depressed.[5] Unstable people also complain more to their doctors about a whole range of 'non-specific' symptoms, that vary from cold hands to cancer.[6] And men with high levels of emotional instability but 'clean' coronary arteries suffer more pains in the chest than men who have blocked arteries but are emotionally more stable.[7]

So we concluded our brief review by suggesting that the idea of 'saying yes to life' seemed to have enough links to physical health to be worth exploring in greater detail.

Refining the concept

This pilot survey revealed a combination of drive and vigour as a major life-affirming quality. Our respondents described an enthusiastic, ambitious, involved, energetic individual – someone who is 'doing well'. But vigour itself includes the notion of good physical health. This is simply another way of saying what we already know – that health has to do with performance. So unfortunately we can't use a notion like vigour to predict who stays healthy, if vigorous people are healthy by definition. In other words, we need to isolate that part of the 'saying yes' that deals with thinking and feeling before we can ask whether life affirmation has any independent influence on a person's physical health.

So we went back to the idea of saying yes to life and looked at it again. Our pilot study had used the most common of all psychologists' approaches, the open-ended questionnaire. It's based on the belief that, if you want to know what people are thinking, you ask them.

The second phase used perhaps the next most common technique – the in-depth interview. This recognizes the limitations of any 'self-reporting' questionnaire, and encourages the subjects to tell someone else what they *really* think. It is the sort of approach that Daniel Levinson and his colleagues used in their study of the transitions that characterize *The Seasons of a Man's Life*.[8] Levinson's set of forty interviews about the stages of adult development revealed the alternating periods of stability and change that gave his book its title. They showed that most men have a *mid-life transition*, though relatively few have a bad enough time for it to be called a *mid-life crisis*.

We followed a similar, though more modest approach. We asked the same questions as we had before – does the difference between affirming and denying life mean anything to you, and could you give examples that identify each type of person? But this time the respondents didn't write down the first answers that occurred to them on the second page of the questionnaire. Instead, the interviewer talked to them, often for an hour or more, constantly seeking and probing to get as exact an idea as possible of what life-affirming qualities the respondent was actually thinking about. This time we deliberately concentrated on mental, emotional and even spiritual aspects. In this way, we started to build up a more three-dimensional picture of what they meant by 'saying yes to life'.

And in that respect it worked beyond my expectations. Not only did most people again instantly recognize and accept the distinction. They also showed a surprising degree of overlap in what they thought the differences were, this time at a more mental level. On probing, the core characteristics of life-affirmers seemed to be much the same to all those who thought the idea was real.

In one respect though, the question was naive. Many of our interviewees pointed out that people are not either affirmers or deniers. Life is simply not so black and white. It is better to imagine some sort of curve or continuum, with the strongest affirmers at one end and the strongest deniers at the other. Everyone has his own position on the line at any moment. And in time their positions might change.

They were right, of course. I used the either/or to simplify the question. Most of our physical characteristics, like height and weight, blood pressure and cholesterol, fall on a continuous curve like this. So do many of our mental features. My question simply aimed to compare one end of the curve with the other. And remember that people can move about on it, either up or down.

Seven ways to life-enhancement

What came out of the in-depth questioning? What are the life-affirming characteristics that ordinary people, when questioned in detail, believe life-enhancers to have in abundance? Leaving aside those that relate directly to physical health, energy or stamina, there appear to be seven that most of our interviewees agreed about.

(1) Life-affirming people are emotionally stable. They are not easily upset. As one respondent put it, 'They don't pour out their emotions all over you.' They don't get buried in emotional turmoil themselves either. They decide on a course of action after examining the pros and cons of any situation for a sufficient, but not an agonizing length of time. They then carry it through. Whether it proves right or wrong in retrospect they don't spend long in looking back, either to congratulate themselves on doing it well or to flagellate themselves about getting it wrong.

(2) Life-affirming people are sociable. They are perfectly capable of being on their own, even for long periods when they have to work through things that can only be done alone. But they choose when possible to be with other people. They're sociable but they're not gregarious – fond of crowds. They may often prefer to be with only a few people rather than many, so as to achieve deeper levels of contact. They are emotionally out-going, trying to reach out to others and genuinely share feelings and ideas with them. But in large or small groups they are capable of expressing themselves to others, not only through words, but also through gestures and looks. Without striving for it, without demanding other people's attention, they have 'presence', sometimes even 'charisma'.

(3) Life-affirming people are self-confident. That's to say that they feel a strong sense of self-esteem or self-worth. This doesn't mean that they are either arrogant or complacent. Nor do they believe that they have gone as far as they can towards fulfilling themselves. But it does mean that they are generally confident about their own actions and their own set of values. They have reached a point, usually through a good deal of effort, and sometimes through considerable suffering, where they feel that their lives are worthwhile. As a result, they trust their own opinions and take full responsibility for what they do. Because they know that they are acting in ways which for them are both honest and authentic, they have very few feelings of guilt. Because they trust their own judgement and don't find it necessary to impress other people, their actions are spontaneous. They do what they believe to be appropriate, rather than what they think other people expect of them.

(4) Life-affirming people are in control of their lives. They believe that they can influence the world, that what they do has some effect on what happens 'out there'. Of course, there are limits. No sane person believes that he can run the universe, or even his own life, completely to suit himself. But life-affirmers believe they have the capacity to bring about what they judge to be realistic changes in their world. Because of this sense of control they can tolerate those occasions when they get mixed signals or conflicting messages from their environment. So they can live with situations that are ambiguous, when the best course of action is not at all clear.

(5) Life-affirming people have a sense of purpose. They believe that they can see some order, some design in the world, some

path that they want to follow. Because of this, they feel a sense of commitment to what they are doing. They feel fully engaged and involved in their jobs, their hobbies and the other activities that make up their lives as a whole. This doesn't necessarily mean that they see any grand design in the universe, or that they feel that some God has revealed his divine plan for them. They may not believe that the universe as a whole has any plan. But they are certain that the part of it that they live in is predictable and coherent enough for them to feel confident in pursuing a particular plan for their own lives. For some this involves trying to discover the purpose they feel is out there already, one that is greater than them and that holds the world together. For others, coming to grips with this question of meaning is more immediate. They simply *create* their *own* plan, their *own* sense of purpose by involving themselves in the things that they believe to be important and enduring. Wherever the plan comes from, inside or outside, is not important. The essential feature is that they feel committed to it and allow it to guide their lives.

(6) Life-affirming people are optimistic. They welcome the future and the changes it will bring as opportunities or challenges, chances to experience new ways of living. This doesn't mean that they constantly expect things to get better. They recognize that change can bring difficulties and they accept the effort and re-adjustment that may have to be made to experience the opportunities that come as a result. This means that they avoid developing so great a commitment to their present lives that the idea of change becomes frightening. Instead they keep themselves open to experience, welcoming rather than dreading what the future might bring.

(7) Life-affirming people have a capacity to feel pleasure and deliberately to pursue the pleasures in life. For them, there is nothing shameful about that. Beyond pleasure, they try to feel satisfied and grateful by what they do. This active pursuit of satisfaction is very important to them. And beyond satisfaction comes the capacity to feel joy. Life-affirmers know that the sense of joy can't be conjured out of nothing and can't simply be switched on at will. It has to be worked for, and even then it may not appear. But they try to live so that joy can come into their lives, even though they cannot predict when or even how it will arrive. Their openness to pleasure, satisfaction and joy is like their openness to experience. It sometimes leaves them vulnerable, but for them the rewards that it can bring outweigh the hurt that

they might feel, the hurt that life-denying people strive at all costs to avoid.

Here then is our life-affirmer, someone who doesn't easily get upset and who doesn't spend hours worrying about past or future decisions. She is socially outgoing, confident about her self-worth and happy about her set of values. She believes in her own capabilities and feels able to exert some control over her surroundings. Life-affirmers feel engaged, committed and have a sense of purpose. Rather than hanging on to the present they welcome the opportunities that the future might bring. And, perhaps most characteristically, they actively pursue pleasure, satisfaction and joy, leaving themselves open to experience, even though doing so may increase their risk of feeling pain.

Rediscovering mental health

Once we had put these features in place, once we had mapped this outline of what people meant by saying yes to life, the floodgates suddenly opened. Once I knew what I was looking for, I found that each of these facets had been recognized for years, though not usually with regard to health, at least not physical health. To my great satisfaction I found something else too. Taking all these characteristics together, the affirmation of life came very close to what psychologists mean when they talk about *mental health*.

Like the character in Molière's play, who suddenly discovered that he had been talking for the last forty years in prose, I suddenly saw what I'd been *feeling* as the affirmation of life without being able to define it. On the physical side the life-affirmer can be recognized by his energy, vigour and vitality. And on the other side of life-affirmation is mental health. We usually experience the two as so closely mixed that we don't separate them, until a study like this concentrates our minds so that we have to.

How many of you, I wonder, wrote down a mixture of physical and mental features in your replies? Most of you did, I suspect. Certainly I have found that when you ask a group of people at a seminar to shout out the qualities that they associate with an idea like 'health' you get both the physical (say strength and resilience) and the emotional (say cheerfulness and fortitude) lumped together. Most people don't stop to separate them.

But does this bring us any closer to looking at the way that one influences the other, at integrating the two sides of saying yes to life?

In 1979 a research report appeared that deals precisely with this question. It represented a follow-up over a period of no less than forty years of a group of about 200 men whose physical and mental health were assessed continuously, first when they were adolescents and then at regular periods throughout their lives.[9] Of fifty-nine who had the best mental health between the ages of twenty-one and forty-six, only two became chronically ill or died by the time they reached fifty-three. But of the forty-eight with the worst mental health between their twenties and their forties, eighteen were dead or had suffered a chronic illness by their fifties.

The findings were put through a battery of statistical tests to control for the effects of other important influences like alcohol and tobacco, bodyweight and the longevity of their relatives. The links remained after all of these allowances had been made. The author of the report, George Vaillant of Harvard University, drew a simple conclusion. The results, he said, showed that 'Good mental health retards mid-life deterioration in physical health.'

Simple perhaps, but immensely important.

Mental health or value judgement?

By today's standards, Vaillant's ideas about mental health are showing their age. But then this study of adult development among Harvard University students, known as the Grant Study because of the philanthropist who funded it, did begin back in 1939. By 1975, physical problems were much more common in those men who were described as having 'poor adjustment' as students and in their later lives as adults. Their illnesses ranged across the board. They included cancer, hypertension and coronary disease, as well as cirrhosis and chronic back problems.

Vaillant's ideas are old-fashioned for two reasons. First, he used rather 'rough' measures to get his data – information from college reports and self-reports of health from the subjects themselves. More striking was the fact that mental health was regarded as an aspect of the successes – personal, marital, social – that his subjects achieved. He believed that the results of being well adapted were obvious enough. No need for any more elaborate measures.

But what exactly was he measuring?

As Vaillant himself remarked, 'it is hard to separate mental health from value judgement'. The signs of adjustment that he chose to use reflect general concepts like overall *soundness*, rather than the sort of measures of mental well-being like proneness to depression that we see psychologists using today. But Vaillant would argue that his rather gross, practical and obvious measures take these other more detailed features into account. And interestingly enough, he has since shown that they give very similar results to those achieved with more modern forms of assessment.[10]

As each man left the University, the staff rated him as being either unusually well integrated, of average stability or else emotionally unstable. In interviews conducted over the next thirty years, continued attempts were made to judge each man's degree of emotional maturity by assessing how he had actually reacted at times of crisis or conflict in his life. Had he responded by what Vaillant described as 'immature defences', like fantasy or an attack of hypochondria? Had he perhaps reacted by trying to repress events from his mind? Or had he rather used the more 'mature' defences of anticipation and good humour, to keep his perspective? If so, he had a better chance of stopping any problem from gaining an overwhelming importance that prevented him from getting on with the normal tasks of living.

In the interviews, conducted over three decades, each of the men was given a score on a scale that measured his adjustment in relation to his career and social life. The same questionnaire also tapped into his mental and physical health. So, for career adjustment, it recorded whether the Grant men had shown a steady advance in their careers with time, and whether they had become more successful than their fathers had been. For social adjustment, the survey team recorded how often each man had been divorced, and whether he thought he had any friends. Psychological adjustment included recording any psychiatric illness that he had suffered since the last interview. The men were also asked whether they enjoyed their jobs and whether they took regular vacations.

Vaillant's reason for putting together all of these different items was a practical and immediate one. In his view 'Behavior over [a] period of time offers a better index of mental health than pencil-and-paper tests or assessment at a single interview.' And certainly he found that the men who were well adjusted in their careers also seemed to enjoy good social adjustment *and* psychological adjustment *and* physical health. Success was not won at the expense of their personal lives. They functioned well in all of these areas.

The results went completely against the idea that mental health might only be achieved 'at the price of a more creative and spontaneous type of personality organization'. On the contrary 'mental health is anything but dull. Whether the criteria are enjoyable vacations and sex lives, creativity in academic and business life, or charm and vitality during the interview, the relatively healthy enjoyed life more and were more enjoyed by others'. In short, they had many of the characteristics that we would call life-affirming.

For the Grant Study investigators, the best assessment of mental health could be made from 'the tangible evidence of success in areas of working and loving' (back to Sigmund Freud). So close was the link, in Vaillant's view, between mental health and 'concrete, externally observable items, [such as] stable marriage ... salary, visits to physicians, long vacations, drug abuse and objective evidence of friends', that these obvious, observable features of a person's life could be used to measure his mental status.

Though we may take exception to some of his methods, Vaillant's conclusions fit exactly with the most recent ideas that have developed about mental stability. When he says that 'ingenious adaptation to stress (call it good mental health or mature coping mechanisms) facilitates our survival', he is describing exactly the importance of appraisal and coping, processes that many modern specialists now accept as *the* major protective factor that breaks the link between stress and disease. It is also the crucial feature that many aspects of life-enhancement have in common.

The men in the Grant Study were not typical of the general population. In their late forties they had only half the death rate and had taken only half the amount of sick leave of other Americans of the same age. But it takes more than a privileged upbringing to become a healthy adult. Despite their background, some of them went downhill in their middle years.

Other research on the same men found that warm relationships with their parents produced adults who were capable of forming close bonds with people in their later lives. In contrast, long-term childhood stresses led to poor mental health in later years. But parenting was not the whole answer. The way that each man came to *respond* to the crises in his life didn't simply result from his childhood. It was much more the result of what he developed into.

And what was the single quality that made his healthy development most likely? Of twenty-five different aspects of personality measured when the men were students, the one that best reflected mental health at age forty-seven was not 'inhibited' or 'humanistic' or even 'friendly' but *practical and organized*.

So the Grant Study offers us a no-nonsense demonstration that healthy mid-life adjustment is a very practical concept with a very practical pay-off. And mental health can be recognized in a very practical way. These early findings have now been revitalized by more recent research. As we will see in Chapter Five, the bottom line, the key quality promoting survival among the Grant Study men, appears to be sheer, simple optimism.

A problem with the original study is that the scales used to measure mental health sometimes contained measures of physical health as well, like how often a subject visited his doctor and the number of days' sick leave that he had per year. There is nothing unusual about this. Many scales intended primarily to measure mental health are 'contaminated' (as the statisticians put it) with physical health measures. You will remember that our own survey of life-affirming characteristics also threw up features that related to both mental and physical well-being. And if scales like this are being used to get some overall measure of 'wellness' then there is no problem.

However, if we want to study the effects of mental health on physical health then we need to use a 'pure' mental-health measure. One such scale is the Mental Health Inventory or MHI developed by Clarice Veit and John Ware Jr of the Rand Corporation in California.[11] It also has a sound practical use. People's scores on the MHI predict the extent to which they use mental-health facilities.

Veit and Ware started with the commonsense notion that to measure mental health in ordinary people (rather than in hospital cases, where much of this work has been done) you have to tap into the mental distress, anxiety and depression that are so common in the general population. But you also have to go beyond these negative dimensions and consider aspects of well-being like cheerfulness, interest and enjoyment of life, the positive side of mental health.

They constructed their MHI with this in mind. In all it contains thirty-five questions. In the negative direction, respondents were asked if they ever felt tense or highly strung, whether they ever felt downhearted and under stress, and if they ever felt that they would be better off dead. On the other hand, they were also asked if they expected to have an interesting day, whether they regarded living as a wonderful adventure, and whether they felt loved and wanted.

The questionnaire was field-tested on a group of over 5,000 people in six different parts of the United States. Some complicated statistics showed that it did measure the underlying mental health of the population, and was free from items that related to their physical health. The statistics also showed that the single factor that the researchers called *mental health* was made up of two separate components – *psychological distress* and *psychological well-being*.

Further divisions were also possible, because both distress and well-being were themselves made up of other factors. For example, distress contained elements of both anxiety and depression, approached by questions like 'Are you restless, fidgety and impatient?' and 'Have you recently been moody and brooded over things?' A third feature of distress was a fear of losing control over your actions and emotions.

On the positive side, mental health was also found to have two components. High scorers on the first, called *positive affect* ('affect' is the psychologists' word for emotion), spent a good deal of their time feeling calm and peaceful. They were generally able to enjoy their lives. Those scoring high on the second feature, which measured emotional ties, felt that their loving relationships were full and complete, and rarely felt lonely.

So the MHI describes mental health at three different levels. First it maps a single, over-arching mental-health factor. Then come two secondary factors – distress and well-being – and finally five sub-factors. All three are valid measures of mental health; they simply give different levels of detail.

When answered by over 4,000 people in four different states, those scoring in the bottom third of the MHI responses spent on average three times more on mental-health services than those in the top third. This excess spending was independent of their physical health, which was measured at the same time. The MHI picks out those most in need of mental-health care. When they do find their way into the medical system, they need more intensive, and hence more expensive, treatment than the rest.

So mental health is tangible. It translates into money. And it looks more like life-affirmation all the time. But the MHI isn't the last word on the subject.

Psychologists have identified other key features that mentally healthy people have in common. Peter Warr at the University of Sheffield thinks that there are five of them.[12] First comes a positive balance of feelings – 'affective well-being'. This is having an excess of positive over negative emotions. We will see later that most people do. Notice how closely this concept of affective well-being relates to the life-affirmer's capacity for feeling pleasure, satisfaction and joy.

Then comes 'competence', the ability to achieve an acceptable degree of success in various areas of your life. This has obvious parallels with the life-affirmer's ability to exert some degree of control over what is happening to her. Warr suggests, 'The competent person is one who has adequate psychological resources to deal with experienced pressures.' Of course, mental health doesn't mean competence in all possible spheres. Everyone is incompetent in some respect.

Third on the list comes 'autonomy' – the ability to formulate your own opinions and actions. It has echoes of our third life-affirming feature, a strong sense of self-worth. However, it is important to get the balance right. Being excessively independent – going entirely your own way – is a sign of mental illness. The goal to strive for is one of successful interdependence with other people.

Fourth in this scheme is 'aspiration', the ability to set goals and then to achieve them. Respondents in our study saw this as part of control. But it overlaps with self-worth as well, because setting realistic goals that are neither too high to achieve nor too low to be worth achieving is one way of maintaining our belief in ourselves as effective human beings.

We will see how mentally healthy people constantly bias their goals upwards, taking themselves close to the limit of their abilities. Remember how Maslow's whole notion of self-actualization and psychological growth had to do with striving to achieve our full potential. Warr points out that striving towards the goals that we value is healthy for its own sake. It is the reverse of the disengagement and apathy that sets in if we duck our problems rather than face them.

Finally, Peter Warr talks about 'integrated functioning', the ability to put all these other features together to achieve 'balance, harmony and inner relatedness'. The opposite happens in neurotic disorders like anxiety and depression. When they strike us, not only do we feel bad, but our feelings of competence, autonomy and aspiration all start to slip away as well. Being able to integrate these qualities across the major areas of our lives – love, work and play – creates the coherent pattern that contributes to our whole sense of identity and individuality.

I had not read Peter Warr's book on mental health when I began to ask questions about the affirmation of life. He hadn't even written it when I first started rubbing these ideas together. Nor had I read Albert Ellis's description of what he, as perhaps the most famous psychotherapist in New York, was trying to achieve with his clients. But I later discovered that in his attempts to change their ways of thinking he aimed, among other things, to help the client assume responsibility for his own life; to accept the fact that we live in an uncertain world; to remain open to the possibilities of change; to become committed to the things that he is doing and to accept himself simply because he exists. For Ellis, these are important goals that the therapist tries to bring about.[13] For us, they are the qualities that the life-affirmer has developed, often for himself.

Overwhelmingly then, what the respondents in our study were describing, out of their own experience and intuition, were the capacities that the professionals attribute to mentally healthy people. The overlap was not complete. But I could hardly miss the fact that saying yes to life means being well adjusted, practical and organized. The obvious question is: why aren't we all like that?

CHAPTER 4

A Question of Personality

―――

Feeling bad most of the time

I get a sinking feeling when I try to find a questionnaire to measure some aspect of our personality. There are just so many to choose from. Fortunately, many of the psychological questionnaires published over the last thirty years all measure the same thing. They assess the tendency which some of us have to feel dissatisfied and upset with our lives.

I have said that psychologists refer to emotion as *affect*. And in 1984, David Watson and Lee Anna Clark, then at the Washington University School of Medicine, described this dissatisfied way of responding to the world as *negative affectivity*, or NA. Those who score high on the scales that measure it are nervous, tense and worried; they are quick to feel angry, guilty and rejected; they magnify and dwell on their mistakes, their disappointments and their frustrations.

Now of course, all of us feel like this at times. We all get anxious or frustrated in response to problems, either real or imaginary. But people high on NA are disposed to react like this *all the time*, whether they have an outside trigger or not. For them, negative affect is a constant and enduring feature. It is what psychologists call a *trait* – 'such individuals are, in any given situation, *more likely* to experience a significant level of distress ... even in the absence of a major, externally obvious stressor'.[1]

In contrast to this 'pervasive disposition to experience distress', people scoring low on the NA dimension view themselves and

1. Do you sometimes feel happy, sometimes depressed, without any apparent reason?
2. Do you have frequent ups and downs in mood, either with or without apparent cause?
3. Are you inclined to be moody?
4. Does your mind often wander when you are trying to concentrate?
5. Are you frequently 'lost in thought' even when supposed to be taking part in a conversation?
6. Are you sometimes bubbling over with energy and sometimes very sluggish?

Box 2.   *Six questions to reveal more about your emotional balance.*

their problems in a more favourable light. They are more satisfied with life. They focus less on themselves, and when they do so they are more pleased with what they find. They also have a more positive view of other people.

Here then is the first of our life-affirming characteristics. Life-affirmers will score low on negative affectivity; life-deniers will score high. The difference reflects a built-in tendency to react emotionally in a particular way.

Let us take a closer look. To start with, examine the questions in Box 2.

These six items come from one of the most widely used of all personality questionnaires. Called the Eysenck Personality Questionnaire or EPQ,[2] it was devised by Hans and Sybil Eysenck when Hans was Professor of Psychology at the Institute of Psychiatry in London. The questions tap straight into negative affectivity, and people answering yes to more than half of them fall on the negative side. But the complete scale consists of twenty-three items. So, although these six are important markers, they are not enough to give you a complete personality score.

The Eysencks called the dimension that this scale measures *neuroticism* or N, because high N scorers have a tendency to develop neurotic illnesses, like anxiety and depression, when they are placed under a lot of pressure. Indeed, the whole concept of neuroticism came out of a thirty-year attempt to discover which types of personality were most likely to suffer from different forms of mental breakdown.

Neuroticism is also the best predictor of how well people will *recover* after a bout of depression. It predicts their chances of getting back to normal even better than the number of times they have been depressed in the past; better even than their number of attempts at suicide. This link exists because, as we will see, high-N individuals have thinking patterns which make them unusually susceptible to the disturbing effects of life events.[3]

It is important to understand that neuroticism is not simply a form of mild depression. High-N people can function quite effectively until something knocks them off balance. What they lack is the ability to bounce back. Neuroticism *predicts* depression because both are based on faulty thinking. But depression is an illness, whilst neuroticism is a psychological trait.

Just as Veit and Ware found that mental health could be divided into various sub-factors, so too can the different facets of personality. High N scorers have a tendency, not only towards depression and anxiety, but also to experience feelings of guilt. They have low self-esteem. They tend to be tense, irrational, shy and moody as well as emotionally unstable.

The opposite pole of neuroticism is called *emotional stability*. The stable person is one who 'tends to respond emotionally only slowly and generally weakly and to return to baseline quickly after emotional arousal; he is usually calm, even-tempered, controlled and unworried'.

Of course, being high on negative affectivity only describes a *tendency* for people to act in a particular way. It doesn't predict their behaviour exactly. The situations that we get ourselves into are constantly changing. So too are our responses. But I think there is little doubt that all of us do have consistent tendencies, enduring patterns, in the way that we respond to the outside world. Some experts believe that they result from a genetic programme influencing the emotional centres in our brain. But even specialists who don't think that personality has much to do with what is happening inside our nervous system still find the idea a useful one.

For example, Robert Hogan, at the University of Tulsa, suggests that what we call *personality* is simply the label that people in any group use to describe the social conduct of others.[4] In any human society, people will try to maximize both their status and their popularity. We all have to conform to social rules, but within these rules we will try to act in ways that the rest of the group see as being consistent. Our behaviour is saying 'This is me, and this is how I want you to see me.'

Human behaviour is very variable. People constantly have to

change their patterns as they deal with other people. But they show consistent tendencies to be, say, conforming or rebellious, sociable or withdrawn, well adjusted or emotional. And the rest of the group respond by giving them a particular role that is appropriate for each person's presentation of himself. As Hogan says, 'the lackadaisical should not be left to guard the flock, the lecherous should not guard the harem, nor the larcenous guard the treasury'.

Other psychologists believe that what we call personality goes much deeper than this social role-playing. They see it as a biologically based tendency to behave in particular ways. Such behaviours have a strong genetic basis. They result from individual differences in the wiring of our nervous system and the way our hormones are balanced. For example, neuroticism is said to depend on an increased sensitivity in our sympathetic nervous system, the region responsible for emergency reactions. High-N individuals may have sympathetic reactions that are switched on easily. They may respond to events that wouldn't be challenging enough to produce any reaction in low-N people, who simply have a higher threshold.

Fortunately we don't have to take sides about how much of personality is genetic and how much is due to the environment that has shaped our lives. Just because some of our capacities may be hereditary doesn't mean that we can't change them. I was born with a particular heart and lungs. But within limits I can improve their performance and get fitter with each aerobic class.

Extravert, psychotic or conscientious?

Now try another six questions in Box 3.

They come from the same questionnaire and there are no prizes for guessing what they measure. Partly it is *sociability*, the second of our life-enhancing characteristics. But the whole twenty-one item scale from which these questions come actually measures a broader trait called *extraversion* or E. As well as being sociable, extraverts are lively, active, assertive, carefree, dominant and eager to seek out new and stimulating situations. People low on these traits, particularly on sociability, are known as *introverts*.

The EPQ also has a third personality dimension, one which

1. Do you prefer action to planning for action?
2. Are you happiest when you get involved in some project that calls for rapid action?
3. Do you usually take the initiative in making new friends?
4. Are you inclined to be quick and sure in your actions?
5. Would you rate yourself as a lively individual?
6. Would you be very unhappy if you were prevented from making numerous social contacts?

Box 3.   *Six questions that tell us something about how outgoing you are.*

measures 'tough-mindedness'. It is called *psychoticism* or P. High-P scorers are cold, aggressive and anti-social. They're self-centred, they lack empathy and they have little regard for others.

Eysenck's three-dimensional model of personality is among the simplest of the many that have been produced. The dimensions were chosen by looking at thousands of replies to questionnaire items, and then establishing statistically which characteristics go together – anxiety with guilt, sociability with self-assertion, impulsiveness with anti-social behaviour. The two major factors – neuroticism and extraversion – shake out of any analysis like this, whoever devised it. They are our first two life-affirming characteristics, two personality dimensions that seem beyond dispute.

But there are more complicated personality schemes, like the framework devised by Paul Costa Jr and Robert McCrae of the National Institute on Aging in Baltimore.[5] In their five-factor model they identify neuroticism, which they describe in terms of adjustment or emotional stability. Their scheme also includes extraversion, which describes the 'quality and intensity of inter-personal interaction; activity levels; and the need for excitement and stimulation'.

In addition, Costa and McCrae describe an attribute that they describe as *openness*, the 'seeking out and appreciation of experience for its own sake; a toleration for and exploration of the unfamiliar'. This trait reminds us of those life-affirmers who see the future as a challenge and welcome the opportunities it might bring.

They also describe a quality which they call *agreeableness*. Highly agreeable people are trusting, helpful and forgiving. At the opposite pole, those low on agreeableness are cynical, suspicious and manipulative (just the sort of pattern which, as we shall see, leads to coronary heart disease).

Finally, the Baltimore team believe that *conscientiousness* is also a basic personality dimension. At the positive end it consists of being organized, reliable and self-disciplined. People at the negative end are lazy, careless and unreliable. If that rings a bell in your mind it is because of George Vaillant's work on mental health. You will remember that the single personality characteristics shown by young men that most strongly predicted their adjustment in later life was the capacity to be 'practical and organized'.

Personalities that endure

The main reason why personality is so important to health is that its traits are extremely stable over time. Situations come and go but our personalities stay much the same (unless we make the effort to change them) for most of our lifetime. For example, in 1965 Costa and McCrae[6] gave a personality questionnaire to several hundred men of different ages. And when they repeated the same measurements on the same group of men in 1975, they found the results to be strikingly similar the second time around. Indeed, they reported finding 'about as high an agreement [as] we would expect if the tests had been given a few weeks apart instead of ten years'.

To make quite sure that the results were not just a lucky accident, they repeated the study using a different group of nearly 400 men. This time they also used a different personality scale. Testing the same men on two occasions six years apart showed a remarkable similarity in their scores for factors like sociability and emotional stability. Six years later still they performed the same tests for a third time. Comparing this last set of responses to the original replies they found that, even after twelve years, the men's personality measures remained very similar, though many aspects of their lives had changed. They summed up their conclusions in six words: 'stability, not change, typifies personality traits'.

As a rule then, people don't become more depressed, more introverted or more conservative with age. But then they don't become wiser or more mellow or emotionally better adjusted, either. Personality can be changed and life can be affirmed. But it is not an inevitable result of age or maturity. It takes work.

From cold hands to cancer

People who are psychologically distressed perceive their physical health to be bad as well. However healthy they really are, high N scorers expect the worst.

Some years ago groups of adults, students and prison inmates were asked how they had been feeling.[7] The simple question was 'Would you say your physical health this past year was excellent, good, fair, poor or very poor?' Their replies were then related to their degree of emotional distress, assessed through a series of different questions about whether they had been feeling lonely, depressed, restless or uneasy without knowing why.

Perceived health was reported to be worse among older people, among the poorly educated and among the unmarried. People's *actual* health status, judged from a list of symptoms that they were experiencing, had the strongest effect on how healthy they reported themselves to be (the results would have been suspect otherwise). But psychological distress (measured as unhappiness, nervousness or negative affect) was also found to predict poor perceptions of health, even after allowing for these other, more obvious features.

The researchers emphasized the link between the way we feel about our health and the way that we feel generally. Perceiving that we have a health problem creates a more general sense of emotional distress. And the same happens in reverse. Distressed people see their health as worse than it is. So when we are asked about our health, we 'respond to [our] total sense of well-being'. How we feel about our physical health both affects and is affected by how we feel psychologically. Or, to put it another way, we only have a sense of positive health when we are both feeling well and doing well.

Paul Costa and his co-workers[8] have also studied the reporting of physical symptoms over a wide range of complaints, including problems with the respiratory, cardiovascular and digestive systems. They were interested to see how these complaints increased with age. They also measured neuroticism. When they compared the two they found a striking association.

Among men with little neuroticism, cardiovascular symptoms

and problems with sight and hearing increased with age. But these emotionally stable men didn't complain of suffering from other illnesses. In contrast, the unstable men did. They reported more symptoms across the board. Their complaints showed no particular pattern, just a general tendency to say they felt ill. The researchers concluded that 'any manifestation of neuroticism – hostility, depression, anxiety, vulnerability to stress – is likely to be associated with diffuse psychosomatic complaints'. They also agree with earlier investigators who found that 'resentment, frustration, depression, anxiety and helplessness can be associated with a wide range of ailments from 'cold hands to cancer'. One of the most dramatic symptoms that they complain about is chest pain. Studies on both sides of the Atlantic have identified a group (mostly of men) who visit their doctors because of anginal pain. When their hearts are examined under X-ray they show no signs of coronary artery disease. But they do have high neuroticism scores. Indeed, high-N patients with clean coronary arteries may complain more about chest pain than low-N subjects whose arteries are badly damaged.[9]

So before patients with chest pain have their coronary arteries examined, a procedure which is neither pleasant nor without its hazards (to say nothing of the time and expense involved) it might make sense to measure their emotional stability. These N scores could then be incorporated in the patients' overall profile of risk factors, and they might help in deciding who should go for an invasive X-ray examination and who shouldn't.

Emotional instability doesn't have much in its favour. It distorts our perceptions of our health and also makes us unhappy. But interestingly enough, emotional over-control may have its hazards too. Those who score very low on N also seem to have an increased risk of developing cancer. I discussed this question with Hans Eysenck, a calm, rational man who rarely gets ruffled. He has a very low score on his own neuroticism measure, and he admitted to me that, as he approached seventy, he was starting to get a little concerned about it.

CHAPTER 5

Accentuate the Positive: Biased Thinking and Feeling

Positive affect; negative affect

By now you may have some ideas about your personality. But what about your feelings – how are they most of the time? To look at them more closely, try answering the questions in Box 4.

Score one point for 'yes', zero for 'no'. I'm not going to ask you to add the two halves together because they obviously measure different things. The first five questions tap into your positive sense of well–being. If you score 3 or more then things are going well for you and you feel good about yourself. The second five are just the reverse.

I have already said that when psychologists talk about emotion, they often refer to it as *affect*. And what we have here is a scale to measure positive and negative affect. Because it was devised by Norman Bradburn in the 1960s, it bears his name. Although it is only short, the Bradburn Affect Scale tells a lot about our emotional lives, and some of its conclusions are surprising.[1]

Most surprising of all, perhaps, is that most of us feel positive for most of the time. Most normal people answer yes to the positive items (except perhaps for being on top of the world) more often than they do to the negative ones. In other words, most people show more positive emotions than negative ones.

If we subtract someone's negative score from the score he gets on the positive questions we will end up with his 'affect balance'

During the past few weeks did you ever feel:

1. Pleased about having accomplished something?
2. That things were going your way?
3. Proud because someone had complimented you on something that you had done?
4. Particularly excited or interested in something?
5. On top of the world?

6. So restless you couldn't sit long in a chair?
7. Bored?
8. Depressed or very unhappy?
9. Very lonely or remote from other people?
10. Upset because someone criticized you?

Box 4. *We all have positive and negative feelings going on at the same time. How do they balance for you?*

– a single measure that sums up how he feels at that particular moment. To see how this relates to other aspects of their well-being, we could ask people to tell us how happy they were feeling at the same time that they completed the Bradburn Scale. We would expect those with a high score to say that they were happy, whilst people low on positive and high on negative feelings (low affect balance) might say that they weren't.

And this is exactly what Bradburn found when several thousand people were asked about their happiness and affect together. These findings have since been confirmed many times. So affect balance is a good indicator of a person's current level of psychological well-being, better than either the positive or negative feelings taken on their own.

Satisfied with life?

Positive affect relates to being involved with people. Sociability and positive emotions go together. Negative affect goes with worry, tension and the reporting of 'psychosomatic' symptoms. But interestingly enough, positive emotions seem to have little effect on say, anxiety, any more than negative affects seem to predict sociability. The two seem to be largely independent of each other.

Affect balance isn't purely an American invention. People react in a similar way in Great Britain. The Bradburn Scale was given to nearly a thousand randomly chosen people in the United Kingdom in the mid-1970s.[2] British subjects also said yes more often to the positive than to the negative items.

In the British sample too, positive and negative affect were not related to each other. But as we could expect by now, negative affect was strongly related to anxiety and to aches and pains, headaches and palpitations. There was a particularly strong link between negative affect and people describing themselves as 'feeling generally run down'.

Positive affect wasn't related to any of these problems. But it was higher in people belonging to some sort of group, like a sports or social club. And, as Bradburn had found, it was strongly associated with a person's social status. Money may not buy well-being, but it certainly helps.

Women had more negative affect than men and younger people had higher levels of both positive and negative emotion than their elders. It seems that as we get older 'life becomes progressively more bland'.

The British survey also included questions about happiness. People were asked how happy they were these days, how far they were managing to get the things they wanted out of life, and how satisfied they were with their lives as a whole. Affect balance was found to be a strong predictor of both happiness and satisfaction.

Two dimensions of mood

A rather different way to study emotions is to have people look at a list of adjectives that describe various moods and to ask them to check off the ones that correspond to how they are feeling right now.

When people's moods are recorded every day, then examined by computer, it becomes clear that they fall on two different dimensions.[3] One axis of 'positive affect' has, at its high end, mood words that people check off, like *interested*, *delighted*, *enthusiastic* and *excited*. At the low end come moods like *sleepy*, *sluggish*, and *tired*. In contrast, a second axis of 'negative affect' runs from moods like *hostile*, *disturbed* and *upset* to those with less negative content, like *at ease* and *calm*. These two dimensions are separate from each other. There is little correlation between them.

Analyses of literally hundreds of responses to various mood questionnaires confirms the existence of these two major emotional factors.[4] Positive affect relates to pleasurable, aroused, engaged mood states – 'the extent to which a person avows a zest for life'. In some studies the high pole of positive affect is high energy; in others it is sociability – notice just how closely these two are linked. At the lower pole of the positive dimension are words like *sleepy, tired* and *sluggish*.

Negative affect emerges as the second and independent factor. People at the high end feel upset or unpleasantly aroused. At the lower pole we find words like *calm, placid* and *carefree*. Notice too that low positive and high negative ends are not the same. One is relaxed, the other is uptight.

We can draw a map of these mood dimensions. The angle between two dimension lines shows how close the link is between them. The smaller the angle the greater the similarity. The angle disappears altogether when they overlap completely. But when two factors do not correlate at all we draw them at right angles, and this is exactly what we see in Box 5.

The axes of positive and negative affect intersect. Each has a high and a low end, and the mood words associated with each end are shown around the edge. Times when we feel high positive and low negative affect together will be experienced as pleasant. We feel happy or satisfied. By contrast, high negative and low positive affect combine to give us an unpleasant time, when we may feel sorry, or lonely, or simply unhappy.

These two dimensions also act as a map to locate the four human temperaments – the personality types that were first described by the ancient Greeks. It doesn't take too much imagination to see sanguine people as experiencing a lot of high positive affect while the melancholics feel low levels of positive affect most of the time. In contrast, choleric and phlegmatic types spend most of their lives feeling high or low levels of negative emotion.

This old Greek idea has been brought up to date. Box 6 shows the personality dimensions from the EPQ. Since extraversion and neuroticism are also largely independent of each other, they are drawn here at right angles. On this scheme the sanguine person comes out as the stable extravert. The adjectives around the edge of his quadrant describe his particular characteristics – sociable,

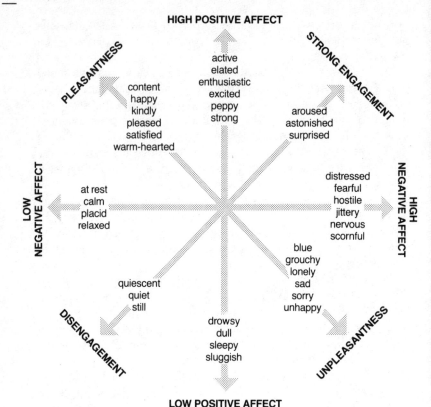

Box 5. *Recording people's daily moods shows that they fall along two separate dimensions corresponding to positive and negative affect. The way that any of us are feeling right now can be located in this two-dimensional space.*

easy-going, carefree and so on. In contrast, melancholics are now seen to be unstable introverts, moody, pessimistic and unsociable.

Independent emotions

So it takes not one, but two dimensions to pin down how we are feeling. For example, some people will describe being happy as having a zest for life and a joy in living. Others will equate happiness with contentment, and still others with relief. Obviously, the simple-minded notion of a single dimension running from feeling good to feeling bad just doesn't fit.

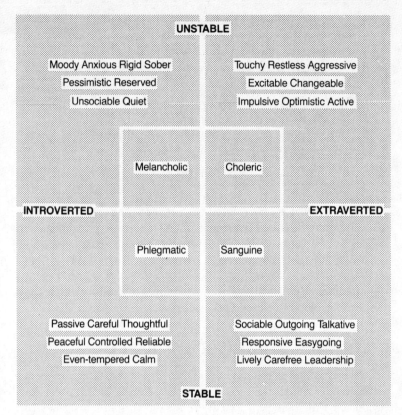

Box 6. *The four temperaments of the ancient Greeks are different combinations of neuroticism and extraversion. Although our actual behaviour depends on the situation we are in, stable extraverts, for example, will generally be more easygoing than pessimistic, unstable introverts. And, although we do shift around in this space, most of us spend most of our time in one quadrant or another.*

But why should the positive and negative feelings in people's lives be independent? To some extent it is because our emotional reactions depend on the events that are happening to us. We react positively to those life events that we want to happen, and negatively to those that we don't. But the events themselves are largely independent, for most of us at least. So our reaction to them will be independent as well.

Peter Warr and his colleagues in Sheffield confirmed this idea.[5] Desirable life events were found to relate to positive but not negative affect. In contrast, negative affect went with negative events.

1. In uncertain times, I usually expect the best.
2. I always look on the bright side of things.
3. I'm always optimistic about my future.
4. I'm a believer in the idea that 'every cloud has a silver lining'.
5. If something can go wrong for me, it will.
6. I hardly ever expect things to go my way.
7. Things rarely work out the way I want them to.
8. I rarely count on good things happening to me.

Box 7.   *Are you an optimist?*

Of course, affect is also related to personality. Running the tests together, the Sheffield team confirmed that positive and negative affect were strongly related to extraversion and neuroticism. But extraversion had no influence on negative emotions. Nor did neuroticism influence positive feelings. So emotional reactions are also independent because the personality dimensions on which they depend are not correlated with each other.

Are you an optimist?

We have talked a lot about the health consequences of neuroticism. But what about extraversion? What is the greatest contribution that being an extravert makes to mind–body-health? No prizes for guessing. It is the fact that most of the time extraverts are optimistic. Box 7 shows a set of eight statements that you may or may not agree with. Try them. They are designed to find out whether you too are an optimist or not.

The first four are obviously endorsed by optimistic people. The second four, where the statement is deliberately turned round, are denied by those of us with an optimistic bias. And most people, when we tap into their optimism with a scale like this, come out on the positive side.

The researchers who devised it, Michael Scheier from Carnegie-Mellon and Charles Carver from the University of Miami, believe that optimism is a built-in feature of many people's personalities.[6] Optimists expect the best to occur most of the time and in most situations. And this expectation stays with them as they get older.

The scale is not designed to assess *why* optimistic people think as they do. Perhaps they believe that they have skills or resources to deal with any difficulty. They may simply think that they are lucky, or that the Lord will provide. But whatever the reason, their optimism gives them an edge.

As we go through life, Scheier and Carver argue, we are constantly faced with situations that are not what we expect. They call for some action on our part to get our lives back in line. People with an optimistic outlook persist longer before they finally give up. They tend to clock up more successes. They also find changes less disruptive to their daily routine.

Of course, their optimism is partly due to a history of successes in the past, to a mastery of different situations. So it is not a surprise that people scoring high on the optimism scale also feel more in control of their lives and have more self-esteem than those scoring low. And when measures are taken to assess their feelings of hopelessness, depression, anxiety and the perception of stress, optimistic people come out lower.

There may be other reasons, too, why optimists have more success in minimizing the difficulties in their lives. One is that in going after what they want, and in dealing with situations that go wrong, they don't try to achieve their long-term aims at a stroke. Instead, they break down what they have to do into a series of tasks (what psychologists call 'sub-goals') and deal with them one at a time. Their optimism helps them in seeing each of these sub-goals through. This approach is far more likely to work for most of us than pursuing the vision of some perfect and completed goal that may be almost impossible to achieve. Looking that far ahead simply provides more opportunities for discouragement and, as we shall see, for unhappiness.

Finally, of course, optimists may be more successful in dealing with their problems simply because they face them early on, before they have had time to build up. They use an early-warning system and an active form of coping, instead of retreating from their difficulties and denying their existence.

Summing up the way that people high on the optimism scale approach their lives in general, Scheier and Carver suggest that 'optimists employ the approach to coping that in most life circumstances is most adaptive, least dysfunctional'.

Stamina in later life

This is borne out if we look at what happens to people in later life. We all know old people who suffer as a consequence of their years, who will tell you that there is nothing graceful about growing old. But there are others who remain active and involved, who function well and who enjoy their lives despite their age.

It would be too simplistic to point to any single factor and say *that* is what marks out the active optimistic elderly from the rest. Even so, some factors are more obvious than others. Elizabeth Colerick at Duke University Medical Center suggests that 'although physical strength often wanes in later life, internal stamina reflects well-tested convictions that obstacles are surmountable and that personal growth is an outcome of personal struggle'.[7]

She studied a group of men and women aged seventy to eighty, dividing them, according to the opinions of people who knew them well, and then as a result of an interview, into those with high stamina and those whose levels of stamina were low.

Of course, 'stamina' is a difficult term to define. In this study it was thought to be made up of several features. They included the capacity for personal growth, involving self-expression and curiosity; self awareness; the capacity to draw on past experience when dealing with current problems and the ability to carry on daily living undaunted by setbacks.

Psychologists interviewed these people in depth, to discover how they dealt with the problems in their lives. Those with high stamina stood out. They said things like 'Don't let . . . problems sit out there in front of you blinding your vision. Use them to drive you forward. Use hardship in a positive way.' Another commented that 'setbacks are a part of the game. I've had 'em, I have them now and I've got plenty more ahead of me. Seeing this – the big picture – puts it all into perspective, no matter how bad things get.'

The life histories of these high-stamina old people, compared to those who simply fell apart, showed that they had not experienced *more* adversity in their lives. Rather they had been able to view these bad periods with a feeling of *triumph*, a 'sense of mastery, of personal control or efficacy, of optimism about the course of difficult times. A triumphant outlook belongs to individuals who believe in their ability to surmount life problems posed by changing circumstances.'

And what gives them the stamina that allows them to feel triumphant in this way? Analysis of the interviews showed that it is linked to marriage, to higher education and to good health. The connection with marriage won't surprise anyone who has seen figures on the disruptive effects of divorce or separation on both mental and physical health. The link with education is less expected, but it is very strong and recalls other data that show poor education to be one of the most powerful factors predicting a heart attack.

And, of course, the link with good health in the past is also clear enough. A person's physical capacity sets limits on her stamina. It does so, says Colerick, by 'shaping personal patterns of appraisal'. In other words, the way we see events and our ability to influence them is affected by our perception of how much vigour and energy we have at our disposal.

Physical health is feeling well and doing well.

So these findings show that old people with high stamina have come to regard change as inevitable, challenging and manageable – a life-affirming quality that is one component of personality 'hardiness'. Their view of change is part of a more general ability to see events with 'an optimistic, triumphant outlook ... which increases coping resourcefulness in old age'. But good health is essential. A history of poor health 'increases vulnerability by triggering a 'defeated' orientation to later life change'.

Unfortunately, in this sort of study it is simply not possible to say whether good health creates a sense of triumph or *vice versa*. But there are other findings that link optimism with health and they strongly suggest that it is optimism that comes first. We have glanced at them already when we looked at college men who were 'practical and organized'. But the Grant Study has had a new lease of life since that report appeared in 1979. And its most recent findings are in many ways the most intriguing.

Internal, stable and global

Martin Seligman ('Marty' to his friends) is everyone's idea of a successful psychologist. As a lecturer he is quick and witty. I have seen him hold huge audiences spellbound. As a researcher, his group at the University of Pennsylvania have contributed probably more than any other single team to our understanding of why some people can persevere, even when they are faced with massive problems, whilst others simply become hopeless and give up trying.

The work goes back two decades. It started with animal experiments in which dogs were exposed to small but uncontrollable electric shocks. They simply couldn't escape from them. Very soon they stopped trying, and even when they were given an escape route they didn't take it. They had developed what Seligman's group called 'learned helplessness'. Some human beings too, when faced with situations that they can't control, rapidly lose their motivation even to try to get on top of them. They lose the ability to learn new approaches that might get them out of trouble, and as a result they show a huge drop in self-esteem.

The question is why some of us feel this sense of personal inadequacy while others don't. Seligman and his colleagues suggest that the people who go under most quickly are those who make three assumptions about the problems that they face.

For example, let's assume that a well-qualified young man goes for a job interview and gets rejected. He asks himself, 'Why didn't I get it?' Either he thinks, 'It's because they didn't like the look of me', or he may say, 'It's probably because they haven't got the money to take on any more people at my level.' How will it affect his future? He may decide, 'It's always going to be like this, I'll never get a job,' or he may console himself with the thought that 'The problem's only short-term. The demand for my sort of skills will take off in the next few months.' Finally, he may think, 'If I can't even impress people at an interview, there's not much I can do in the rest of my life either.' Or he may decide, 'Failing a job interview doesn't have to ruin everything else that I do.'

Note the difference between these two ways of looking at failure. In the first, he believes that the reasons are *internal* ('it's my fault'), *stable* ('it will always be like this') and *global* ('it affects my whole life'). But the second way of looking at the problem is much more healthy. The failure is seen as *external* ('they can't take me on though they want to'), *unstable* ('it won't last for long') and *specific* ('it only affects part of my life').

In a now famous research paper Seligman and his colleagues suggested that the way that people habitually explain such bad events to themselves (in technical language, the 'attributions' that they make for failure) strongly influence who becomes helpless and loses her self-esteem.[8] It is those who attribute bad events to internal, stable and global causes – those with a *pessimistic* explanatory style – who get depressed[9] and go under.

Into the CAVE

But who are the vulnerable ones? How are we to tell one person's explanatory style from another's?

There are two ways. One is to ask them questions about how they would react to a series of hypothetical events and what they would be thinking at the time. The other is much more immediate. It involves actually examining what people said or wrote about a real bad event at the time that it was actually happening.

This method looks at people's diaries or old letters or what they said at interviews about a particular problem that they had experienced and *why* they thought it had occurred. The procedure is called the 'content analysis of verbatim explanations' or CAVE. Though it hardly seems a reliable method of getting at people's attributions, the Philadelphia group claim that different listeners can reach surprisingly close agreement about the speaker's explanatory style when they have short extracts of his comments about success and failure to work with.

They have also found that, like his personality traits, someone's explanatory style is extremely stable over the years. They interviewed a group of elderly people and asked them about their current lives. They also examined diaries or letters that they had written fifty years or so earlier. They found that the subject's explanatory style for negative events was surprisingly similar on the two occasions, half a century apart. So they concluded that our way of explaining bad events is an enduring risk factor, say for depression, and one that persists over our whole life-span.

But more interesting still is the link between this type of pessimistic explanatory style and physical health.

Maintaining the habit

Studies that we will describe later on the survival of breast-cancer patients have clearly shown how a helpless and hopeless attitude is associated with a shorter survival. Seligman's group were impressed by this work but were more interested in knowing how pessimism influences other aspects of health.

So one of his associates, Christopher Peterson, looked at how habitual styles of attribution affected the reporting of health complaints in a group of college students.[10] He gave them a questionnaire to measure their attributional styles. He then recorded their illness reports over the next month and their visits to the doctor during the following year.

Peterson found that those students who viewed their failures in a stable and global (i.e. a hopeless) way had more health complaints over the next month and paid more visits to the doctor during the following year. And this was true even allowing for any levels of ill-health or depression at the time when the initial measurements were being made.

Where did this link between style and health actually come from? He examined the students' health habits, like whether they ate breakfast, whether they exercised and whether they smoked or drank heavily. He found that those who offered stable and global explanations for the bad events in their lives were less likely to look after themselves, perhaps because they simply felt less able to change their bad habits.

But interesting as they are, these findings are no more than suggestive. They only relate to self-reports of illness, and we have seen how illness reporting is influenced by factors like neuroticism. And practically all the illnesses that were reported were minor infections – colds, flu and sore throats. But to rank as an important factor in the mind–body equation helplessness (as measured by explanatory style) has to be more than just a risk factor for the reporting of minor infections.

And it is. Which brings us back to the Grant Study.

Thirty-five years on

You will remember that the men in the Grant Study were students at Harvard in the early 1940s. In 1946 many of them answered a series of questions about their war-time experiences, particularly about how successful or otherwise they had been in handling difficult situations. Forty-odd years later the replies provided by ninety-nine of them were given the CAVE technique to establish how far the attributions that they held about their problems were stable, global and internal.

Their ratings on all three features were combined to form a single score that reflected the men's overall attributional style. High scorers had the most negative attributions. In 1946 they said things like 'What I feel is characterized more by confusion than by sense.' At the other (low) extreme, one man who had been accused of betraying a confidence in the army said simply that the problem had arisen not through any fault of his, but because 'The officer had not bothered to get all the facts.' Each man received his attribution rating on the basis of these sample interview replies (using on average about ten statements per subject).

The great advantage of the Grant Study is that each man had also been examined by his doctor every five years from age twenty-five to fifty, and all of these records were still available.

Comparing the explanatory-style scores with the health records was most revealing.[11] From age thirty to forty there was no particular relation between style and health. It's hardly surprising that psychological factors don't show their effects in such a young, healthy population. Biological effects swamp them out. However, by age forty-five the picture was quite different. There was a strong association between the two. Men with a pessimistic style had distinctly more illness than those who had found more optimistic explanations for their problems. And, though the link got weaker in the fifties and beyond, it was still positive.

Seligman and Vaillant decided to apply an even more stringent test to their data. Everyone's health as it is measured right now depends quite strongly on how healthy they were, say, five years ago. But – making allowances for the influence of the last five yearly health report, the study team still found a link between pessimism and health for men aged thirty-five and forty. The results were a convincing demonstration of what Vaillant himself had meant ten years earlier when he said 'Good mental health retards mid-life deterioration in physical health.'

What links pessimism with illness?

Remember that the complaints that the unhealthy men suffered from were of all kinds – back trouble and gout, diabetes and arthritis, heart disease and cancer. Their pessimism wasn't linked to any particular disease. Somehow it was affecting their physical health as a whole.

But how?

As the investigators themselves put it, 'We do not know the mechanism by which pessimistic explanatory style puts one at risk for eventual poor health.' But like Carver and Scheier they saw several possibilities. Perhaps people with a pessimistic outlook simply become more passive when they get ill, and don't seek medical advice. Or perhaps they don't look after themselves in the first place (remember Peterson's students). Maybe they don't realize that they can do things to keep healthy. Or maybe they simply feel that more or less anything they do will prove to be useless.

Then again, people with negative explanations tend to be lonely and socially isolated. But we will see how social support is almost essential to stay healthy. So perhaps explanatory style affects long-term health by damaging their chance of making relationships.

There are other possibilities as well. A joint investigation between researchers in Philadelphia and Yale has found that a pessimistic style is linked with disturbances in the immune system. So too is being in poor health and being depressed, features that often go with it. But pessimism exerts its effects even when these other influences are allowed for.

Can a pessimistic outlook influence our immune system directly? The answer must be yes. The way that we assess situations determines our emotional responses to them. Emotions release hormones and hormones can influence immunity. But it is important to realize that this process doesn't happen (or *needn't* happen) automatically, without our knowing about it. In the last analysis it is the way that we think and feel that triggers the immune change. This is why Seligman's team are the first to admit that the disturbance in their patient's lymphocytes might actually be due to passivity or isolation or a lack of self-care.

Impractical and disorganized

Which brings us to the final, and I think most likely, explanation. People with stable, global and internal explanations for their problems are simply poor problem-solvers. As a result, they may suffer more adverse life-events than optimists, simply because they don't see them coming and act soon enough to avoid them. And when the events do arrive they may have a greater impact, simply because the pessimist has little idea how to deal with them. What these people lack is the ability to be 'practical and organized'.

Having said that, I doubt very much whether any *single* mechanism will explain the increased risk of ill-health that the pessimist runs, though I believe that his failure to cope will emerge as the main contender.

But, even before the explanations are all in, a more pressing question is whether this pessimistic explanatory style can be changed. Seligman, Vaillant and a host of therapists believe that it can, though they haven't succeeded in demonstrating it yet. And so do I, or I wouldn't have begun this book. Boosting our optimism is a key part of what I've called 'life-enhancement'. There are many groups of researchers currently trying to put together a 'treatment package' intended to do just that.

But to understand how, we need to know more about why optimism fails in the first place. To begin with, we need to know why people get depressed.

CHAPTER 6

In and Out of Depression

―――――

Take a look at the list of statements in Box 8.

How many of them refer to you, and the way that you are feeling right at this moment?

I feel blue or sad.
I feel I have nothing to look forward to.
As I look back on my life all I can see is a lot of failures.
I am dissatisfied with everything.
I am disgusted with myself.
I feel I would be better off dead.

Box 8. *Six questions from one of the best-known questionnaires to tell you if you are depressed.*

Measuring depression

The chances are that most of you reading this won't agree with all of these items. But, if you do, you may be suffering from a mild form of depression. I say 'may be' because no one can have their mental state diagnosed from only six items like this. The statements themselves come from a larger questionnaire that is used to assess whether people are depressed or not, and if so then how bad their problem is. Since it was devised by Aaron T. Beck ('Tim' to those who work with him) of the University of Pennsylvania, it is called the *Beck Depression Inventory* or BDI.[1]

Looking at the BDI and how it was put together tells us a lot about the nature of depression.

In the early 1960s the most influential view about why people get depressed was provided by psychoanalysts. Put crudely, they maintain that depression is the result of anger turned inwards, something that children do to avoid the rejection which they fear may result if they let it out on other people, and particularly their parents. This analytic view is still alive and well, though it exists in many different forms, all of them expressed in much more complicated terms than this. Critics of this analytic approach point out that its concern with events that occurred a long time ago doesn't help in diagnosing the problem in the here and now. What Beck (then very much a psychoanalytic therapist himself) wanted to do was to learn more about the features that go with depression – to make them more easily observable and even measurable. He selected a set of the symptoms that he found among depressed patients in his practice and produced a questionnaire to measure each of them, on a scale of 0 to 3. It consists of twenty-one different items that distinguish depressed people from normals.

Box 8 only shows the questions that relate to sadness, pessimism, lack of satisfaction with life, self-hate and the wish to punish oneself. But in addition the BDI measures crying, irritability and withdrawal from people, the inability to make decisions, sleep disturbances, lack of energy, loss of weight and loss of any interest in sex. It is only one of several ways of assessing a person's depression. But it has been so successful because its authors were able to observe very carefully just how their depressed patients differed from more normal people.

What does depression mean?

'Depression' is a much abused word. Many people say 'God, I'm so depressed' when they simply mean that they are feeling sad. And certainly low spirits are often a part of depression. But a depressed patient's moods often centre around a loss of interest in things, a sense of grey emotional flatness or emptiness rather than feelings of sadness.

Depressed people not only experience an *emotional* distortion, a slippage in how they feel. Their patterns of *thinking* change too. The BDI shows just how depressed people reproach themselves for what they have done (or failed to do). Beck himself identified three separate patterns of distorted thinking that they suffer from. They have a sense of personal failure, a feeling that the whole world is in chaos and a belief that this whole awful situation is going to drag on into the future with no hope of it changing. This sense of being helpless to alter things at present and hopeless about being able to do so in future is the very crux of depressive thinking. And of course it's very similar to Seligman's idea of pessimistic attribution. As we go on we will find other areas where the two overlap.

But even a flat emotional state and a pattern of hopeless thinking are not enough to diagnose someone as having a depressive illness. Many of us suffer from short-lived periods of painful thinking and feeling, but they quickly clear up again. For a diagnosis of clinical depression to be made by a psychiatrist, there have to be other problems as well. Common ones are a sense of irritation and a feeling of not being able to concentrate on things, together with a 'washed-out' feeling of having no energy – being tired all the time. Sleep problems are also common, either difficulties with getting to sleep or else waking early in the morning and not being able to drop off again. At the same time, people disturbed enough to be described as clinically depressed are usually slow in everything they do. Some experts even believe that depression is essentially a problem that all stems from this slowing down or 'retardation'.

There are two other factors that clinicians look for before they make the diagnosis. The first is that the impairment must interfere with the patients' normal social life. Depressives become withdrawn into themselves. The second is that the problem should have gone on for some time – at least two weeks, and some specialists say at least a month. When, and only when, most of these criteria are fulfilled, can the person be said to be suffering from clinical depression. Any problem with thinking and feeling that doesn't have at least some of these associated features may be very unpleasant for us to go through. But in technical language it doesn't constitute what psychiatrists call a 'case'.

How many kinds of depression?

There have been many attempts over the last twenty years to divide depression into various types, in the hope that they may have different causes that can be treated in different ways. One approach separates those people who vary between being depressed and being 'normal' from those whose mood swings are wider. As well as going into depression this latter group also swing as far in the opposite direction. They show periods of excitement and elation known as *hypomania*, or in extreme cases mania itself. During their hypomanic episodes, sufferers are thinking things like 'Nothing can hold me back; I can do anything I set my mind to; I am filled with energy; my powers are unlimited.'

Until recently, hypomania has had a bad press. Psychiatrists have emphasized its impatient, explosive nature. Certainly the patient's family and friends become stressed and exhausted trying to deal with the blast of energy that they receive. As one specialist puts it, 'hypomania is a nuisance; mania is a bloody nuisance', both for the therapist and the relatives.

In the last few years this view has changed a little. Some manic episodes are terrifying even for the patient himself, and the excessive generosity that manics show can well bankrupt their family. But it is sometimes said that mania, or at least hypomania, isn't all bad. The energy that it releases may allow the hypomanic to work intensely for a long time and to have flashes of creative inspiration. Salesmen, performers and others who have to appear before the public may find the extra lift just what they need to get their message across successfully. Unfortunately real creativity has to be structured to achieve anything, and so these bursts of frantic, over-aroused, disorganized activity are unlikely to produce much of lasting value.

Even so, there is no doubt that 'bipolar' patients themselves (those who swing between the two extremes) do value their upbeat moods.[2] One study in Los Angeles found that 90 per cent regarded their sensitivity to be increased because of their mood swings and more than three-quarters said that their productivity was boosted as a result. Two out of three also felt that their sexual intensity was increased during their manic phases, and I have known the wives of hypomanic patients who also would certainly agree.

So hypomanics love their highs. I remember a general practitioner in her early thirties once telling me that she had gone through a very grey winter. It wasn't the sense of depression that bothered her so much as the lack of even a single burst of mania. Many manics are reluctant to take any medication that brings them down. And when they want to feel sharp – perhaps to deal with some important event in their lives – they may come off it altogether. The consequences can be disastrous.

'Bipolar' depression is clearly different from the 'unipolar' illness (where the patient only varies between being depressed and being normal). Another distinction that is sometimes made is between 'endogenous' depression, which is believed to be due to some biochemical disturbance in the brain, and the so-called 'exogenous' form, where the trigger is thought to lie in the outside world.

The symptoms in endogenous depression more often respond to treatment with anti-depressant drugs or electroconvulsive therapy. With exogenous (sometimes called *reactive*) depression, where external events are thought to cause the depressive episodes, the response to medical treatment may not be so good. What the patient has to do is to deal with the events. And they certainly take their toll. Reactive depression is ten times more common than the endogenous and bipolar varieties put together.[3]

Triggers for depression

But it is pointless to ask 'What causes depression?' and expect to get any simple answer like faulty brain chemistry (though bipolar and endogenous depression have a major 'biological' aspect) or faulty thinking (though much depression is associated with distorted cognitions) or life events (though disturbing events are common before the onset of many depressive episodes). We now know that there are multiple triggers for depression and that they combine together in various ways.

For example, depressed people may feel helpless because of their sense of being rejected by others.[4] This feeling triggers a particular programme in their brains that slows down their behaviour and leads to the usual pattern of depressed activity. This may be a very old pathway, arising early in our evolutionary history. It may have been designed to conserve our energy at a time when we are most vulnerable because of our social disconnection. This is an interesting idea because of what it says about the *interaction* between our social environment and our brain biochemistry. Neither might cause depression on their own, but the combination certainly can.

Others believe that the lack of pleasure that depressives feel results from a different kind of interaction. Some aspect of the particular person's make-up, like having standards that are too high or finding difficulty in joining social groups, combines with life events like having to face extra demands at work or losing a loved one. Each affects him in the area where he is most vulnerable because of the other.[5]

There are many examples of this type of interactive effect. But what about the individual features that are involved in the mix? There is a long list of them. It starts with a change in the season.

Spring sickness

Despite folklore about the young man's fancy, there is not much evidence that human beings copulate more in the spring than at other times of the year. According to workers at the Clarke Institute of Psychiatry in Toronto, the thing that does peak in spring is not sex, but depression.[6] Recording the frequency of depression over a period of six years consistently showed a peak (seemingly of *endogenous* depression) in the spring with a second peak (apparently of *reactive* depression) in the autumn.

They claim to have found ninety-day cycles in human mood for both uni- and bipolar depressives, as well as similar cycles in 'normal' people. It seems that we all have regular mood swings. Those people whom we call 'depressed' simply swing further. It is sunlight that apparently drives the cycles, and, in those people who are more genetically disposed, it can drive them into clinical depression.

Feeling ill, feeling bad

A more obvious cause of depression, but one that is often overlooked, is physical illness. When we feel ill, we feel bad. A breakdown in physical health can cause psychological problems directly by causing changes in the brain, say altering its blood supply or the balance of neurohormones. Alternatively, it can change our sleep patterns or our pain threshold.

But a physical illness can also have a less direct influence on our perception of what we are capable of doing. The realization that we don't function as well as we did, that there are things that we can't do any more, and that we are not as productive as we would like to be, can itself be extremely depressing. So too can the thought that our illness restricts our social lives – reducing the number of people we make contact with and perhaps changing the strength of those relationships that we do manage to maintain.

This is particularly true for serious diseases like coronary problems, cancer and arthritis. But I personally believe that a great deal of minor illness often leads to people getting mildly depressed as well.

Depression and post-viral syndrome

Some years ago a very detailed study of physical illness and depression was carried out in a group of over 700 volunteers in Los Angeles by Carol Aneshensel and colleagues.[7] They interviewed all of these people four times in the course of a year. At each interview they asked them about the physical complaints they had been feeling during the previous week. The research team used several questionnaires for depression. By doing these interviews repeatedly they could assess how far being ill was related to being depressed on each visit, and how it related to the chance of becoming depressed in the future. They could also look at the reverse problem – at whether being depressed led the volunteer to report more physical illness.

They found that even minor illnesses like colds and flu, aches and pains, led to an instant increase in feelings of depression, compared to previous visits when the subjects were interviewed and found to have no physical symptoms. By contrast, being depressed led to a slight increase in the reporting of physical ill-health, but not on the same occasion. Depression was only linked to physical symptoms at the next interview.

The Los Angeles team concluded that a depressed mood may frequently result from even mild and common forms of physical disturbance. They stressed the way that having our activity restricted as a result of not being well can disrupt our ability to earn a living and can also affect the way that we relate to other people.

We can take these ideas a stage further. We may suffer from physical disorders that are so slight that we may not realize we have them. But our bodies are aware of the fact and communicate the information to our brain. The result is that we feel mildly depressed without ever knowing why.

For example, there is much current interest in the so-called post-viral fatigue syndrome. This complaint arises in those (fortunately few) individuals who suffer from a viral illness but who for some reason don't make a full recovery. The virus leaves them 'washed out' and generally weakened, often for weeks or months.

In Britain there is a well-recognized post-viral complaint called myalgic encephalomyopathy or ME – literally nerve, brain and muscle disease – that attacks several thousand people a year. It is thought to be due to a group of enteroviruses, viruses usually found in the gut. The best known is Coxsackie, named after a town in New York State where the first outbreak was reported.[8] Sufferers from ME feel tired or exhausted, especially after making any effort. They also have trouble concentrating and are very likely to feel depressed. In the United States a similar syndrome has been reported though the virus to blame is thought to be Epstein-Barr, the organisms that cause infectious mononucleosis.[9]

Though distressing, the depression associated with post-viral syndrome is easy to understand. It usually begins with a spell of illness and results directly from it. So post-viral fatigue syndrome represents a clearly definable problem. Fortunately, it is comparatively rare.

Perhaps I should explain what I mean. Specialists involved in the treatment of ME-sufferers estimate that there may be perhaps 100,000 sufferers in Britain, with say 10,000 new cases every year. I know of no similar estimate for the United States, but let us assume that it represents the same percentage of the population.

The problem is that we simply do not know how many of these patients were actually infected by a virus in the first place. The symptoms don't prove anything in this respect. *Proving* a viral origin requires complicated and expensive testing. As we will see in the last chapter, this is why the emphasis is shifting. Experts are now talking about patients with the *chronic fatigue syndrome* (CFS). They recognize that the patients are suffering from a seriously debilitating complaint but they do not necessarily link it to an earlier viral infection. In other words, when we look at fatigue as a whole, there are certainly far more people suffering from CFS than there are sufferers from 'pure' ME.

But there must be many occasions when we are fighting off a different viral infection, say flu or the common cold, when the complaint doesn't 'come out' and we suffer from what physicians call mild or 'sub-clinical' infection. Aneshensel found that depression follows after respiratory infections, but what about those occasions when we are not sure that we have such a problem? What we feel is a general draining of energy, a difficulty in coming to grips with what we have to do. But we don't know why until the cold breaks and we recognize the problem for what it is. Alternatively the episode may pass without us ever knowing what has caused it.

If physical health means 'doing well' then the sense that we aren't doing well for reasons that we don't understand is very likely to depress our mood. Once we start sneezing or shaking we almost experience a sense of relief. Now at least we know what is causing our depression. It's a viral infection and not some vague apprehension about the future.

And we don't need to stop at infection. There must be dozens of other reasons why our bodies feel vaguely uneasy and why we sense that we are not functioning as well as we would like to. For example, some therapists on the fringe of orthodox medicine believe that our blood sugar may fall to levels which are too low for us to function properly. However, they suggest that the levels we need vary for each one of us. So it is possible for you or me to have too little sugar in our blood to meet our individual needs. But at the same time it wouldn't be diagnosed because we would fall within the 'normal range' measured for the population as a whole.

The condition that results from this fall has been called 'functional hypoglycaemia'. Our capacity to function is reduced, though blood tests would not pick up the reason why. However, the sense of reduced capacity that goes with it might well affect our mood. If there is anything in this notion (which has yet to be proved), then low levels of blood sugar could also affect our brains directly. The resulting confusion, irritation and failure of concentration is likely to depress us all the more.

But why stop at blood sugar either? There is now a whole

subject called 'nutritional medicine' which deals with the effects of food, vitamins and trace elements on health and disease. A major concern of workers in this field is that although, in theory, we may be receiving adequate amounts of everything in our diet, we may nonetheless not be absorbing it all properly. So we may have functional deficiencies which again are difficult to detect. But our bodies may detect them as a mismatch between what we want to do and what we are capable of – as a feeling of not doing well.

Those people who sense this mismatch most severely will be those who most commonly feel lethargic, those who most frequently feel out of sorts, those who generally experience a wide range of bodily symptoms. In short, they are people who display high levels of neuroticism.

Back to personality

People with high scores on N are more prone to become depressed than those who score low. The reason is clear enough. If depression results from a feeling of incapacity (itself the consequence of some physical problem) then people high on negative affectivity will be the ones who feel their inadequacy in its most acute form. Their personality predisposes them to take a pessimistic view, and the lens through which they see the world will magnify any loss of power that they feel into a major problem.

Some specialists who don't accept ideas about personality as an enduring, biologically based reaction to the world often object that neuroticism predicts depression simply because the questions that are used to measure each of them are rather similar. The Eysenck Personality Questionnaire and the Beck Depression Inventory, for example, both enquire about unhappiness and the perception that life is getting out of control. So we should beware of inflating the relationship between them.

Even so, the connection between N and depression is a real one. One very careful study of over 1,000 women in New Zealand found that perhaps a quarter of the depression process could be explained by the women's neuroticism score.[10] And it is worth remembering that few of the well-known risk factors for disease, like hypertension or raised cholesterol, explain more than 10 or 15 per cent of the coronary risk. Seen in this light, neuroticism emerges as a powerful psychological predictor.

The same New Zealand study revealed another very interesting fact. High scores on N we're also linked to life events. As the authors put it, 'subjects scoring high on N have a tendency to report more adversity'. This may be because high N scorers actually *have* more life crises. It is easy to believe that high scorers attract more events by constantly creating difficulties for themselves. But there is another explanation too. Perhaps high N scorers *experience* their life events as being more negative. What are minor problems to other people tend to be disasters for them.

And it's life events themselves that have been the subject of some of the most elegant work on depression and its causes.

Social origins of depression

George Brown is a professor of sociology at London University. Because of his sociological background, he believes strongly that much depression is caused by the awful circumstances in which many people are forced to live their lives. And his own work has gone a long way towards proving it. His best-known results were published in 1978 in a book with his co-worker Tirril Harris. *Social Origins of Depression*[11] describes their study of over 400 working-class women in Camberwell in London.

Selected at random, these women took part in a detailed interview designed to explore their living conditions and to look for any significant life events that had happened to them over the course of the previous year. They also had a detailed psychological examination, to see how many of them had become clinically depressed during the same time period. The start of their depression was dated as accurately as possible. Links were explored between the time that it appeared and both major life events and what Brown calls *on-going difficulties* in the woman's life – situations like her husband's constant drinking.

To express their results very briefly, they found that one woman in twelve developed a clinical depression during the year in question. Of those who did, nearly 90 per cent were found to have had some severe life event or major difficulty during the nine months or so before the interview, compared with only 30 per cent of the 'non-cases', women free of depression. So life events seemed to play a major role.

Brown's team adopted a form of interview where the events were recorded as the women described them. But their seriousness or otherwise was decided upon, not by the woman herself, but by a panel of expert raters who agreed on how significant such an occurrence (say a death or serious illness in the family, or a major problem with the house) would be for an average woman living under these conditions.

This type of approach represents an enormous amount of work for the research team. But it was thought to be necessary to minimize the memory biases that can creep in so easily when people were asked how significant a particular life event was in their past.

Severe events or major difficulties (so-called *provoking factors*) didn't on their own predict who would become depressed. They only did so if the woman was also the victim of one or more *vulnerability factors*. These factors were a strange group. They consisted of either not having anyone, particularly a man, to confide in; of having three children under the age of fourteen still at home or of the woman herself having lost her own mother before the age of eleven. Later findings showed that a husband's unemployment might also be a factor increasing the wife's vulnerability to depression.

Confounding the critics

Just how well does this combination of provocation and vulnerability really predict who will become depressed? And how does this curious collection of features in a woman's life hang together? In other words what, if anything, do they have in common?

George Brown himself is very conscious of the fact that, even among women experiencing serious events, only one in five becomes depressed enough to be called a psychiatric case. He agrees that it is very difficult to predict what will happen to any particular individual because people vary so much. For example, if we look at the risk of cancer developing in a cigarette-smoker, we find that most smokers, even heavy smokers, don't get the disease. On the basis of the usual statistics, smoking explains less than one-hundredth of 1 per cent of the cancer risk. That doesn't mean that it's not important. All it does is stress the difficulty of predicting it for you or me.[12]

In the same way, provoking agents *don't* produce depression in most people. But a large proportion of the women who did become depressed *had* suffered a serious event before their break-down and this finding has now been confirmed among literally thousands of women in England, Scotland, Canada and Australia.

Troubles, they say, never come singly, and some combinations have a devastating effect on our morale. For example, women suffering a severe loss and at the same time experiencing a serious on-going difficulty were *fifteen* times more likely to become depressed than those with no losses and no long-term problems. [13]

I keep referring to women, because they have been studied most closely. But other research is starting to show that some-thing similar may happen in men. [14] Sometimes aspects of our lives that we can deal with one at a time simply come together like a conjunction of planets. The combined blow is too much for us to take. We find ourselves suddenly helpless in the face of an overwhelming mixture of circumstances.

For example, Brown's team talked to one woman, a widow with three children in their teens living at home, in a house with-out electricity or gas because she couldn't pay the bills. Her six-teen year-old son was on probation for violence. But the event that finally crashed her into depression was being told that she could get sixty days in jail if she fell behind with paying his £400 fine. She saw no way to find the money: she was left completely without hope.

Helpless and hopeless

And hopelessness is the *key* feature that all these provocations and vulnerabilities have in common. At one time Brown and Harris thought that vulnerability factors acted by reducing our self-esteem. People with high self-esteem who feel that they can master situations are much less vulnerable to provoking factors than those who don't. But their ideas have now gone further.

I asked George Brown what he currently thought were the key features that led to depression. [15] He said that each of the vulnerability factors that they had discovered certainly might act to lower a woman's sense of self-esteem. But, if she could call on support from other people, then she might still be able to avoid getting depressed. Having someone to talk to might stop her from feeling hopeless.

Often the seeds of hopelessness are sown a long way back in

the past. The final jolt is devastating simply because it makes us see a reality that we have long chosen to ignore. As Brown puts it, 'Life events may be finally bringing home to us things that we have realized but failed to acknowledge for years – that our marriage is not a success, that we are not on top of our job, that we have been rejected.' It is only when a particular set of life events finally forces us up against the full implications of this reality that we are likely to slide into hopelessness.

For most of the time, Brown suggests, 'we are all hopelessly optimistic'. But sometimes our optimism needs to be re-examined. We need to look again at the assumptions on which our lives are based. 'The emotion of sadness or depression . . . tells us there is something wrong. . . . Depression helps to break through the unrealistic level of optimism that many of us use to evaluate the world. It concentrates our attention on the fact that something needs to be changed.'

A role for brain chemistry?

As a sociologist, concerned with the way that our environment moulds our day-to-day lives, George Brown believes that the most important factor affecting recovery from depression is the 'sheer weight of difficulties that a woman is carrying'. In any community, he believes, the largest group of depressed people are those who find difficulties surrounding almost all aspects of their lives.

I was sympathetic to this idea that depression is nature's way of telling us that something is wrong with the way that we've been living. No one can deny the crushing weight of the events that bear down on many people.

But as a biologist I had to point out that most psychiatrists see depression as a malfunction in the chemistry of our brains. Didn't he agree that much of it had a biological basis? Of course he did. But he thought that vulnerability factors might also be involved, even in many of these patients suffering from brain-disordered depression.

Many psychiatrists are tempted to hive off those patients who respond well to anti-depressant or electroconvulsive therapy into a special group who are said to have an 'endogenous' complaint. But it would be a mistake to see even their problem as a purely 'organic' brain disturbance. Why? Because at the moment we still know so little about what it is in the brain that is being disturbed.

From amines to receptors

What we do know is that depression is sometimes associated with a fall in the level of compounds called *amines* in the brain. These substances (like dopamine and noradrenaline) are involved in the passage of electrical impulses from one nerve to the next. Nerve cells in the brain have tiny gaps called *synapses* between them. Electrical messages pass down one nerve, across a synapse and into another. The result of this meshwork is that the messages can travel along tens of thousands of different routes. This almost infinitely flexible routing arrangement permits the immense complexity in our thinking and feeling that we tend to take for granted.

But the electrical impulse itself can't cross the synapse. Instead, the nerve cell carrying the signal releases a tiny amount of the amine which acts as a transmitter. It flows across the synapse and stimulates the signal to be generated again in the next neurone in the network.

In the mid-1960s some depressed people were found to have reduced levels of amines in their brains. Later research showed that certain drugs would relieve many cases of depression. And what these drugs seemed to have in common was their ability to enhance brain amine levels. So-called *tricyclic anti-depressants* like amitriptyline and imipramine slow the rate at which the amines are reabsorbed from the synapse, and so increase the length of their stay there. Substances called *monoamine oxidase inhibitors*, like tranylcypromine, act by slowing the rate at which the amines are broken down. And so the biochemical pathways for depression, involving a shortage of amines in the synapse, seemed to be quite straightforward.

Except that they are not. Because there is now a 'second generation' of anti-depressants like nomifensine which relieve depression but don't have any significant effect on the amine levels. As well as the amines, there are also other compounds involved in communication between nerve cells that may also be involved. And to make the matter even more complicated, these various transmitters may interact with each other.

The latest attempt to explain the action of anti-depressant

drugs goes like this. It suggests, not so much that they influence events in the synapse (though they may do), but that they affect the surface of the nerve cells itself. We now know that many cells have *receptors* on their surface, regions specifically designed to receive transmitter molecules, much as a lock receives a key with a particular shape. Nerve cells in the brain have receptors for amines and for other transmitters. Depression may occur when this lock and key mechanism fails to work.

Anti-depressant drugs somehow correct the problem. They ensure that the receptors on the cell surface function as they should, and that the right message is transmitted from the receptor to the machinery inside the cell. As a result, the victim starts to think more rationally.

Cognitions and cognitive therapy

Perhaps the most important breakthrough in the study of depression over the last twenty years is the realization that depressed people have a very characteristic way of thinking. They have 'faulty' cognitions, which make them depressed in the first place and which maintain their depression once it has started. Indeed, anyone scanning the host of recent paperbacks on mental health might believe that the problem of depression has finally been understood and even solved. The treatment, it seems, simply involves the therapist and patient working together to correct the sufferer's thinking problems.

For example, in his most entertaining and readable best-seller *Feeling Good – The New Mood Therapy* (which I strongly recommend) David Burns, an author with impeccable credentials and a one-time colleague of Aaron Beck, says quite clearly that 'the negative thoughts that flood your mind are the actual *cause* of your self-defeating emotions'.[16]

If so, it is difficult to see why people get depressed when they are ill, and why depression is more common in those who are deprived. I wonder what the women in George Brown's study would make of Burns's conclusion.

The fact that the cognitive view has been 'oversold' in this way is a pity, because thinking does have an important part to play in depression and 'talking therapy' based on the cognitive approach certainly helps some people to recover. To a large extent it was pioneered by Aaron Beck, and the story of how he came to realize the importance of thoughts in depression is a fascinating one.[17]

Trained as a psychoanalyst and practising in Philadelphia in the 1960s Beck found that some patients seemed to have things happening inside their heads which psychoanalysis wasn't tapping in to.

For example, one client had been critical of his therapist and confessed afterwards that he felt guilty. A simple enough connection, it seemed. Many analysts believe that hostility and guilt are linked together in the subconscious. But this particular patient confessed that as soon as his anger had subsided he found himself thinking, 'I shouldn't have said that ... he won't like me ... I have no excuse for being so mean.' In other words, the guilt resulted from a series of thoughts – fleeting, transient thoughts – that the patient had about his anger and its possible consequences. They centred around the possibility of losing his therapist's respect.

This case and many like it persuaded Beck that we are all constantly engaging in a series of 'automatic thoughts'. They are so rapid that we are scarcely aware of them, but they strongly colour our perceptions of the world. They reflect a set of underlying rules or assumptions that we have all developed for living by, rules that we have built up over the years. They include ideas like 'I should show proper respect to people in authority', or its opposite, 'No one tells *me* what to do.' We measure our life experience against these rules.

Our fleeting automatic thoughts ('He won't like me if I do that') are the result of comparing what is happening to us with what our rules tell us *should* be happening. The emotions that follow – depression if it seems that we are losing something important; elation if we feel that we are gaining; anxiety if we feel under threat – are the direct result of this rapid stream of thinking, this continuous update that tells us what is happening to us and how we ought to feel about it.

Distorted thoughts

It was the Greek philosopher Epictetus who said, 'Men are not moved by things but the view which they take of them,' and his ideas largely sum up the cognitive approach: thinking first, feeling later.

But cognitive therapists have gone further than simply examining our internal rules. They have looked as well at the way we think, and discovered a series of distorted ways of thinking that are linked to emotional disturbances generally and particularly to being depressed.

One is called 'over-generalization' – assuming that because something is not the way I want it, then *everything* is a disaster. For example, I notice that I have a leaky tap in the kitchen. The central heating is old and giving problems. And there is a wet patch on the wall. I conclude that 'The whole house is falling apart. Nothing works any more.' Or perhaps I get behind with a piece of work. I can't make time to see my friends. The garden is getting out of hand and I conclude that 'I can't get anything done. I'm never going to be able to get myself organized.'

Just look at the attributions.

Another faulty thinking pattern is one which Beck calls 'selective abstraction'. I put some tiles on the bathroom wall. One – only one – is cracked, but that is the only one I ever see. And I see it every time I go in there. The rest of the wall, gleaming and perfect, is invisible to me as I concentrate on the one offensive detail. Or I go to a party where everyone is warm and friendly. Well, almost everyone. There is one woman there who treats me with disdain, or so it seems to me. Her indifference to what I am saying immediately outweighs everyone else's attention. I concentrate on this one problem area ('What have I done wrong?'), oblivious to all the rest that is going on and that I could be enjoying.

A third type of cognitive error is 'arbitrary inference'. At the same party I conclude that the woman in question obviously finds me lacking in some respect. Her indifference results from some defect on my part ('Is it the tie; do I smell; am I shouting, or what?'). It never occurs to me that her child is at a private school and she only came to meet someone who might be able to help her with the debts that she has run up since her husband walked out. It doesn't occur to me that she may be so wrapped up in her own problems that she can't give anyone her full attention.

These patterns of faulty thinking only disturb me because they impact on areas where I am particularly vulnerable – my pride in my home, my commitment to working effectively, my need to be liked. I get hit where it hurts. Each of us have different areas of vulnerability that relate to being accepted or rejected, to success or failure, to being well or being ill, to winning or losing.

When our distorted thoughts impinge on these particular areas that are important to us the result is a mood of unhappiness. Unless we can pull out of it, there follows a more prolonged period of depression. We get depressed about the world, about the future and most importantly about ourselves.

There are now dozens of studies that show how depressives selectively concentrate on negative information about themselves. They recall their mistakes more quickly than their successes, unhappy memories more quickly than happy ones. People scoring high on neuroticism do the same, which is one reason why high N scores predict who will get depressed.[18] Oddly enough, their view of other people isn't biased in this way. They have no problem in recalling the positive features of others. Their negative outlook is reserved for themselves.

Faulty thinking – cause or effect?

The idea that thinking can lead to mental disturbance is very attractive, which no doubt accounts for its great popularity in recent years. When I first came across it, it felt so 'right' that I thought I suddenly understood what depression was – a consequence of the way that I chose to look at the world.

But, as with so many ideas that take off like a rocket, two decades of research have tended to show up its shortcomings. The major problem with the cognitive approach is in its basic assumption that errors in thinking *cause* changes of mood and eventually *result* in depression. It is certainly true that depressed people do show the 'cognitive distortions' like over-generalization and arbitrary inference. It is also true that they feel bad about themselves, their world and their future.

But it is not at all clear that their thinking *leads* to their depression.[19] It is possible that patients may think that way *because* they are depressed. Depression may cause distorted thinking, rather than *vice versa*. Even Aaron Beck himself has recently conceded that the original theory was too simplistic.[20] While still emphasizing the link between negative thinking and depression which he first discovered by looking at nearly 1,000 psychiatric patients in the late 1960s, he now agrees that many other factors might be involved. In short, he believes in the existence of further interactions.

For example, one of the most obvious features of severely depressed patients is their extreme reluctance to do anything that requires any effort. But it now seems that our ability to motivate ourselves to make an effort may depend on our having intact amine pathways in the brain. Any malfunction in these pathways (and we have seen that in depression they are often disturbed) might create a set of negative cognitions that render it psychologically very difficult for us to make concentrated effort. They rob us of the ability to think clearly enough to test whether our view of the world is really true or not. Believing that it is, we get locked into a negative downward spiral.

Points on a circle

Helping patients to change their distorted thinking patterns is called 'cognitive therapy'. Whether the disturbed thoughts came first or not, such therapy certainly works. But there is still some doubt whether cognitive therapy works better than drugs for treating depression. Some trials have found that it does so in the short term, but that over a period of months drug-treated patients improve to the same extent.[21] One group of therapists believe that if cognitive therapy shows no effect in two to four weeks then the patient should be switched to a drug regime. They also found that in hospital patients a *combination* of drug and cognitive therapy produced a greater improvement than either of them used alone.[22]

The striking fact about any treatment is that, if the patient's depression responds at all, then it does so across the board. Successful drug therapy will not only improve her symptoms, like sleeping problems. It will also lift her moods, as well as correcting her low self-esteem, her pessimism about her world and her feelings of hopelessness about her future. And cognitive therapy, if it works at all, not only corrects her faulty thinking but improves her other symptoms as well. So 'depressed mood is associated with changes in neurotransmitter levels, in cognitive distortions and in reduced social behaviour. Each of these may serve to maintain the others in a circular fashion. If so, then treatment interventions that change any of the factors will also tend to change the others and the end result will appear the same'.[23]

Conserving our resources

We still have to ask one final but very fundamental question. Being depressed feels awful. It reduces our productivity and greatly increases our risk of suicide. Yet it persists in the human species. Over the span of time for which there are written records, people have always got depressed, and if we look at many animal species they show a similar retardation when exposed to highly stressful environments.

The question is: why is it still with us? Specialists in evolutionary theory believe that any feature that persists like this must have some survival value, at least for the species as a whole, otherwise it would have died out. So what is the survival value of depression?

We have looked at the suggestion that there is a biologically based programme in the brain that makes us slow all systems down so as to conserve our vital resources at times when we feel deserted or rejected by our fellows. At such times we can't depend on anyone for food or warmth or shelter, and so we have to be very sparing with our own resources until we can depend on their support again.

This may be true, but I think there is another, perhaps more important, explanation as well. Like George Brown, I believe mild depression is nature's way of correcting our positive biases if they have gone too far in the manic direction. And severe depression is what happens when mild depression gets out of hand.

Sadder but wiser

Researchers in Oregon asked depressed patients and normal people to join a group of others whom they hadn't met before and make a short speech about themselves. At the end of the meetings they were asked to rate how well they had performed, how friendly, popular, assertive and attractive they thought they had been. The groups were overlooked through a one-way mirror by observers who also rated them on these same characteristics.

The depressed individuals rated themselves low on social skills. And the observers agreed with them. The non-depressed did just the opposite. They rated themselves high. Indeed their own ratings were higher than the observers rated them on their social performance. They had what the researchers call a 'halo' or 'glow' that gave them a self-enhanced illusion about their own capabilities. Whilst the depressed patients were accurate and realistic in their self-perceptions, the normals biased their self-image upwards.

The Oregon team suggested several reasons why this 'warm glow' that people feel about themselves may be important. It perpetuates our favourable self-image. It may also make us feel more accepting of other people. In contrast, mildly depressed people seem to be 'sadder but wiser'. They are certainly more realistic in their view of the world.

The researchers' conclusions bear directly on our whole idea of the affirmation of life. They say that 'a key to avoiding depression is to see oneself less stringently and more favourably than others see one ...'. Or, to put it another way, 'to feel good about ourselves we may have to judge ourselves more kindly than we are judged'.[24]

Pushing the buttons

This notion that mildly depressed people are more realistic than the rest of us is becoming inescapable. In a now classic investigation of how much control people believe they have over situations, volunteers were asked to sit in front of a piece of apparatus with two coloured bulbs and a push-button. When the yellow bulb lit up they could opt either to push the button or not. On some occasions, the second green bulb also lit up. The volunteers had to decide to what extent their button-pushing (or deliberate non-pushing) controlled the green light. The results were then related to the BDI scores.[25]

In the first experiment, when the rate of button-pushing actually did influence the green light, both normal and depressed people were able to predict their levels of control very accurately. But the experimenters then changed the rules. They set things up so that they, and not the subjects, controlled the light, arranging events so that it went on 25 per cent or 50 per cent of the time. Pushing the button had no effect on how often it would light. But the subjects didn't know this when they were asked to estimate how frequently it lit up and how much they thought they were controlling it.

The depressed subjects were still very accurate in estimating the amount of control they seemed to be exerting. By contrast, the normals overestimated their control in trials where they seemed to be doing well, and underestimated it when things were going badly. What they were experiencing was a set of illusions, both about control and no control, that the depressives didn't share.

Why should this happen? Perhaps depressed people are not particularly concerned with trying to maintain their sense of self-esteem. So they don't bias upwards their perceptions of their world. They are not motivated to regain their self-regard either, because the mechanisms that maintain their self-deception have broken down. So-called normal people, by contrast, take the credit when things are going well. But when they are going badly they attribute their failures to other, outside factors – exactly the pattern of attribution that maintains their optimism.

So while Beck and others have emphasized the cognitive errors of the depressed, perhaps we ought to look at the cognitive distortions that all of us use every day to keep on feeling good about ourselves. We should remember that 'at times depressed people are sadder but wiser . . . . Non-depressed people succumb to cognitive illusions that enable them to see themselves and their environment with a rosy glow.'[26]

Does your world-view need adjusting?

We maintain the glow because we have developed a series of internal pictures about what the world is like. And as long as nothing happens to show us that our schemes aren't working, we continue on automatic pilot, maintaining the positive bias that keep us active, optimistic and motivated to carry out the tasks in hand.

But if some event happens to disturb the pattern – the sort of life event that George Brown talks about – then it has to be attended to. The automatic pattern is no longer adequate. Reality can't be taken for granted any more. It has to be scanned and searched to see what has gone wrong. The result is a feeling of mild depression for as long as the confusion persists. Most frequently it resolves. The new information is taken on board. Changes are made to account for the new situation. Normality (that is to say the warm glow, the self-enhancing illusion) returns.

But sometimes it doesn't. Sometimes we see no way to resolve the problem. There is no possibility of recreating a self-enhancing image. The result is a slide into severe depression and the feelings of hopelessness and despair that go with it.

So the crucial question is not where does depression come from? We have seen that it comes from many sources. More important is the question of how mild depression resolves itself – or, to put it another way, what stops the mild depressive slipping off the edge into severe depression?

And the answer depends on the remarkable ability that most of us have for facing our problems squarely, or if that doesn't work of maintaining the illusion that we aren't totally hopeless, that we can still maintain some measure of control over some aspects of our lives.

Restored by illusions

Shelley Taylor in Los Angeles has done as much as anyone to explain this remarkable resilience of the human psyche.[27]

She agrees that, in George Brown's phrase, 'we are all hopelessly optimistic'. We attribute good outcomes to ourselves, bad outcomes to outside events; we remember ourselves in the past as being more successful and more often correct than we really were; we underestimate the amount of negative reactions that we receive from other people; we reward ourselves more than our actual performance would justify.

But we have a good reason. Self-reinforcement, which, she says, normal people do to excess, keeps us concentrated on what we have to do. 'The effective individual in the face of threat ... seems to be one who permits the development of illusions, nurtures those illusions, and is ultimately restored by those illusions.'

The problem with living that way, it would seem, is that if our illusions are disturbed, or challenged, or destroyed, then we must surely be left open and vulnerable?

Apparently not.

And the reason is that in real life, unlike the psychology laboratory, we have an almost infinite range of options open to us. In the lab, we might give up at a particular task when it becomes clear that we aren't influencing its outcome – like switching on the light. But in life we simply shrug it off, and go and find another task that we feel we can have some influence on.

Shelley Taylor came to this conclusion after talking to cancer victims. Many of them developed their own theories about how their cancer originated, for example that it was the result of the trauma involved in a motor accident. When they were finally convinced by their doctors that this wasn't possible, they simply adopted another theory – for example that it was due to their diet. Some patients changed their diets in an attempt to avoid a recurrence. And many of those whose disease still recurred simply accepted that they must have been wrong that time as well, and devised some other plan.

Taylor believes that people greatly exaggerate how much they think they can accomplish. She points out how many of the items on today's list of 'things to do' get transferred to tomorrow. But, amazingly enough, we don't feel that our lives have failed as a result. We simply accept that this is how things turn out. She talks about a sense of 'cheerful ineptitude' in which, if a particular plan doesn't succeed, most of us regard it as a mild frustration rather than a major disaster. It is only if *all* of our goals are blocked that we start to feel a loss of control.

Her notion of cognitive adaptation sees such people as 'adaptable, self-reflective, and functional in the face of setbacks.'

Most of us have a range of different responses at our disposal. If we are unsuccessful in one area we will turn our frustrated efforts at control, understanding and self-enhancement towards other tasks at which we may be more successful. In her words, 'the process of cognitive adaptation to threat, though often time consuming and not always successful, nonetheless restores many people to their prior level of functioning and inspires others to find new meaning in their lives.'

If life-enhancement is about anything, it is about developing this flexibility, this quality that allows us to keep bouncing back whatever the pressures that threaten to submerge us. The trick is being able to bounce in a different direction each time.

People who can do that, at least most of the time, have a sporting chance of maintaining their mental health. We recognize them as life-affirmers. And we recognize something else about them as well.

They often have a great capacity to be happy.

CHAPTER 7

Strive to be Happy

―――

You are a child of the universe . . .
You have a right to be here . . .
With all its sham, drudgery and broken dreams,
It's still a beautiful world.
Be careful. Strive to be happy.

So ENDS one of the most famous epitaphs of all times, the one that states 'Go placidly among the noise and haste'. It was found, so it is said, on a seventeenth-century tombstone in a country churchyard. It was obviously written by a life-affirmer.

Subjective well-being

Happiness has been a major concern of philosophers since the time of the ancient Greeks. But in the 1960s it became a subject for scientific study as well. It was first looked at by sociologists, curious to know exactly what had to be provided for people (more jobs, better housing, cheaper health care) to improve their quality of life. And the subject has now become a growth industry for social scientists.

Happiness and satisfaction with life are lumped together under one heading which psychologists call *subjective well-being* or SWB.

According to Ed Diener at the University of Illinois at Champaign, who has contributed as much as anyone to this field in recent years, 'subjective well-being (SWB) is concerned with how and why people experience their lives in positive ways – including both cognitive judgements and affective reactions'.[1] And that says it all. Being positive about your life involves both thinking (cognitive judgements) and feeling (affective reactions).

The well-being that you experience will influence your behaviour in the outside world. But basically it is something that occurs inside your head. That's why it's subjective.

What it takes to be happy

Many surveys have set out to discover what people need to increase their subjective well-being.[2] Summarized briefly, they find that most people have to be satisfied with themselves to some degree. A measure of self-esteem seems to be important for most of us to feel satisfied with our lives. We also need to be satisfied with our standard of living (though we have a strong tendency not to be) and with our family lives. Older people are more satisfied than the young in every area except health. Young people feel greater joys but older people, while they have less intense emotional reactions, judge their lives as a whole to be more positive. Women experience both greater joys and greater sorrows than men do, although the difference is marginal. Younger women seem to be happier than younger men, but older men have the advantage over women of their age.

Being unemployed has a dramatic effect on well-being. The unemployed are the least happy group in major surveys, not just because of the effects of reduced income. In contrast, marriage is a strong positive predictor of SWB, often the strongest. However, being a parent does little to increase the well-being in most people's lives.

Sociable, extraverted people are happier than those who choose to have less social contact with others. The most intense form of contact, of course, is being in love, and a satisfying love life is one of the most important of all predictors of SWB.

In some studies, high self-esteem was strongly related to feelings of well-being. Feeling competent, able to cope and having personal resources to call upon also increased it strongly. Finally, our perception of our health has a major effect on the way that we report our levels of happiness.

Theories of happiness

There is no shortage of theories that try to explain just what happiness is. They fall into three groups. The first is the notion that happiness occurs when you achieve some goal that you were aiming for. The second is that it comes from building up a network of happy associations. And the third (and for us the most interesting) is that it results from the way you choose to judge your current situation.

Reaching a particular goal is the most widely held idea of what makes people happy. Abraham Maslow suggested that there is a set of goals and needs that we all share, ranging from the need for shelter to the need to achieve self-actualization. Unfortunately, later research found little evidence for this set of universal needs. If there is any single need that affects everyone, it is probably the need to feel effective, to believe that we can personally influence events rather than being a victim of them.

But this whole question of goals is a subtle one. We all know that once we get something it doesn't give us the same feeling that it did the moment before we got it. One view of happiness suggests that we automatically adapt to whatever we've got. Once acquired, an object or a situation gives us progressively less pleasure. It is only an *improvement* in our situation that gives us any satisfaction, and so we spend our lives constantly trying to improve on what we've done or what we've got.

Canadian researchers took this idea of achieving goals one step further. T. S. Palys and Brian Little asked people about their various 'personal projects', the important things that they were trying to achieve in their lives.[3] Projects could be short- or long-term, easy or difficult, performed alone or with others. They also asked them how satisfied they were with their lives as a whole, right now. Then they matched the information about their projects to their levels of satisfaction, to see what influence the way that people organize their lives has on how satisfied they are.

Those people who reported greater satisfaction were involved in short-term, relatively easy, enjoyable projects, many of which were carried out in collaboration with others. By contrast, those with low life satisfaction had 'placed their bets on the long term'. Their projects were generally more difficult and less enjoyable but more important to them in the long run. They were also less involved in joint projects with others.

So satisfied people organized their lives around a series of enjoyable projects that were not very difficult. Dissatisfied people, by contrast, were pursuing difficult projects that, at that time at least, were not as enjoyable. Perhaps this is why they had difficulty in recruiting others to join them. These results suggest that being able to break life down into a series of short-term objectives, each enjoyable in itself, and most of them carried out in collaboration with other people, could go a long way towards increasing our levels of satisfaction. Remember Carver and Scheier's idea that optimists do the same thing – break life down into manageable chunks.

A related notion has been proposed by Mihaly Czikszentmihalyi of the University of Chicago. He believes that enjoyment results from the process of 'flow'.[4] We constantly have to keep directing our attention to the outside world to deal with what is going on there. And most of the time this drains our energy away. But, he suggests, there is one occasion when to do so is a positive pleasure. Indeed, it gives so much pleasure that it requires no effort at all. This is the situation in which we have something that we must concentrate on, but where we feel that our capability to succeed exactly balances the difficulty involved.

If the job is too hard for us, we experience anxiety. If it is not difficult enough we feel bored. When the two are matched, the activity 'flows' and becomes self-sustaining, a reward in itself. Czikszentmihalyi interviewed many different groups of people – surgeons, climbers, artists – and found that the satisfaction they had gained from the flow experience made it almost addictive. He found that people's levels of happiness were consistently related to how far their challenges and skills were in balance. But any activity can be experienced in the same way. Indeed most flow experiences were felt during people's everyday work.

A related view of happiness suggests that happy people are those who have come to link happy or satisfied reactions to quite ordinary events. So, says Ed Diener, 'certain individuals may have built up a strong network of positive associations and learnt to react habitually in positive ways'.[5] People with a particular bias towards making positive associations are happier than others. But this doesn't mean that their thinking patterns are fixed. They can change as new experiences become incorporated into the pattern.

Then there are the 'judgement theories' of happiness. Essentially they say that people decide whether they are happy or not by judging their situation against some standard. In *social-comparison* theories they judge themselves against other people or compare what they have with what they want, or with what they had in the past. The perceived gap between what a person has and what he wants is a powerful predictor of life satisfaction, but so too is the gap between what he has and what he thinks other people have got.

Ordinary happiness

A final example of a judgement theory is the idea that a person adapts to good times, so that they no longer make her happy. Conversely, she also adapts to bad ones, so that in time she becomes resigned to those as well. An interesting variation on this theme was developed by Alan Parducci of the University of California, Los Angeles. He suggests that people may be happier if they try to arrange their lives so that they experience frequent, minor pleasures rather than waiting for a few ecstatic moments.[6]

Parducci has produced an impressive analysis of the frequency of different events and how they affect people's living, from which he concludes that 'If the best can only come rarely, it is better not to include it in the range of experiences at all. The average level of happiness can be raised by arranging life so that high levels of satisfaction come frequently, even if this requires renunciation of the opportunity for occasional experiences that would be even more gratifying.' In other words, rare moments of ecstasy do less for us than more frequent moments of 'ordinary happiness'.

There is one idea which can hardly be called a theory of happiness, but which sums up many of the ones that we have been looking at. It is the notion, proposed by Jonathan Freedman, that some people simply have a 'talent' for happiness that others lack.[7]

As he says, 'We all know that some people enjoy life more than others, make the most of what they have, see the world through rose-coloured glasses; while others are exactly the opposite, always complaining, never seeming to experience joy, looking on the sour side of everything.' 'Perhaps', he says, 'there are complex personality traits or combinations of them that allow or encourage happiness and others that do the opposite but we do not know what they are.'

But I think we do know. They are sociability and emotional stability, the two life-affirming characteristics that have such an influence on our balance of positive and negative affect.

The Fourteen Fundamentals

If we study the attitudes of happy people and then model our behaviour on theirs, there is a good chance that we will end up being happier as well. That is the philosophy developed by Michael Fordyce, a psychologist at Edison Community College in Florida. For most of the last twenty years he has devoted himself to doing just that, teaching people to adopt such attitudes and then actually measuring the result.

To do so, he devised his own Happiness Measures, a '60 second index of emotional well-being and mental health'. It consists of asking one simple question: 'In general, how happy or unhappy do you usually feel?' People give their replies on an eleven point scale ranging from 'extremely unhappy' (utterly depressed, completely down) to 'extremely happy' (feeling ecstatic, joyous, fantastic), simply by checking the box that most closely reflects how they usually feel. (See Box 9.)

However, Fordyce has gone much further than that. Most measures of happiness tap a person's *feelings* about being happy. But there are other aspects that are relevant as well. He has therefore produced his own *Self-Description Inventory* or SDI, a broadly based personality test designed to give 'a general profile of an individual's progress towards happiness'.

The SDI asks people to assess their happiness in four different ways. The first scale enquires about how much happiness they have *actually achieved*. People who score high derive great happiness from living. They gain rewards from most aspects of their lives and show a great deal of vitality. Low scorers, by contrast, are not at all content with their lives. They experience a lot of stress and personal dissatisfaction and feel unhappy and unsuccessful.

Then comes the *Happy Personality Scale*. Happy scorers come

PART I DIRECTIONS: Use the list below to answer the following question: In general, how happy or unhappy did you feel during this last week? Tick the *one* statement below that best describes *your average happiness*.

- [ ] **10.** Extremely happy (feeling ecstatic, joyous, fantastic)
- [ ] **9.** Very happy (feeling really good, elated)
- [ ] **8.** Pretty happy (spirits high, feeling good)
- [ ] **7.** Mildly happy (feeling fairly good and somewhat cheerful)
- [ ] **6.** Slightly happy (just a bit above neutral)
- [ ] **5.** Neutral (not particularly happy or unhappy)
- [ ] **4.** Slightly unhappy (just a bit below neutral)
- [ ] **3.** Mildly unhappy (just a little low)
- [ ] **2.** Pretty unhappy (somewhat 'blue', spirits down)
- [ ] **1.** Very unhappy (depressed, spirits very low)
- [ ] **0.** Extremely unhappy (utterly depressed, completely down)

PART II DIRECTIONS: Consider your emotions a moment further. *On the average*, what percentage of the time do you feel happy? What percentage of the time do you feel unhappy? What percentage of the time do you feel neutral (neither happy nor unhappy)? Write down your best estimates, as well as you can, in the spaces below. Make sure the three figures add up to equal 100 per cent.

ON THE AVERAGE:

The percentage of time I feel happy	_____	%
The percentage of time I feel unhappy	_____	%
The percentage of time I feel neutral	_____	%
TOTAL	100	%

Box 9.   *This simple questionnaire is known as the Happiness Measures. Devised by Michael Fordyce in Florida, it has proved to be a surprisingly reliable way of measuring people's degree of happiness. He has particularly used it to test the value of his Fourteen Fundamentals programme to boost happiness levels.*

out high on being extraverted, spontaneous and friendly. They have a positive self-image and feel that they know and accept themselves. They feel largely autonomous, self-sufficient and certain of their sense of values and of the direction in which their lives are going.

A third scale measures *Happiness Attitudes and Values*. High scorers have an optimistic outlook on life. They have a modest level of ambition and set realistic goals for themselves. They enjoy living for today and are not unduly worried about the past or future. In addition, they have a strong commitment to their own happiness. Low scorers think pessimistically, set themselves difficult goals and do not value their happiness highly enough.

Finally, in the SDI, Fordyce has devised his *Happiness Lifestyle*, which assesses the way that people actually live their lives. Those scoring high lead an exciting, involved, robust life. They are active and busy, spending most of their time in activities that are enjoyable and exciting. They find their work meaningful and rewarding. People scoring low have lives which are less active, less rewarding, less sociable and less enjoyable.

Putting all this together he says that 'high scoring individuals in the SDI could be described from their . . . personality test profile as having: a high degree of personal happiness, a lower degree of depression, hostility, tension, anxiety, guilt and a variety of other negative emotions; a high level of energy, vitality and activity; a generally self-actualized . . . emotionally healthy personality and a personality that is outgoing, spontaneous, extraverted and socially orientated'.

But this is far more than a description of a group of remarkably fortunate people. For the SDI, which has now been given to several thousand subjects, actually forms the basis for a programme of change – the *Fourteen Fundamentals*. It is a set of prescriptions for happier living, which not only concentrates on our feelings, but also attempts to alter the personality, values and lifestyle that do so much to determine how happy we will be.[8]

Increase your own happiness

Let us take the prescriptions that come out of the *Happy Personality Scale* first. Fordyce doesn't believe that we should creep up on any of these issues. He confronts them all squarely, convinced that happiness comes from directly willing it to occur, rather than hoping that it will somehow arrive while we are busy doing something else.

So his first fundamental is 'work on a healthy personality'. Happy people, he says, like themselves and have high self-esteem. This comes from productive work on worthwhile projects; from developing and enhancing one's skills, from setting moderate goals and achieving them, and from making a conscious decision that 'I deserve to like myself; I don't need an excuse to do it.' Happy people also accept themselves, together with their shortcomings. They have learnt to be less than perfectionist and don't punish themselves for their inadequacies.

In addition, happy people know themselves. They spend time gaining insight into their own motives. They also help themselves, trusting their own instincts and trying to become self-sufficient, rather than having to rely excessively on others. Finally, they try to live for themselves, not being too concerned about what others think and about always having to gain their approval. Those who would be happier should do the same – work on all of these areas and increase the health of their own personality as a result.

His second recommendation, since happy people are outgoing and extraverted, is to try to develop an outgoing social personality, by joining a club, by talking to people, by going out of your way to make new friends. Since happy people are also spontaneous, he suggests that you also try to be yourself and accept that not everyone is going to like you. It is only by coming to this realization that you can stop censoring what you say and do for fear of giving offence. Finally under the heading of personality, Fordyce suggests that we try to eliminate negative feelings and problems, both by letting them out rather than bottling them up, and by seeking professional help when the need arises.

We saw that the SDI has a scale to measure *Happy Attitudes and Values*, and five of the *Fourteen Fundamentals* are designed to work at this level.

First among them is to stop worrying and to stop confusing worrying with planning. As Fordyce puts it, 'if there's nothing you can do to avoid your worry right now it's not worth worrying about'. He suggests that the majority of things that people do worry about never actually occur. He challenges his readers to prove this for themselves by noting down their various worries in a diary for several weeks and afterwards recording just how many of them actually happened.

More controversial is his suggestion that we should lower our expectations and aspirations. This is based on the view that high expectations lead to disappointment, but lower expectations lead to pleasant surprises. In this we hear echoes of Parducci. Fordyce also suggests that happiness is a way to travel, rather than a place to arrive. What is important is to be happy *now*. We have more chance of doing so by setting ourselves short-term, modest goals, a conclusion that Palys and Little also came to.

In the category of *Attitudes and Values*, he lists the needs to develop positive and optimistic thinking. Since 'optimism may be the most fundamental difference between happy and unhappy people', he encourages his pupils to focus on the positive. One way to do so is regularly to check your thoughts. If the thought that you are currently having is negative, then switch it immediately to some more pleasant scene or happy memory.

Related to this is the need to become present-oriented, to live mostly for today. This he describes as a need to avoid living out old disasters or old triumphs. They are past. In the same way, waiting for an ideal future or dreading what the future might bring are equally inappropriate. As a typical exercise he suggests we should try to 'make this week the best week you've ever had in your life'. But just as importantly among attitudes and values, is his reminder that close personal relationships have perhaps the greatest effect of all on happiness. Enriching such relationships could therefore be the very best happiness investment.

Finally we come to the question of *lifestyles*. The *Fourteen Fundamentals* calls for their practitioners to be more active and to keep busy, preferably with some of the time being spent in particularly enjoyable activities. Those who would be happy should also spend time being productive at meaningful work. To do so they need to be better organized at planning things out. 'You are in a much better place to get what you want if you know what you want.'

And underpinning all these other suggestions for happiness is the 'secret fundamental', which is simply to think about and value your happiness, to pursue it actively, and to give it a high priority. It is by acting upon it directly that happiness will come.

So what can we make of this wealth of advice, full as it is of begged questions (how can I actually find some meaningful work?) and its overtones of the 1960s' 'doing your own thing'? It is repetitive and oversimplified, and many of its categories are overlapping. But nonetheless it is important. Fordyce has published seven different sets of results in which he shows that the *Fundamentals* programme does actually boost levels of happiness, as assessed by his *Happiness Measures*.

For example, in his early research he compared the effects of administering the programme to a group of students over a two-week period with the effects of telling a similar group that they would become happier simply as a result of the course that they were enrolled in. The *Fundamentals* programme produced an increase in happiness greater than any mere suggestion.

Loading the odds against himself, he then gave one class of students complete instructions in the *Fundamentals* programme while a second group received an outline of what it contained, without any particular suggestion that they should use it. On a whole range of happiness measures, students receiving full instructions gained more in happiness over an eleven–week period.

In summary, Fordyce claims that, in seven studies taken together, 80 per cent of people who received the programme said that it made them happier. For about a third of those the response was very positive. He admits that the enthusiasm with which he presents the programme may have been partly responsible for its success, but nonetheless he believes that 'thinking about one's happiness regularly, pursuing it actively, and placing it as a top priority are some of the main ways to increase it'.[9]

If we cut across the set of categories – personality, attitudes and so on – that he presents in the SDI, then I think we can simplify his scheme. And in doing so, something new emerges.

Keeping busy, being productive and getting organized are key features that relate to active involvement in the things that we are doing. In other words they relate to *commitment*. Spending time socializing, developing an outgoing personality and realizing the importance of close relationships all have to do with involvement with other people – *sociability*. Giving up worrying, developing an optimistic outlook and eliminating negative thinking all relate to changing your emotional balance to produce more *positive affect*. And finally, living in the present, working on a healthy personality and being yourself all relate to self-knowledge and *self-esteem*.

In short then, we have commitment, sociability, positive affect and self-esteem as the four pillars of happiness, with a built-in, self-monitoring function to make sure that we are actually attending to them.

It is surely no coincidence that they are four of our life-affirming characteristics as well. No coincidence at all, because, in the last analysis, happiness results from mental health.

Research by Fordyce and those like him shows that happiness can be increased if mental health can be boosted. This is certainly a worthwhile aim in itself – some would say the highest that we can aspire to. Happiness is its own reward.

But what about that other vague though widely held idea that happy people are also somehow physically healthier as well?

Are happy people healthier?

In 1984, Alex Zautra and Ann Hempel, two psychologists at Arizona State University, wrote that 'For quality of life there are no greater needs than health and happiness. That these are related in a person's mind should surprise no one.[10] In short, it's easy for us to believe that people who are happier also have better physical health.

The two Arizona psychologists examined no less that eighty-one separate studies which looked at possible links between the two. And the links were certainly there. They said that they had to hunt for studies which failed to find some relationship between physical health and mental well-being. However, the link wasn't very strong. Secondly, a lot depends on which measures of health you decide to take. And thirdly, it is not at all clear whether it is health or happiness that comes first.

Let us take the three in turn. Firstly, how strong is the link? The answer is a statistical number that doesn't mean much to most people, a correlation of about 10 per cent, the sort of link that is often seen in mind–body investigations. Being translated, it shows that someone who tells us that he is in good health is twice as likely to report that he is experiencing 'good well-being' as someone who says that his health is poor.

Unfortunately, the problem revolves around the word 'report'. It is people's reports of their health that relate to the extent of their well-being. When we take more 'objective' health indicators, based for example on a physician's examination or on laboratory data, then the relationship is usually much weaker.

It seems to be satisfaction with life rather than positive

emotional feelings that are linked both to objective health and to the perception of how healthy you are. And this leads us up against the central unresolved dilemma. Are happy people healthier, or does the arrow point in the opposite direction? Is it rather that healthy people are happier? The sort of studies that have been done so far only show relationships – one thing appears when the other does. They can't say anything about which comes first.

Of course, the two factors influence each other. Remember the research by Carol Aneshensel, who found that bad health produced depression very quickly. Depression also led to ill-health symptoms, but much more slowly. Of the two, physical health had the more powerful effect. This happens time and again, and we shouldn't be surprised if this proves to be true for the health–happiness link as well.

Satisfaction with health is certainly a powerful predictor of satisfaction with life as a whole. But on balance it seems people are happy because they are healthy, rather than the reverse.

If this is true, where does it leave us? It means that while happiness is still what most of us aspire to, we should seek it, using the *Fourteen Fundamentals* or however else, as an aim in itself. Being happy doesn't necessarily mean that you are going to be physically healthy as well.

That's one of the results I was hinting at, right back in the first chapter, when I warned you not to expect too much from mind–body-health. If life-affirmers do succeed in being healthier, it isn't because they generate the right cosmic energies. It isn't necessarily because they have a mental hotline to their immune system either. It's largely because they simply value their health and do their best to preserve it.

CHAPTER 8

Mind–Body-Health: Only Connect

Two enormous shifts have occurred in the way that people have come to think about health and illness over the last decade. We have already looked at the first – the idea that being healthy means being at your functional best, being fully yourself, pushing yourself to the limit. This capacity to function (I call it 'doing well') is certainly one of the hallmarks of a healthy person. It is one of the key features of vitality or vigour. But it is only one of three. It goes with 'feeling well' and 'staying well'. It would be a mistake to believe that it's the whole story.

There are people with serious injuries, confined to wheelchairs, who, when you ask them how they are, will say, 'Fine, thanks; never felt better.' They're the sort who feel good enough about themselves to compete in the Para-Olympic Games. So not being able to function up to everybody else's norm doesn't automatically stop us from feeling healthy. And it also seems to me that the constant feeling of *having* to push yourself to the limit ('empty heat') shows a distinct lack of autonomy or control – a shortage of one of our basic life-affirming features.

The other major shift in our perceptions about health is the inescapable realization that the mind and the body interact, that (to some degree at least) the health of each depends on the other. This is hardly a discovery. It's not even a rediscovery because the idea, going back at least to the ancient Greek notion of a healthy mind and a healthy body, was never completely lost. However, it had been progressively ignored and obscured by a medical technology that has concentrated increasingly on physical measurements (blood biochemistry, radio-tracers, body scans) to assess whether we are healthy or not.

The move to put the mind back into the medicine of the body was driven by a number of forces. First perhaps was the discontent felt by an increasing number of patients about just how little 'orthodox' medicine could do for them. There has been a strong 'consumer' tendency, on both sides of the Atlantic, to see orthodox medicine as increasingly impersonal, expensive and unable to solve many health problems. In tandem with this public disillusion has been the rise of types of medicine offering a more personal and more integrated approach.

For example, the British Holistic Medical Association was founded in 1984 with, as its first declared aim, the education of doctors, medical students and other allied professions in the principles and practice of holistic medicine. And we have already mentioned its sister organization, the American Holistic Medical Association, which has a similar role in the USA. The setting up of the BHMA represented one branch of the medical profession trying to put its house in order. Later the membership broadened to include people interested in the health field but without a medical degree. Holism was expanding its territory.

At the same time, the whole set of 'alternative' therapies like acupuncture, homoeopathy and osteopathy, which had existed for decades but had kept a low profile, suddenly started to become more respectable.

Holistic medicine itself has always claimed to be about approaching the treatment of illness at three different levels – physical, mental and spiritual. It tries to see the person in the broad context of his surroundings. Holistic treatments for physical complaints take notice of the patient's emotional state, the problems in his life and his social network, as well as his blood pressure and serum cholesterol.

Holism in Britain has recently tried to distance itself from 'alternative' therapies. One reason is that the principles on which many of them are based are difficult even for holistic doctors to take seriously. Another reason, as I heard a BHMA spokesman admit recently, is that no form of alternative medicine has ever been shown to alter the course of any major, life-threatening disease. Though it may use alternative approaches, holism doesn't reject orthodox medical techniques, only the way that they are sometimes applied.

Beware of buying labels

For those of you who have come this far, mind–body links are no surprise. Many of you will have read Norman Cousins's account, in *Anatomy of an Illness*,[1] of how he treated a severe spinal problem with a combination of medication and laughter – high doses of vitamin C and the Marx Brothers. Many of you will also know about the cancer treatments that Carl and Stephanie Simonton, then a husband and wife therapy team working in Texas, described in *Getting Well Again*.[2] They were among the first to use imagery, guiding your imagination to picture your white blood cells going into battle against the tumour.

These books mark the spirit of the times in the late 1970s. They reflected the emerging belief that there simply *must* be some effective alternative to orthodox medical technology with all of its shortcomings. And this belief has continued to get stronger. Cousins and the Simontons are still active. They have written a lot more since then, but in retrospect their original paperbacks, full of hope and enthusiasm, now look a little like history books.

For all of these reasons then – disenchantment with the orthodox, the new age of holism and a wave of inspirational paperbacks – an increasing number of people have come to believe in the mind–body connection. The majority of any group of people whom you ask in Britain or the United States will tell you that their mental attitudes play an important part in keeping them healthy, or in getting them back to health when they are ill. Probe a little further and you will find that most of them can't say exactly how this is supposed to happen. But they certainly believe it, or at least they want to believe it.

And wanting is the problem. So great is our need to believe in the connections that are summed up by that current buzz-word *mind–body-health* that we risk taking on board a set of ideas that we *feel* to be right, without ever looking at what is behind them. So eager are we to embrace the whole person and the holistic approach that I think we run the risk of simply buying a label.

Since the mid-1970s I have wanted to know whether the label has anything attached to it. As a physiologist, trained to understand how the body works, but also sympathetic to the ideas of holistic health, I was disappointed by most of the work that was published on mind–body connections. I still am. I saw the link between mental and physical health as the result of brain biochemistry interacting with body cells, and *vice versa*. I still do.

If that process happens at all, then it should be measurable. But very few reliable measurements have been made. I once asked a staff member at a foundation that promotes alternative therapies if there were any published studies to justify the claims that were often made for this type of treatment. She looked at me with some irritation. 'My God', she said, 'you always want numbers, don't you?'

And she was right. I do, though I now understand that we sometimes have to use more creative ways of getting them than the classic 'double-blind' clinical trial that we use to test new drugs. But to look at mind–body links scientists still need data for the analytical left side of their brains to work on, although they have to use more right-brain thinking as well. One of the leading lights in the holistic movement in Britain once offered me a job as a 'token left hemisphere', because he too realized the pressing need to distinguish the fact from the speculation. In part this book came of my attempts to do just that.

Unfortunately much that is written about the mind–body area has more to do with prejudice than assessment. I discovered for myself, quite early on, that there were two contrasting attitudes in the way that health professionals thought about possible links between mental and physical health. The contrast still persists. If anything the attitudes have moved further apart in the last ten years. I have described one of them as 'open-eyed acceptance', the other as 'close-minded rejection'.

Diverging views

Two examples, both published in major scientific journals, show up the contrast. In 1981 Susan Birchfield and a research group at the University of Washington (including Thomas Holmes, whom we will hear more about later) looked at personality differences between people who are sick and others who are rarely sick.[3] They gave a battery of tests to patients who were attending a medical centre, either for their annual health check-up or because they had been referred there by their physicians. The patients had the usual physical examination and lab studies. They also provided details of their health histories, from which the researchers could distinguish the sick from the rarely sick.

At the same time this particular group of patients answered a series of questions about their feelings. They completed a set of short psychological questionnaires, designed to measure how satisfied or frustrated they were with their lives. Included were questions like 'Do you enjoy the work that you are doing?', 'Do you have close friends in whom you can confide?', 'Do you feel frustrated because you feel prevented from doing things properly?' and 'Do you ever wish you were dead?'

By comparing the answers with the subjects' actual health records the research team built up a composite picture of the person who, they claimed, usually has good health:

> The typically rarely sick individual is a male, aged 20–55, who is happily married. . . . He experiences more satisfaction than frustration from life and enjoys his work, family and friends. . . . He rarely does things that cause trouble for himself or others, he is rarely depressed and he never wishes he were dead. He rarely worries or gets 'uptight'. . . . He tends to be an optimist, feeling that the future will be brighter, while refusing to worry about the past.

So mental and physical well-being go together in a rather straightforward way. Or so it would seem. Susan Birchfield suggests that 'The cardinal sign of "disease" is disability and the cardinal symptom is dissatisfaction/discomfort.' We would agree with that. Only we would call them 'doing badly' and 'feeling badly'.

In contrast 'the cardinal attributes of "health" are productivity and satisfaction'. Again, we would agree, though we would call them 'doing well' and 'feeling well'. Not only that, but she says, 'rarely sick people can be differentiated from the general population and from sick people according to psychological characteristics, especially coping styles and outlook on life'.

So do satisfaction and enjoyment of life, optimism and not dwelling in the past contribute good physical health? They might. Many of us are convinced that they do. But unfortunately this report doesn't prove it one way or the other. All it shows is that healthy people are more satisfied and optimistic than sick people. And that's hardly a surprise. Like the problem of happiness and health, there is simply no way of telling from this kind of study whether not getting uptight is actually good for your body.

To their credit, the Washington team do acknowledge this. They also point out that even taking all the psychological factors together gives us only a slim chance (maybe one in five) of predicting those particular people who will fall sick and those who will stay well. Differences in environment and lifestyle often overshadow any conclusions that we might draw from their psychology.

But if we have to beware of our naivety running away with us, we must also avoid the opposite extreme. A clear case of premature rejection can be found in a now famous guest editorial written by Marcia Angell.[4] It appeared in no less a publication than the *New England Journal of Medicine* in 1985. 'Is cancer more likely in unhappy people?' she asks; '. . . what about heart attacks, peptic ulcers, asthma, rheumatoid arthritis and inflammatory bowel disease? . . . A stranger in this country would not have to be here very long to guess that most Americans think the answer to this question is "yes".'

She rightly blasts the media for putting out a continuous stream of superficial stories about the mind–body link. Then she quotes two scientific studies that suggests there is no link at all. Unfortunately she chooses badly. Both were designed in such a way that they could hardly be expected to show very much. For some reason she ignores the 15,000 reports, just on the question of mind and immunity, that appeared in 200 journals between 1976 and 1982. They were published in summary form by the Institute for the Advancement of Health. Some of them are rather well designed, and point to a different conclusion.[5]

Angell does highlight one real danger that we risk in accepting the mind–body connection. To attribute recovery from illness to the patients' own will to live may mean blaming those who don't recover for not trying hard enough. If treatment is carried out with sensitivity, then the patient who doesn't get better shouldn't feel like a failure. But some cancer patients, for example, certainly do feel that way. And some of their therapists have a lot to answer for.

However, there is something even more damning to Angell's mind than blaming the victim. It is the lack, as she sees it, of any convincing data to establish that the mind–body link even exists. In her view, 'it is time to acknowledge that our belief in disease as a direct reflection of mental state is largely folklore . . .'.

Her remarks typify the views of an increasing number of physicians, some disenchanted, some never very enchanted in the first place, by the links between mind and body. The question has become, quite simply, the most disputed health issue of our time. It is difficult to remain rational and objective about it, and some people, on both sides, have stopped trying.

Norman Cousins himself, now Dean of the Medical School at Los Angeles, has come back into the debate, one which he was instrumental in starting. He sympathizes with physicians who feel increasingly 'pushed by imponderables in the wrong direction', who feel besieged by the flurry of publications on the importance of psychological factors in disease. He draws attention to the very real concern that some people 'may regard positive emotions as a substitute for essential medical attention'.

In an attempt to defuse some of this controversy, Cousins suggests that building feelings of confidence within the patient, giving him a sense of purpose and strengthening his will to live are not alternatives to therapy but rather ways of 'enhancing the environment of treatment'. They are the wise physician's attempt to create a spirit of responsible participation with his patient that should foster the process of recovery.

With consummate good sense he says that 'It would be as much an error to suppose that intangibles dominate human health and disease as it is to suppose that they are altogether absent. The essential issue is whether it is possible to strike a sensible balance between psychological factors and biologic factors in the understanding and management of disease.'[6]

Well, is it possible? Where does such a balance lie? My own view, after looking at the subject for the last ten years, is that the balance is weighted rather heavily on the biological side. If it weren't, if the influences of mental on physical health were as obvious as, say, the role of blood pressure in heart diseases, then there would be no discussion.

Effects of the mind (that's to say the brain) on the body are real; that is beyond dispute. But their relevance to physical health and illness is much less clear. And usually they are not nearly as potent as the force that the body exerts on the mind.

Let me show you what I mean.

Blowing the mind

Recall first the detailed study of the links between physical illness and depression carried out on over 700 volunteers in Los Angeles by Carol Aneshensel and colleagues.[7] At each of four interviews they asked the volunteers about the physical complaints they had been feeling during the previous week and whether they were also feeling depressed.

They found that even minor illnesses like colds and flu, aches and pains, led to an instant increase in feelings of depression compared to previous visits when they had been interviewed and had had no physical symptoms. By contrast, being depressed led to only a slight increase in the reporting of physical ill-health, but not at the same interview. Depression was only linked to physical symptoms that appeared at the *next* interview four months later. And even then the link was not as strong as in the other direction. Interestingly enough, as people got older they showed more illness but were less depressed about it. Men showed less of either than women did, and people with more money were also less likely to be either ill or depressed.

It is not surprising that our mood goes down if our illness stops us from doing things. Doing badly (the opposite of doing well) leads to feeling badly.

More surprising is the way that different people respond to having their activities restricted. In the short term, virtually everyone has a temporary drop in mood. Fortunately, our experience of illness is usually short-term as well. But many people have the ability to adapt quite rapidly, even to long-standing complaints.

For example, patients with chronic pain are now being taught how to accept the fact that the pain will probably always be with them. Having accepted it, they learn how to stop it disrupting their lives. Basically what they learn is the ability to cope with it. Coping is now the most important topic in the whole mind–body area: one of the absolutely crucial features of being able to say yes to life.

So our mood goes down because our activity is restricted. But that's not the only way that physical illness affects our mental health. There are more obvious and more direct links as well.

In the 1960s, Fort Detrick in Maryland was a centre for the US Army Chemical Corp. Groups of volunteers there were exposed to a typhoidal bacterium called *Pasturella*, to see which of them would develop a fever as a result. They also recorded their moods twice a day (using the sort of mood scales we have already seen) from before they were exposed to the organism right through the illness itself. What the investigators discovered was that, after exposure, the volunteers' positive feelings started to fall and their negative moods started to increase. Hardly surprising, you might think. But the unexpected feature is that these mood changes started the day *before* their temperatures started to rise. It seemed that such mood swings might act as predictors of illness, 'sensitive psychologic barometers to biologic states'.[8]

Notice that their moods didn't change because they suddenly felt feverish. The mood swings came before the fever. Feeling bad seemed to result from some direct biochemical change associated with the infection. But it was such an early change that even the men themselves weren't yet aware of it.

There are many diseases that make people feel bad before the complaint itself becomes apparent. Current research is looking at mood changes in HIV positives, those who don't yet show any evidence of AIDS. It may be that the presence of the virus, or its products, or the defence that the body tries to mount against it, have a direct effect on the sufferer's mental health, quite apart from the anxiety and demoralization that is caused even by the possibility of being infected.

There is good evidence that this even happens with flu. One of the responses that the body mounts against infection with the flu virus is the production by white blood cells of the anti-viral substance *interferon*. But if high doses of interferon are given to healthy volunteers, they too start to develop some flu-like symptoms. For example, their reactions get slowed down.

As I said in connection with the post-viral fatigue syndrome, I have often wondered whether minor infections may also account for the type of mood swings that many people describe. Everything is going well, perhaps for days or even weeks, until suddenly and unaccountably you feel anxious, listless and distressed. Suddenly, everything is an effort. When this happens we look around for a cause and it is usually easy enough to find one. We may ask, 'Why can't I do this?' and the answer comes back, 'It's because I'm losing my grip.' We ask, 'What's the matter with me?' and we hear, 'You're just not up to it.' We say, 'I used to be able to do all this okay,' and the voice in your head says, 'Stop fooling yourself. You never did it very well, now you can't do it at all.'

But just as you are spiralling down into increasing gloom about how competent you really are, ever were, or ever will be, you start to sneeze. The headcold breaks and you realize with immense relief that the slide into despondency was physical after all. It was due to the effects of interferon or one of the many other responses that the body makes to being infected.

Box 10 is a scheme of my own, meant to show some of these mind–body links. It also shows the way that our individual personalities act as lenses to magnify or distort the process. We now know well enough that personality dimensions like E and N have a major influence on whether our mood stays buoyant or whether we get depressed when parts of our life start going wrong.

So the body affects the mind, either directly (via some biochemical process) or through our perception that we are not doing things very well. The body–mind effect is strong and unmistakable.

But can we run the film backwards, and see how the mind affects the body?

Psychosomatics up to date

A doctor met one of his patients at a cocktail party. 'How are you?' the doctor asked. 'Oh, I feel great today, doctor,' the patient replied. 'Mind you, I expect it's psychosomatic.'

We are indebted to Fredrick Alexander, the founder of the Alexander Principle (a type of treatment based on the idea that the way we use our bodies physically affects the way that they function) for introducing the word 'psychosomatic'. It has become part of our everyday language. And the idea that it embodies – that specific physical problems have particular psychological causes – is so widely believed that it seems a heresy to suggest that it is wrong.

But it is.

For over fifty years psychosomatic specialists have tried to link different types of emotional disturbance to particular physical complaints. And they have all failed. The idea of someone with a 'cancer-prone' or a 'rheumatism-prone' personality, whose problem is largely due to his particular emotional make-up or thinking patterns, is simply not borne out by the facts.

That doesn't mean (as Marcia Angell would claim) that our psychological state has no bearing on our physical health. But it does mean that the old idea of looking for some sort of one-to-one relationship between mind and body is a thing of the past. More modern therapists now realize this. They have now recast the old psychosomatic principle in a more general form by suggesting

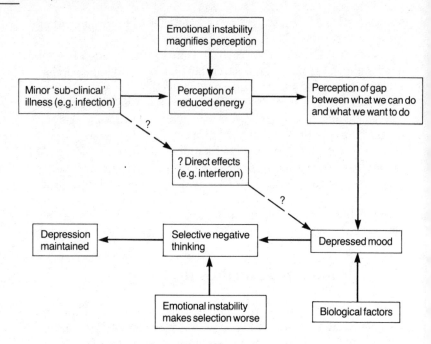

Box 10.   *Some body–mind links.*
The link between illness and depression arises because, before the illness is even apparent, we feel our energy level falling and find we can't do as much as we want to. There may also be a direct effect of the infection itself, due, for example, to the action of interferon. Our depressed mood leads to us concentrating on negative thoughts about ourselves, and unless we have the life-affirming resources to bounce back the depression may be maintained. Emotional instability acts as a distorting lens by selecting only negative information to dwell on.

that 'psychological factors probably influence the outcome of virtually every disease'.[9]

What they don't say is that the influence is often so weak that it's hard to detect. Let me give you a few examples where the mind–body link seems very clear. Then let me tell you what is disappointing about them.

Intimations of mortality

Firstly, how long people live is determined, among other things, by how long they think they are going to live.

In the 1970s researchers asked one simple question of a group of 3,000 elderly Canadians.[10] The question was 'For your age' (they were all sixty-five or more) 'would you say in general that your health is excellent, fair, good or poor?'

For six years after the question was asked their health records were searched to see which of them were still alive and who had died in the interim. By matching these *actual* health outcomes to each person's *perception* of their health, the researchers discovered that the risk of dying was nearly three times greater among those who had rated their health as poor, compared to those who said it was excellent. This 'subjective' estimate of health – the sense of how people felt about themselves – was a better predictor of death than a more 'objective' measurement based on the actual use they had made of health-care facilities in the year before they had answered the question.

And this is not an isolated finding. The same type of survey was carried out in Alameda County. Nearly 7,000 Californians of all ages were also asked in the mid-1960s to rate their health as excellent, good, fair or poor. They were followed up for nine years to see who had died. Men who said their health was poor were more than twice as likely to die over the period as those who, at the outset, said that it was excellent. For women, the risk was increased fivefold.[11]

But how did they know; what was it that put their lives at higher risk?

People who perceived their health as being poor didn't take such good care of themselves. They had fewer social contacts and were less happy than the others. But this wasn't the whole story. There are ways of using statistics to take these other factors into account. And after doing so it was found that neither the volunteers' age, sex nor 'objective' health status at the beginning of the study fully explained away their health perceptions. Neither did how well they looked after themselves, nor how large a social network they were part of. These features were powerful predictors of mortality in themselves. But subjective health taps something beyond them. Interestingly enough, it doesn't seem to be emotional distress that leads to premature death either. Although people with poor health estimates were also higher on measures of depression and low morale, these psychological factors didn't seem to affect longevity at all.

So how does perceived health work? The researchers suggest that people may have knowledge about their own bodies, about their nervous, hormonal and immune systems, that they are hardly aware of, and that certainly don't show up on health examination. But the ability to access this information 'subconsciously' allows them to get a good idea of just how healthy they really are.

And there is a practical lesson to be learned from all of this. The Canadian team conclude that 'increased emphasis on technological medicine has tended to result in less and less attention to what people say about their health'. Doctors should listen more to what their patients are telling them.

If thinking you are ill can influence your health, can other psychological factors do it? The answer, of course, is yes. Redford Williams and his group at Duke University unearthed a series of psychological tests that medical students in North Carolina had completed during their training in the late 1950s. In 1981 they traced 225 of these ex-students (now physicians) and established whether they were still alive (ill or healthy) or whether they were deceased. They then compared this information against the scores that the men obtained as students on one particular psychological scale that measured hostility.[12] The type of hostility they were looking at was not blind rage. Instead it was a cynical distrust of other people and their motives.

They found that men high on this hostility scale twenty-five years before were nearly five times more likely to have developed coronary heart disease in the interim. And when they looked at deaths (from all causes, not just coronaries) they discovered that the high hostiles were six times more likely to have died than those who had more regard for their fellow men. Again, statistical corrections showed that the excess of deaths wasn't due to the fact that the men as students may have smoked or drunk more or had higher levels of cholesterol or blood pressure.

So why did they die sooner? Williams believes that hostility has a direct effect on your coronary arteries. But, in addition, individuals who show an obvious dislike or avoidance of other people get disliked and avoided themselves. Belonging to a support network increases your chance of survival. Not belonging reduces it. So maybe these hostile doctors simply kicked away their life-support systems.

'Nothing I can do'

If heart disease, the major killer of men in Western societies, is influenced by psychological factors, then so too is the number-two killer, cancer. Steven Greer and his group, originally at the Faith Courtauld Institute and later at the Royal Marsden Hospital in London, studied women who had been diagnosed as having breast cancer and who had therefore had a mastectomy. Three months after the operation they were interviewed to determine how they were responding, how they had mentally adjusted to having the disease.[13]

Greer's team found that the women's reactions could be divided into four types. Those whom he described as having a *fighting spirit* said things like 'I won't let cancer beat me; I'm trying everything to get better.' A second group showed what the interviewers described as *denial* of their condition: 'the doctors just took my breast off as a precaution'. Some women showed a *stoic acceptance:* 'I know it's cancer, but I've got to carry on as normal.' Finally, the fourth group seemed to be *helpless and hopeless.* They said things like 'There's nothing I can do, I'm finished.'

To see whether these attitudes had any effect on how long the women survived, Greer's team, in a piece of research that is now famous in cancer circles, followed them up for five years. He found by that time that women showing either denial of their cancer or having a fighting spirit were more likely to have survived and to be free from recurrence of the disease than those who were either stoically accepting their problem or who were helpless and hopeless in the face of it. Even after ten years, the pattern was the same. Only 20 per cent of the helpless/hopeless group were survivors as compared to 80 per cent of those with fighting spirit.

In California researchers carried out similar interviews and did the same sort of follow-up study on patients with malignant melanoma.[14] They found that women showing stoic acceptance and men who were helpless and hopeless had an increased risk of the disease spreading. What was important in both studies is the fact that these psychological factors predicted death or the spread of the disease quite independently of the sort of biological factors that cancer specialists use in predicting survival.

'Do I get infected?'

Let's move on to look at some other examples of how people's psychological make-up influences their physical health – this time how the way we think and feel may increase our risk of infection.

We can start by going back to Fort Detrick and the US Army volunteers. They were often involved in trials to test new vaccines against pathogens like typhus, typhoid and yellow fever. Not surprisingly, some of them reacted to these vaccines, either with local swelling at the point where they had been jabbed or with more general joint pains and fever.[15]

Before the vaccine shots they also completed a battery of psychological questionnaires that included tests of hypochondria, loss of morale and low ego strength. Subjects whose scores came out badly on this combination of tests were described as being 'psychologically vulnerable'. The question was whether they were physically vulnerable as well.

And it won't surprise you to learn that they were. Only about one man in ten showed any reaction to the vaccines. But of those who did, the psychologically vulnerable were three times more likely to respond than those whose psychological tests showed them to be more robust. As a group they seemed to be psychologically 'hypersensitive'. When exposed to infection, they were more physically sensitive as well.

At the Medical Research Council's Common Cold Unit in Wiltshire, volunteers are exposed to respiratory viruses.[16] They receive the virus in the form of nasal drops, after which they are followed for five days to see whether they get cold symptoms like sore noses, how many handkerchiefs they use, and whether they started to shed the virus themselves.

In one trial that looked at the effect of psychological factors, the person's life events didn't predict who would become infected. What did predict who would have more cold symptoms was the volunteer's personality. Introverts had more symptoms than extraverts. And introverts also shed more of the virus while they were ill. So far no one has been able to explain this effect, but workers at the Common Cold Unit (soon alas to be closed down through lack of adequate funding) tell me that they find it happens time and again.

Let's take as a final example susceptibility to another more serious complaint, this time glandular fever, known technically as infectious mononucleosis (or more simply as 'mono'). If you have been exposed to the virus that causes it (called Epstein-Barr virus or EBV) then your immune system develops antibodies against it, and you become immune to future attacks. So it is possible to tell who is susceptible to the disease. They are people with no antibodies in their bloodstream. The process of developing antibodies on coming into contact with the virus is called *seroconversion*. Those who seroconvert may be able to contain the virus, or they may go on to develop mono itself, with its symptoms of fever, sore throat, liver problems and physical exhaustion. Indeed, we saw that the Epstein-Barr virus has been suggested as one of the causes of post-viral syndrome.

Mononucleosis gives researchers an excellent chance to see whether psychological factors are involved in people becoming infected with the virus (and seroconverting) and then actually developing the disease.

Stan Kasl and his colleagues looked at this problem in a class of 1,400 West Point cadets that they followed for four years.[17] When they entered the Academy, about two-thirds of the cadets were immune. They had the antibody already. So attention concentrated on the others. Every year about one in five seroconverted, and a quarter of those developed glandular fever. The question was, what characteristics, measured at their entry to the Point, and before any exposure to the virus, would predict which cadets were susceptible?

They found a combination of factors that predicted not only seroconversion but who would become infected, and how severe their illness would be. They were, firstly, having an 'overachieving' father, one who had done well in life despite having had a poor education. Second was the cadets' strong attachment to a military career. These young men wanted to do well. But the third predictive factor was their poor academic performance. Despite being strongly committed to getting on, and presumably having fathers who pushed them in that direction, the cadets most likely to suffer from mono were simply not very bright. They probably felt trapped and pressured by their desire to succeed, and as a result it seems their distress somehow increased their susceptibility to EBV.

So here are eight clear examples of the mind affecting the body, of the impact of mental health on physical health. And I have been careful to choose only the best. Every one of them measured some psychological factor at the outset and then followed the subjects for months or years to see what happened to them. This is called a 'prospective' design and it is the only type that we can really take seriously.

Unfortunately, the scientific journals are littered with at least ten times the number of what are known as *retrospective* studies. Here the investigator locates people who are ill, or finds the relatives of those who died, and asks them to cast their minds back. Were there perhaps any disturbing events that occurred in the weeks or months before the illness that might account for it?

And the answer of course is always yes. We all have disturbances in our lives. And most people are so convinced that 'stress' causes illness that it is not difficult for them to search back in their memories and come up with possible causes. They may even be right. But we can never be sure by looking back this way, and so retrospective studies have to be put on one side.

But even faced with this array of solid, prospective data I still have to say that mind–body connections are not as strong as those that go in the opposite direction. Let me try to explain why.

Strong links – weak links

Only when groups of people are exposed to some overwhelming disaster like a plague or a famine can we be sure that most of them will fall ill as a consequence. Normally in any group who encounter the sort of unhealthy influences that we normally experience (like a high-fat diet or cigarette smoke or a flu epidemic) only a proportion of them will become ill. Remember that only one in ten of the Fort Detrick volunteers reacted to the vaccines. Remember, too, that we frequently carry round disease-causing or 'pathogenic' organisms without succumbing to them. Not all the seroconverters at West Point developed glandular fever, and only 20–40 per cent of people who have been colonized by streptococci (the bacteria that cause scarlet fever and 'strep throat') actually develop symptoms.

Health specialists years ago explained this by saying that virtually all illness is 'multi-factorial'. It is due to a number of different forces all acting together on the same person. For an infection it is obviously necessary to have an organism present. But unless it is particularly virulent, it is also necessary for the person carrying it to be weakened in some way before the disease will develop. The weakness may be physical, like a shortage of some trace element needed to keep the immune system working properly. Or it may be psychological, like the frustrated need to do well among the West Point cadets. More serious psychological problems are those like the cynical hostility felt by the doctors when they were students in North Carolina, or the helpless reaction to cancer in the women examined by Steven Greer.

There is a whole branch of medical statistics that looks at these multi-factorial causes of illness. It tries to establish just how strong they are. Almost invariably the answer comes back, that for explaining bodily disease biological causes outstrip any others.

This is true even with the mind–body links we have been looking at. In the Alameda Study of self-related health, believing that their health was poor increased the risk of people dying. But their *actual* health status predicted it more strongly, and a measure of how well they looked after themselves physically was stronger still. In the studies of melanoma, psychological attitudes predicted the spread of the disease, but the stage of development which the tumour had reached was the most powerful predictor of all. So psychological factors may only represent the 'fine tuning' in a system where our biological state is the major predictor of illness, and hence the major cause of wellness too.

You will have noticed that I keep talking about *predictors* of illness because all we can usually say about any particular 'risk factor' (physical or mental) is not that it is certain to kill you, but that it increases the chance of your falling ill to some particular extent, measured over so many years.

So, for example, if we take heart disease, we can say that a group of people with a collection of raised risk factors (high cholesterol, high blood pressure and so on) will fall into a 'high-risk' group. They have a 10 per cent chance of having a major heart attack within the next five years. But if we look at the actual figures[18] we find that even in this high-risk group only about one in fifty will actually have an attack, and for members of a low-risk group, with normal risk factors, the figure is nearer to one in 250.

If you multiply it up to the whole population, it represents an enormous toll – one male death in every three in England and Wales; over 150,000 dead every year. Not for nothing is coronary disease called the 'number-one killer of Western man'. What does come as a surprise is how difficult it is to translate these population figures into risks for the individual – for you or me.

All that any doctor can do is to give you an estimate of how likely you are to fall ill, based on what he knows about you. And often that estimate may be much lower than you would think. Few health specialists doubt that cigarettes make a major contribution to lung cancer. One analysis suggests that if the population of England and Wales gave up smoking overnight then 22,000 lung-cancer cases would be prevented every year (to say nothing of 23,000 coronary cases). And 90 per cent of lung-cancer deaths occur in those people who do smoke.[19]

But we saw how knowing that people smoke gives you a less than 1 per cent chance of predicting whether they will get cancer or not.

The reason is simple enough. Although few non-smokers develop lung cancer, many smokers don't get it. People show an enormous variation in their susceptibilities to disease. They have vulnerability factors that make them more prone and resistance resources that protect them. Life-affirming qualities are among the resources that increase their resistance.

But I am not only saying that psychological features produce outcomes that are difficult to predict. A lot of physical ones have this problem of low predictability as well. I'm saying in addition that, as far as the body is concerned, many mental outcomes are completely lost, overwhelmed by a mixture of more powerful biological effects.

A few of the 'psycho-social' risk factors that we know most about, like hostility and being isolated from other people, foretell future disease about as well as any single factor relating to our biology – like blood pressure and cholesterol. At best, cholesterol levels predict only one in every ten cases of coronary disease. But many of the other psychological factors come much further down the list. They predict people falling physically ill at a level of one in twenty or one in fifty or one in 100. Naturally enough, because of their 'mental' nature they often give better predictions for mental breakdown. George Brown could predict depression among one woman in five. But expect to see many other examples where the effect of the mind on the body is so tenuous that for practical purposes you may wonder whether it is there at all.

We have to appreciate another fact as well. Feeling that your health is bad is one predictor of death. How well you look after yourself is another. But the two of them overlap. Although you can separate them in the statistics, part of feeling bad may actually result from the fact that you are not taking care of yourself, or perhaps that you are socially disconnected from other people. Remember how Redford Williams suggested that hostility has a distinct effect on the chemistry that leads to blood clotting in the coronary arteries. In addition it also drives other people away and leaves you lonely and isolated.

Enter PNI

What I've just said will disappoint a lot of people. They will point out that in the last five to ten years we have had a major break-through in the study of mind—body connections. We have learned that there are direct connections between the brain, the nervous system, the glands that produce our hormones and the immune system itself. Surely in the last few years we have seen a mind—body revolution?

The answer is 'yes we have'. We now understand much better than we ever did how emotional disturbances lead to the outflow of a whole series of chemical messengers (hormones) that affect many aspects of our bodily functioning. We have also discovered a series of other substances, known as *neurotransmitters* or *neuropeptides*, that are found in many different parts of the brain and the body, and that are responsible for rapid communication between the two.

And we have come to appreciate how the brain and the immune system are connected with each other. For example, the brain sends out nerves to areas like the thymus gland that is responsible for the growth and maturation of many of the white blood cells (lymphocytes) involved in the immune response. So there are direct 'hard-wired' connections between the nervous and the immune systems.

We have even discovered that many of these lymphocyte cells have areas on their surface called 'receptors', regions that recognize and accept certain chemical molecules in the bloodstream. As we saw with brain chemistry and depression, these molecules fit into the receptor region much as a key fits into a lock. As they do so they 'switch on' biochemical processes inside the lymphocyte itself. The striking fact is that the molecules that activate the lymphocytes are either hormones released from the nervous system (or the glands that it stimulates) or neuropeptides like those produced in the brain.

But there is more. Recently, the lymphocytes and other cells involved in the immune response have come under close scrutiny. As a result we now know that they not only have receptors, so that they can recognize the neuropeptides. They are also able to produce neuropeptides for themselves. The immune system produces the same type of molecules that the brain uses to transmit its own messages.

The implications are staggering, and they have led to the development of a whole new branch of science called *psychoneuroimmunology* (PNI) – literally the study of connections between the mind, the nervous system and our immunity. It is now clear that the brain and the immune system are in full communication with each other, and that the messages are transmitted both ways. Emotional distress can lead to the release of transmitters that will suppress the actions of the immune cells. When the body comes to fight off an infection, the same cells send their chemical messages to the brain, to keep it informed about what is happening.

The nervous and immune systems have been known by generations of specialists but they have always been regarded as quite separate, disconnected systems, running in parallel. Now finally we have come to realize how the function of each has profound effects on the other.

The discoveries of PNI have been said to open a whole new chapter in our understanding of the mind–body link. For example, in a recent book on *The Psychobiology of Mind–Body Healing*[20] its author, Ernest Lawrence Rossi, captures the spirit of the new scientific age when he tells us that 'This messenger molecule and cell-receptor communication system is the psychobiological basis of mind–body healing, therapeutic hypnosis and holistic medicine in general.'

Melancholy occasions

This new science has produced some impressive results. Let us get some sense of what PNI researchers are discovering.

To do so we have to know that our immune system produces two kinds of protective response to the presence of a foreign intruder. Firstly, white cells known *B-lymphocytes* (because they develop in the bone marrow) produce protein molecules called *antibodies* that coat invading materials like bacteria and mark them out for destruction by special cells called *macrophages*. The production of antibodies by B-cells is assisted by the action of lymphocytes called *helper T-cells* (T because they develop in the thymus gland). Another group of T-cells (called *suppressors)* switch the process off when it has gone far enough. Helper and suppressor cells provide a push–pull action and their balance is essential for normal immune functioning. One other cell type that we should know about is the *natural killer* or NK cell that is able to destroy either invading cells or renegade cells arising from the body itself, such as early tumours. Unlike the macrophages, NK cells seem to be able to recognize 'foreign' material without needing an antibody marker to point it out.

So this, in one paragraph, is an outline of immunity – a scheme that it takes whole textbooks to describe properly. It is over-simplified but it will suffice to give a flavour of some recent findings about the links between mind and immunity.

For example, one of the most disturbing events that can happen to anyone is to lose their spouse. We will see how lists of life events put bereavement right at the top, with a maximum possible score of 100. And some research shows that bereaved spouses, particularly men, suffer from an increase in mortality, usually within a year of losing their loved ones.

What more natural then than to look at the effects of bereavement on immunity? Several investigations have found that, within a matter of weeks of bereavement, T-cells show a fall in their normal activity.[21] And this has been linked to the premature death of widowers. As long ago as 1884 the *British Medical Journal*,[22] talking about funerals, suggested that 'the depression of spirits under which the chief mourners labour at these melancholy occasions particularly disposes them to some of the worst effects of chill'. It seems to have needed the discovery of PNI nearly a century later to show how this might happen.

But before we conclude that the death of the remaining spouse is due to a direct mind–body link, we ought to remember two facts that do not fit this scheme. The first is that, for most people who are bereaved, immunity recovers within a matter of months. It doesn't stay 'suppressed' for the rest of their lives. The other is that when bereaved spouses do die (and most of them survive) it can be from virtually any cause. It is not generally the result of some massive infection. But it is infectious disease that the immune system protects us against. So the bereavement story may not be the confirmation of mind–body-health that it was thought to be. An alternative explanation is that, rather than succumbing to immunosuppression, the bereaved simply lose their motivation to live, let themselves go, give up and become helpless. Death may be due to simple self-neglect.

Another emotional problem frequently linked with physical illness is depression. We have seen how readily people can become depressed as the result of minor aches and pains. There is even some evidence that links depression to the progression of cancer. So it is natural to enquire whether depressed people also show reduced immunity.

The answer is that they do. Patients in hospital with major depressive disorders have fewer lymphocytes, and those that they do have are reduced in activity.[23] They also have higher circulating levels of the hormone *cortisol*, which itself has a suppressive effect on the immune system. And these alterations are not caused by simply being in hospital, because they are not found in schizophrenic patients who have been there for the same length of time.

So depressed people may also show immune disturbances. Another mind–body link? Yes. But, interesting as it is, the disturbance is only seen in the severely depressed. People with only mild depressions have a perfectly normal immune system.

Separation, divorce and Alzheimer's disease

Let us complete this whistle-stop tour of some of the more striking PNI findings by considering the work of one of the most influential research groups in this field.[24] Janice Kiecolt-Glaser is a psychologist, an elegant, affable and clear-sighted woman who works at Ohio State University. In the same research team is her husband Ronald Glaser, an immunologist of wide experience. Between them they combine the many skills necessary for looking at the integration of the mind and the immune system. They have examined all sorts of measures of immunity in people undergoing all sorts of emotional disturbance.

For example, they found that at examination time medical students show a fall in the number of helper T-cells and in their activity, and a fall in natural killer cells too. In addition, antibodies that the students had developed against *herpes simplex* (the virus causing cold sores) also increased, suggesting that the virus (which stays with you once you have caught it, lying dormant in your nerve cells) was becoming activated again. They also found that lonely students had more immune problems than those who felt that they had friends, and the same was true for lonely psychiatric patients. So suffering short-term stresses and being dissatisfied with our personal relationships is linked to changes in our immunity.

What about long-term problems?

The Ohio group looked at people who were recently separated or divorced. Women who had separated from their partners had fewer lymphocytes. Those who had been separated for less than a year had fewer T-helper and NK cells and also had higher antibody levels against Epstein-Barr virus. It seemed that during the particularly stressful period of early separation the virus was starting to show itself.

But, as I heard Janice Kiecolt-Glaser say at a conference in Washington, 'The mere presence of a partner is not equivalent to a supportive relationship.' (Her remark, though not meant to be funny, nearly brought the house down. Most of the audience knew just what she meant first-hand.)

What it means in immune terms is that women who were unhappily married were found to be more emotionally depressed, to have lymphocytes that were depressed as well, and to have antibodies that were working harder to suppress EBV. And though men are generally believed to adapt to separation more easily than women, the Ohio team also found more emotional distress and very striking increases in antibodies against herpes and mononucleosis in men who had split up.

Finally, what about really long-term stress? Maybe people eventually adapt to it and their immunity returns to normal?

Alzheimer's disease attacks the brain in such a way that the victim eventually becomes completely helpless and needs to be looked after the whole time. Doing so puts an extreme strain on the relatives who have to do the caring. And since they may have to do so for ten years or more, the strain is certainly chronic.

The Glasers looked at the mental and physical health of Alzheimer care-givers. These people who looked after their demented relatives showed much more emotional distress than people of the same age who didn't have this cross to bear. They also had fewer lymphocytes and a lower ratio of helper to suppressor T-cells (an important ratio for normal immunity, and one which becomes badly disturbed in diseases like AIDS). They also had higher antibody levels against EBV. Most striking of all perhaps was the fact that these immune disturbances had been going on for years. Care-giving relatives didn't have the capacity to adapt to their role and get their immunity back to normal.

This work from Ohio together with many similar investigations shows how psychological distress can increase our susceptibility to infection. The emotional disturbances don't induce the infection directly. But they may lower our immune resistance to it (remember the psychological vulnerables at Fort Detrick and the not-so-bright students at West Point). Other possibilities relate to cancer. Perhaps immunosuppression reduces the surveillance carried out by NK cells and early cancerous changes are not detected and destroyed. Instead, they proliferate.

The PNI manifesto

Put all this together and we have what we might call the PNI manifesto, a set of beliefs about the effects of the mind on the body that resembles the humanistic manifesto that Abraham Maslow put forward thirty years ago. It is certainly held with the same conviction by many health specialists.

But I am not one of them; at least not yet. And the reason is twofold.

There is no doubt that emotional distress causes bodily changes – nervous, hormonal and immune. For millions of years, that's what anxiety and fear have been meant to do. And particular patterns of emotion may be linked with illness, either with the way that it starts or at least with its spread once it gets a hold.

But what is crucially lacking are studies where all of these elements – distress, disturbance and disease – are found in the same person. It is certainly possible that immune changes – a fall in the number of lymphocytes or in their activity may lead to illness. But do they? We simply don't know. Lymphocyte numbers vary, even in the blood of 'normal' people, so it is difficult to judge the importance of any fall in the immunity of people in distress. Often their disturbances seem to be rather minor (well within the normal range) and rather short-lived. Remember how bereaved lymphocyte activities usually returned to normal within a year or less.

Emotional distress may lead to infection by disturbing our immune responses, but it will take a lot more data than we have at present to prove that it happens consistently. And even the idea of cancer being due to an immune breakdown seems much less credible than it did ten years ago when many of these studies were started. Very few types of cancer, it now seems, go by this route.

But, above all, we have to realize that it is not a series of mysterious messages carried by nerves or neuropeptides that decides whether we fall ill. Those are only the *pathways* to illness. If emotional disturbance does lead to physical disease then it's our failure to come to grips with our life situation that switches on the emotional response that alters the physiology that leads to the dysfunction that creates the complaint. It is our appraisal of the situation and our response to it that decide if the pathways are activated or not.

Saying yes to life means meeting our situation head on, defusing our distress and limiting our dysfunction. Most illnesses don't creep up without our knowing, and life-affirmers increase their chances of feeling well, doing well and staying well by the way that they deal with reality.

But leaving aside the whole question of mind–body links for a moment, they also do it by simply looking after their bodies more directly. They seek out the latest health advice and, if it seems credible to them, they absorb it into their own way of life.

CHAPTER 9

Look to the Body

T HE great problem with health education is that most people find it boring. Putting over a simple health message, for instance that cigarettes increase your risk of both lung cancer and heart disease, is surprisingly difficult. You might think that everyone is interested enough in maintaining their health to listen to new advice when it first appears and then to act on it. But that's not what actually happens.

A boring education

Instead, when a new piece of health-related advice becomes available, it is taken up and acted upon very quickly by a minority group of what have been called 'health innovators'. Two features mark these people out. They are the ones who have a special interest in keeping healthy. But, more particularly, they are also the group who believe that the state of their health depends on what they do about it. They are convinced that they can exert some control over how healthy they are. In short, they are our life-affirmers.

Remember the *inner-directed* people in the UK market surveys, a growing sector who profoundly *disagree* when you put to them ideas like 'There is little I can do to prevent disease'? Remember the health *confidents* in the United States – a quarter of the population in that telephone survey – who strongly *agreed* with the suggestion that they could control their own health?

These are the innovators, the people to whom the new health message gets across very quickly. Not only do they think that it might work. More importantly, they believe that they can get it to work for them.

Following the innovators, often quite a long way behind, are a much larger group of people – call them the health *conservatives*. You can recognize them by the fact that they don't start shifting their own behaviour until they see some other groups taking the lead. As the benefits of the change become apparent, they start to jump aboard. They too become convinced that they can help themselves, but others have to prove it for them first.

Finally, there remain the group who have been called the health *indifferents*. They have little interest in changing their ways at all. When you ask them why not, they may perhaps challenge your facts ('My grandad smoked sixty a day and he lived to be eighty-four'). But more often they give you a fatalistic reply ('You've got to die of something'). Deep down, you get a strong hint that they don't really believe that there is much they can do to stay healthy. Their physical well-being seems to be largely outside their own control.

And this is why health education is boring. A new campaign starts, and after a short time the innovators don't need to have the message endlessly repeated. They are already doing it. However long it goes on for, the indifferents will disregard it altogether. What's left are the conservatives in the middle, hearing it time and again, and slowly changing, not so much because of what they hear, as because of what they see other people doing.

Today's health educators are coming to realize that simply presenting the facts about illness or death isn't enough to change people's behaviour. There also has to be the stronger message that 'You can get it to work for you'. This is something that manufacturers in the health area and their advertising agencies have known for years.

Ironically, we owe a debt to the AIDS outbreak for forcing health education to adopt the more 'consumerist' feel that their messages need if they are to be effective. But huge problems remain. For example, three out of five middle-aged men in Britain still have a cholesterol level that doubles their risk of a heart attack, compared to achievable, 'safe' levels.[1] What message is going to have an impact on that situation?

This isn't a book about health education, so I don't want to get side-tracked into the question of how to sell good health at a national level. But what I am concerned about is what life-affirmers actually do for themselves. They clearly believe that what they do will make a difference. Their other great strength is that they aren't put off even if the message isn't very exciting. Because, in general, it's not.

Enormous health gains can be made by following the most elementary set of principles that have been known about for years. Life-affirmers appreciate that we don't always need more discovery and innovations, though they are interested in some of the more innovative ideas that we will consider at the end of the chapter. They realize that they can add years to their lives by just doing the boring things that everyone knows about.

And there are solid figures to prove it.

Seven pillars of health

We have already mentioned a large-scale American study in which the health of a group of about 7,000 people was followed over a period of nine years.[2] They lived in Alameda County, California, and I shall refer to this Alameda Study several times, because it tells us a lot about staying healthy. In the next chapter we will see how it showed that being in a social network increases your chances of survival. But for now I want to concentrate on what the Alameda Study tells us about helping ourselves.

The Californian investigators were interested to know how far subjects in the survey followed a series of simple, self-help procedures. So they took nearly 5,000 of their volunteers and asked them. The 'health practices' that they were interested in are listed in Box 11.

Let's look at a few of them individually.

Smoking is something we already know about. Suffice it to say that when current smokers in the Alameda County were compared with those who had never smoked, the risk of death was at least doubled, and increased fourfold in some groups. Drinking heavily also produced an up to twofold difference in the death rate, when people only having a drink every other day were compared to those having more than one a day.

For being overweight (even 30 per cent over ideal weight for height) the difference was not so dramatic. More recently there's been a good deal of controversy about whether obesity is a serious mortality risk. Some specialists feel that being moderately overweight doesn't in itself seriously increase your risk of death. And I have heard cynics suggest that the reason why both the Government's health advisers and the medical profession go after obesity is that it is a 'soft' target. It isn't protected by the same vested interests that surround the tobacco industry.

Even so, there isn't much that obesity has in its favour. Fat people run a higher risk of having increased blood pressure, and their blood fats may also be disturbed. Add to that the increased risk of diabetes, gout and arthritis, and you shouldn't need mortality figures to persuade you to get your weight down within normal limits.

With physical activity (of which more in a minute) there was no such doubt in the Alameda findings. The most active men had only half the risk of dying as those who were lest active, and active women reduced their risk threefold.

When all seven of these health practices were put together into a single index, men who practised six or seven of them had half the mortality risk of those who used less than five. For women, the difference was similar.

And we will see in the next chapter that there's another twist to this story. Because if women practised less than five and were also isolated from other people, their risk went up to threefold. For isolated men who didn't look after themselves, the chance of dying was *five times* as great as for well-connected men who did.

It's worth just repeating these figures, to drive them home. Over a period of say ten years, you are only half as likely to die if you take care of yourself in this ultra-simple way, even if your network of friends and relatives is rich and rewarding. But if your social position is more marginal, then it is even more important not to let yourself go. How best to get that message across to people who already regard themselves as living on the social margins is a real challenge for health educators. Fortunately, it is a message that life-affirmers have already taken on board.

Four o'clock in the morning

The Alameda Study also had a question about sleep. People's sleeping patterns are closely bound up with both their mental and physical health.

Do you:

1. Not smoke cigarettes?
2. Drink only moderately (not more than four drinks at a sitting)?
3. Stay inside the normal weight limit for your height?
4. Eat breakfast regularly?
5. Not usually eat between meals?
6. Sleep seven to eight hours per night?
7. Take regular exercise?

Box 11.   *The seven basic health practices that were looked at in the Alameda County Study. Despite being so simple, most of them on their own will reduce your chance of dying over the next eight years, and when practised together they have an even stronger impact on reducing the death rate.*

Disturbed sleep (especially waking up early in the morning and not being able to get to sleep again) is one of the characteristics of depression. It seems to be an 'endogenous' feature – one due to biological factors more than what is going on in the patient's life. By contrast (as most of us know) not being able to *fall* asleep for a long time is one of the characteristics of anxiety.

Paradoxically enough, some depressions lift if the patient is deprived of a night's sleep, but the improvement is only temporary. At a more practical level, psychiatrists are often asked by patients what they can do about their sleeping problems – 'I just lie there, tossing and turning and worrying about things.' The best advice I ever heard for a patient with depression was 'Well, don't just lie there. Get up and do something useful, even if it is four o'clock in the morning. If you feel tired later you can make your sleep up during the day. Getting something done, even if it's only the dusting, may help you to realize that you're more capable than you thought.'

But disturbed sleep is a problem that goes beyond anxiety and depression. It can have a much greater impact on our lives.

Sleep and death

Several large-scale surveys leave no doubt about the fact that how long we sleep is related to how long we live. The earliest was a massive questionnaire study organized by the American

Cancer Society in 1960. It asked over a million Americans about various aspects of their lifestyle, then followed them up for six years to see what happened to them. By the end of that time, people who said that they slept for six hours or less had a higher death rate than those who said that they slept for seven to eight hours.[3] Similar results have been found in Finland, and the Alameda Study also reported that people who sleep for six hours or less have their chance of dying over nine years increased by a third, even when we make allowance for the effects of smoking, alcohol and so on.

As yet, no one can explain why this should be. Perhaps some people who are already ill, and who sleep badly as a result, get included in the surveys and bias the figures. A similar problem may occur with studies on bodyweight. People who are seriously underweight seem to run similar health risks to those who are obese. Perhaps they are simply ill to start with.

But these sampling problems don't explain the connection as a whole. People sleeping for less than six hours really do seem to have an increased risk, and the link is all the more remarkable because it was found, not by actually measuring how long they slept, but simply by asking them. Doing it this way, one has to live with the fact that poor sleepers are terribly inaccurate in their estimates of how long they actually stay asleep.

Suspecting this, specialists in Edinburgh examined eighteen middle-aged people who said they slept well and compared them with a similar number who in others ways were very similar but who said that they slept poorly.[4] They took them into the sleep laboratory for five consecutive nights and actually measured their sleeping patterns. The self-declared poor sleepers slept much longer than they thought. Even so, they did lose half-an-hour a night compared to the self-confessed good sleepers, and they woke up twice as often in the early part of the night.

So people who say that they sleep poorly do have some basis for their complaint. When the poor sleepers in Edinburgh were looked at more closely, three interesting facts emerged. Firstly, they were more anxious. And this link between poor sleep and an anxious temperament has been found repeatedly. We can guess that they would come out higher on other measures of negative affectivity as well. Secondly, when overnight urine samples were taken, they were found to excrete more adrenaline than the good sleeper.

And thirdly, they were simply hotter. Their body temperature was higher, not only during the night, but during the day as well. This might give some clue about their higher death rates. Perhaps people who sleep poorly have a biochemical profile that means that their sleep doesn't restore them properly.

Restoring the tissues

Why do we sleep at all? The widely held belief is that we need to reverse the breakdown of our tissues that occurs during the day. In our waking state we are constantly aroused and alert. Our sympathetic nervous system is switched on and we produce hormones like adrenaline and corticosteroids from our adrenal glands. These are 'catabolic' hormones – they increase the rate of tissue breakdown to produce the energy we need to keep going. But these hormone levels fall when we are asleep. When we are sleeping there is also a rise in growth hormones and testosterone, so-called 'anabolic' hormones which help to build our tissues up again.

It is possible that poor sleepers don't get enough of this anabolic, tissue-building phase. So their bodies suffer over the years, and the result is premature death. Higher body temperature and higher adrenaline excretion are both linked to higher rates of catabolism. And adrenaline output is boosted when we get anxious. So we may have another mind–body link here for poor sleepers, with anxiety altering their hormone profile to raise their metabolic rate (mirrored by an increase in their body temperature). This over-aroused state, even while they are asleep, may stop their bodies from ever fully recovering. The final result is the excess mortality that we see in the surveys.

If this is true then the remedy seems obvious enough. It's to get their anxiety levels down. It seems that we can never get away from the mind–body links. In later chapters we will look at how they can go about it.

But other specialists doubt that the whole sleep-and-restoration story is that simple. After all, they point out, there are no other findings linking anxiety or neuroticism with an increased risk of death (except perhaps deaths from suicide and accidents). Other experts even question whether sleep itself is necessary to restore our tissues. They believe that the physical rest that goes with lying down for the night will do it just as well, whether we are sleeping or not.

But perhaps our need to sleep isn't so much to allow our bodies to recover as to restore our brains. After all, for every moment that we stay awake, we have to remain vigilant. Our brains are constantly scanning the world outside, as well as continually processing the messages coming up from our bodies. In computer terms, the brain never goes 'off line'. Except when we sleep.

So there is now a growing view that the real reason that we sleep is to restore our psychological functions. There has been a huge amount of work done on dreaming, which happens during the rapid-eye movement (or REM) stage of the sleep cycle. Yet it now seems that the important sleep phase for restoring the brain isn't the REM phase, but rather the period of slow-wave sleep (SWS), the deepest sleep stage, when our brain waves are at their slowest.

Dysthymia, asthenia and all that

If this is true, then we might expect one of the results of sleeping poorly to be a psychological change. And psychiatrists do recognize a condition where patients have a mildly depressed mood, not serious enough to be called clinical depression. Disturbed sleep is one of its characteristic features. They call it *dysthymia*, which literally means 'disturbed mood', but there is more than just mood involved. Dysthymic patients often find it difficult to concentrate or make decisions. They have low self-esteem and may frequently feel quite hopeless. And very often they have only low levels of energy. They feel 'tired all the time'.

There is a name for this sort of fatigue as well. It is called *asthenia*, a very old term in psychiatry that may now be making a comeback. The link between asthenia and dysthymia is an interesting one. It certainly isn't unexpected. If I can't function properly then my mood and self-esteem will obviously plummet. I'll be feeling badly because I'm doing badly.

Recently some sleep specialists have started to explore the idea that, apart from asthenia and dysthymia being linked to one another, they may both be linked to poor sleep. The notion is that if sleep is impaired and brain function isn't restored, then our performance the following day will suffer as well. Dysthymia and asthenia may both result from a loss of (particularly slow-wave) sleep. There are even efforts being made to increase SWS by using appropriate drugs (though certainly not the benzodiazepine tranquillizers, like Librium and Valium, which actually reduce it).

But drugs would be a last resort. Before that, we could try taking all the 'sensible' precautions designed to help us sleep, like not having a heavy meal before we go to bed, not sleeping in a room that is too hot or cold and, quite simply, spending enough hours lying in bed to get the chance of seven hours' sleep.

If all this fails, and we still lie awake with our motors running, then we should look at what we can do to bring our anxiety levels down, preferably for ourselves. But there are certainly times when we are almost overwhelmed by some major, but short-term worry, and it makes sense to give ourselves a respite, by changing our brain chemistry with a drug prescribed by our GP.

Going for the high

Many people say that they started to sleep longer when they took up exercise, if only because they began to feel better about themselves. Some long-distance runners say that once they get over the initial pain, running gives them a feeling of enormous well-being. It may be a sense of peace and tranquillity. Alternatively, it may be something much more exciting, the sort of buzz that other people get from (definitely non-prescription) drugs. It is known as the 'runner's high'. And the parallel with drug effects is close, because some exercisers get addicted to it. When they can't run, for example because of an injury, they suffer real withdrawal symptoms.

Now we know that drugs like heroin act by releasing peptide messengers inside the brain. There has been a lot of interest in whether heavy exercise does the same, by releasing *beta-endorphins*, molecules that are involved in switching off the body's perception of pain. Typical of such reports is one from Germany where volunteers were studied after taking a ten-kilometre run. Their levels of beta-endorphin (or some compound like it) increased after the run. The runners also felt better about the world in general, and felt more self-reliant than they had before.[5]

So it seems that we might have an interesting chain here, with a change in behaviour (exercise) leading to a change in biochemistry (release of endorphins) to give a positive shift in feelings. Unfortunately other investigators haven't been able to confirm this link between mood change and endorphins.[6] But though the links are not properly understood, the mood change is definitely there. As a result (as we shall see presently) exercise can be used to treat emotional disturbances like anxiety and depression.

Of course, we usually think of exercising more in the context of physical health. In Alameda County, men who took vigorous exercise had half the mortality risk of those who didn't, and women benefited even more.

Exercisers have never doubted that what they are doing is good for them. If they looked at any of the data at all, it was only to confirm their beliefs. So it may come as a surprise to many exercise buffs to hear that most of the firm evidence that links exercise with longevity is really rather recent.

Do exercisers live longer?

The problem with showing that exercise is good for you has to do with self-selection. Say you look at a group of people who exercise and a group who don't. And say you find that the exercisers have some advantage, like being thinner. On its own, that doesn't show that exercise gets your weight down. It may simply be that thinner people exercise more.

This type of self-selection was a great problem for the early exercise researchers. As long ago as the 1950s, they compared the rates of heart disease among London bus drivers, who sat at the wheel all day, with those of bus conductors, who spent the day running up and down stairs collecting fares. The conductors had lower coronary rates, but a later examination of their uniform trousers also showed that they were thinner to start with. Studies with all sorts of other physically active people like postmen, labourers and dockers were all dogged with this problem – do thinner or fitter or healthier people 'select themselves' into more physically demanding jobs, or is it the experience on the job that makes them healthier?

The problem was finally resolved with the publication in 1984 (the year of the Los Angeles Olympics) of a long-term study of students who had been at Harvard University between 1916 and 1950.[7] A little like the Grant Study in design, this investigation examined the entry records of nearly 1,700 Harvard alumni. Information was also collected about various aspects of their lifestyle, through questionnaires that they had completed in the mid-1960s. Among other subjects covered, these questions asked about the amount of exercise which they had regularly been taking since they had left the University. How often did they climb flights of stairs, how many city blocks did they walk a day, and did they take part in active sports?

Finally, in the early 1970s the Harvard men also answered questions about their more recent health, particularly about whether their doctor had diagnosed any signs of heart disease. And for those men who had died, the time and cause of death was established from official death certificates.

What did this impressively thorough investigation reveal? It showed that whether or not the alumni took part in sports when they were students had no effect on their chances of having a heart attack in later life, unless their exercise was maintained. In contrast, the activity pattern that the men habitually followed after leaving college was strongly linked to their coronary risk. Indeed, for the group as a whole, taking little exercise was the strongest predictor of having a heart attack, stronger even than smoking or high blood pressure. And exercise actually offset the risk caused by these other factors. For example, even heavy smokers who also took vigorous exercise had only half the coronary risk of those smokers who didn't.

In an analysis of all these multiple risk factors, the investigators calculated that the frequency of heart disease would have been reduced by a quarter if all of the alumni had been exercisers. If, in addition, they had been thin non-smokers with normal blood pressure and no parental history of the disease, then their overall risk would have been reduced to only a third of what was actually found. And with the exception of the genes that we inherit (which at the moment we can't do much about) it isn't too fanciful to imagine that people who take regular exercise may be more inclined to get these other risks down too.

Because when they become committed to an exercise programme, they often take up other health habits as well. Their desire to smoke is frequently reduced; appetite is more controlled and so bodyweight may fall. And though exercise doesn't have much of a direct effect on blood pressure, the general sense of 'thinking healthy' that goes with it often makes them more blood-pressure conscious, and eager to control it by other means. Some studies even suggest that while fit and unfit people produce the same amount of hormones like noradrenaline in response to stress, the fit ones break it down faster and so it doesn't produce so much tissue damage.

The Harvard Study has now been followed by other investigations that also show how exercise reduces the total death rate by reducing the rate of coronary heart disease. It doesn't seem to affect the rate of deaths from say, cancer. But since heart disease accounts for one death in three among middle-aged men, just getting the coronary rate down can have a significant impact on our survival.

Better than chocolate

So much for death. But does exercise have any other (perhaps less dramatic) advantage? It certainly does, and they are especially interesting for anyone concerned with the connections between the mind and the body. After several decades concentrating on exercise and physical health, it is now becoming clear that physical fitness is intimately bound up with mental health as well.

For example, exercisers often report that they have more energy.

What do you do when your energy starts to flag in the middle of the day? Some people grab a bar of chocolate, in an attempt to put their blood sugar back up again. But a better way of achieving the same effect is to take a brisk, ten-minute walk.

Groups of students were asked to record how energetic and how tense they felt at a particular time of the day. Then they rolled a dice, and depending on the number that came up, they either ate a bar of chocolate or went for a walk. They recorded their energy and tension levels immediately afterwards, and one and two hours later. By repeating the experiment on twelve different days, it was possible to compare the effects of the two treatments for each individual.[8]

The results showed that they felt much more energetic after the walk than after the sugar snack, both immediately afterwards and for the next two hours. With the chocolate, they felt more energy straight after eating it than before, but they felt even more tired an hour later. The chocolate also made them tense, and the feeling of being both tense and tired was particularly unpleasant. It contrasted with the increase of energy with a fall in tension that they felt on days when they went for a walk instead.

So it seems that up to two hours of increased energy and

reduced tension can be achieved with surprising ease. But the psychological benefits of exercise go much further than that. Because physical activity seems to be a particularly good way to treat depression.

Running through your mind

In the late 1960s in Wisconsin, a group of patients suffering from moderate depression were given psychotherapy. But a second and otherwise similar group in the same clinical setting received a more unusual treatment. Three times a week for ten weeks they went walking and jogging in the company of a therapist. And at the end of that time they had done at least as well with their emotional problem as those who had received more conventional treatment. In their report of the work entitled *Running through Your Mind*, John Greist and his colleagues concluded that exercise is at least as effective as psychotherapy for the treatment of depression, at only a quarter of the cost.[9]

Since that time these findings have been repeated. In one striking example, E. W. Martinssen and his colleagues in Norway took a group of quite severely depressed psychiatric in-patients and guided them through a nine-week training programme, one hour a day, three days a week. They compared the results with what happened to a similar group receiving occupational therapy.[10]

The results depended on how hard the patients had worked at their exercise. Those who didn't get physically fit were no different from the control group. But those who did became significantly less depressed, despite the fact that they may have had their problem for years.

And you don't have to be an in-patient to derive the benefit. There are now many studies that show how exercise lifts the mood of quite ordinary people who are feeling dejected because of some event in their life. Scores on the Beck Inventory improve as we get fitter.[11]

There are two obvious questions about this exercise-induced anti-depressive effect. The first is why it happens, and the second is how hard you have to train to achieve it.

As to the first, no one is quite sure. It would be very satisfying for biochemists like me to believe that exercise shifts brain endorphins and triggers a chemically induced change in our mood. This may happen, but, as we've already seen, the evidence isn't very convincing.

The effect is probably more general than that, and depends on several factors. For example, while you are actually exercising it's difficult to think about the problems that were depressing you in the first place. And this simple 'distraction' is a method that many therapists use to stop their depressed patients from turning their minds inwards. Then again, most organized exercise programmes involve working out with other people. Friendships are often forged in such a group, and certainly the members frequently offer help and support to each other. So a secondary effect of being in an exercise group may be the social support that comes from it.

Probably most important is the fact that exercise is really a form of training in pleasure and mastery. The activity itself is fun. But more than that, people who once believed that they couldn't do anything properly, much less being able to run or move to music, slowly discover that they can. I remember the satisfaction that I got myself when, after a long lay-off, I found that I could get round the track again without stopping. It encouraged me to do two laps, and then more.

As the result of their exercise programme, depressed people find themselves slowly achieving something that they thought was far too difficult for them. And often this spills over into other aspects of their lives. If they can get themselves fit, then perhaps they can achieve some other goals as well.

What does 'fitness' really mean?

Which brings us to the question of what we mean by 'fitness' and how hard we have to work to achieve it.

There are lots of mistaken ideas about what exercise does for you – like making your heart or lungs bigger. It doesn't do either, to any noticeable extent.

What regular exercise does is to train the muscle in your heart to contract more efficiently. This means that every heartbeat in a fit person pumps out more blood to their tissues than when they aren't fit. That's why the first effect that we see with training is that our heart rate goes down. We don't need to pump so often if we are pumping more vigorously.

There are other changes that come with training as well. Our blood takes up more oxygen and our muscle cells use it more effectively. So basically being physically fit simply means being able to take in and utilize more oxygen than before. That's why fitness is actually measured by the rate of our maximum oxygen uptake. It is interesting that among Martinssen's patients only those whose fitness increased showed falls in depression, and other studies too have found that little is gained if we work so gently that our oxygen uptake isn't increased.

How do we get this training effect?

When I lecture to exercise teachers I explain that we need three sessions a week, each lasting for an hour, to get us started. Once you are fit, you can maintain it with rather less, but we should never fall below two weekly sessions of half an hour. And I explain that for at least half of that time we should be working hard enough to push our heart rate up to 70 per cent or more of its maximum value. This maximum varies with your age. At twenty it is about 200. By the time you get to sixty it is down to 155. You can get a chart that gives your maximum heart rate and also shows you the 70 per cent to 90 per cent value – the zone to aim at (Box 12). Most exercise teachers will stop the class several times and encourage you to take your pulse, to see if you are working hard enough.

But that, quite emphatically, doesn't mean exhausting yourself.

And this is one of the reasons why, when I'm lecturing to would-be exercisers (rather than their teachers), I recommend aerobic classes to get fit. Moving to music in a supportive atmosphere with a competent teacher who understands about your heart strikes me as the most effective and certainly the most enjoyable way of going about it.

Of course, tens of thousands of people choose to run instead, and here the advice about working hard enough without exhausting yourself is to run so that you have just enough breath to carry on a conversation with someone running with you. If you can do that, then your heart is going at just about the right rate.

What about walking? For years, general practitioners have suggested that their more sedentary patients get fit by taking walks. And for years some exercise specialists (including myself) have doubted whether walking pushes your heart rate high enough to put you into the training zone.

Well, we were wrong. Some very elegant studies from the University of Massachusetts have recently shown that at least two people out of every three can get their heart rate up to 70 per cent of its maximum by briskly walking for a mile.[12] They have even devised a one-mile walking test (like the old aerobic one-mile running test) that shows how fit you are and what you have to do to improve.

This finding that 'the vast majority of adults can attain heart rates during brisk walking that are considered to be above the training threshold' may revitalize the whole exercise business. We may see an end to the stress fractures and pulled muscles that can result from bringing your feet down too heavily and too often, if people take up fast walking instead.

I confess that, for me, serious fast walking still looks a little strange – like a duck accelerating for take-off that it can't quite manage. But I'm sure that feeling will pass. Fast walking is here to stay. So much so that in 1988 the American Medical Association was involved in a nationwide programme called 'Walk with your doc'. Physicians and their patients walked together in about a hundred cities throughout the United States. For some patients, it gave them their first chance to really talk to their doctors as well.

Orthodox advice

We have looked at some of the simple things that life-affirmers do to take care of their bodies – at health practices, sleep and exercise. But what have we missed? The one huge remaining subject, of course, is diet. Whole libraries have been written about the importance of diet on a macro-scale (the right balance of fats, proteins and carbohydrates) and at a micro-level (getting enough essential vitamins and trace elements). And we simply don't have space to dissect this dietary question.

But there is an awful lot that people take on trust. For example, despite what the colour supplements tell you about the benefits of reducing serum cholesterol, most people don't realize that solid evidence that cholesterol reduction saves lives was only obtained in 1984.[13] Earlier trials, costing hundreds of millions of dollars, failed to show any benefits at all. So for years we may have been doing it right. But our successes have often been based more on beliefs than on data.

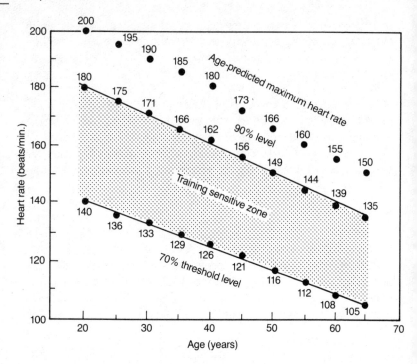

Box 12. *To gain a training effect, our hearts must beat at 70 per cent or more of our maximum heart rate. The chart shows how this maximum rate varies with our age and calculates the rate to aim at during an exercise session to achieve a long-term training effect.*

The general recommendations of official bodies like the UK Committee on Medical Aspects of Food Policy,[14] and the British Cardiac Society Working Group on Coronary Disease Prevention,[15] with their advice about eating less fat and more fibre, are generally on the right lines, though some of us believe that their recommendations about reducing salt have been overdone.[16] The details still need a lot of fine tuning, but anyone looking for 'orthodox' dietary advice can now get it without much problem.

More alarming to some health specialists is the sudden upsurge in 'unorthodox' advice about food that has appeared in the last few years. We are told that many of our health problems result from what we eat, not because of its nutritional content, nor even because of its effects on our coronary arteries, but rather because we are allergic to it.

Allergic to everything?

Clinical ecology is one of the most recent branches of medicine or (as many orthodox doctors would suggest) of fringe medicine. Its practitioners are concerned with the very wide range of 'non-specific' symptoms that many people take to their GPs. We have seen that very often the doctor is at a loss to explain them. But clinical ecologists (who also describe themselves as specialists in 'environmental medicine') feel that they can be explained quite easily. Depression and fatigue, arthritis and hypertension, problems in the respiratory, intestinal and urinary systems, may all be traced back to the patient's 'sensitivity' to substances in her environment – food and water, chemicals and pollutants.

Of course, orthodox medicine is also concerned with allergies, with the reactions that some people have to pollen or dust or insect stings. Immunologists understand this process very well. It involves a set of chemical reactions that result in the break-up of particular cells in the body (known as 'mast' cells) that release the irritant chemical *histamine* in the process. There are rather precise tests that can be used to see whether this type of reaction is taking place. In the vast majority of patients who present with symptoms, this type of allergic response isn't involved. But clinical ecologists no longer claim (as some once did) that their patients are 'allergic' in that sense. Instead, they refer to them as having become 'hypersensitive' to different substances or as being 'environmentally ill'.

The model that they use to explain such illness is very like the one used by some stress researchers. When the body is healthy, it can withstand a lot of disturbances from the outside. But as the external pressures accumulate, and it gets weaker as a result, then minor insults that it would have shrugged off in the past start to take their toll. Our immune system becomes sensitive to substances that it wouldn't normally react to, and the result is a wide range of possible symptoms.

Specialists in environmental medicine have even described the detailed immune disturbance that they believe to be responsible. Exposure to 'allergens' (immune stimulants) reduces the number of T-lymphocytes which normally control the production rate of antibodies by another type of lymphocyte, the B-cell. Without this controlling influence the B-cells lose their ability to distinguish one incoming material from another. So they mount immune responses against substances that previously would have been harmless.

Apparently the only treatment for this immune malfunction consists in two parts. It involves removing the patient from the source of the problem, by severely restricting him to the few foods that tests have shown he's not sensitive to, and by radically changing his living environment (no carpets or curtains, they collect dust; no exposure to paint or petrol, they can create chemical sensitivities).

The second part may involve 'desensitizing' him with 'vaccines' that consist of very dilute extracts of the allergens themselves. Exposure to these materials at very low levels (like inoculation against infection) is somehow thought to bring the immune system back into balance. But it all takes time. Treatment for environmental illness can be a long (and expensive) process, with many relapses and setbacks, just as it seems that you are starting to recover.

Back to homoeopathy?

Many of the patients whom I have met while they were receiving this type of treatment were quite convinced that it had completely changed their lives, perhaps even saved their lives. And those who treat them (often 'orthodox' doctors who qualified in a different speciality then moved into clinical ecology) swear by it too. So it may seem heavy-handed to point out that there is no evidence at all that our immune system does get disturbed in this particular way.[17] Nor have I found any published studies in which the desensitizing vaccines were compared with an inert placebo to see whether they have any consistent effect in reducing the patient's symptoms beyond what hope or chance or good luck might achieve.

Since they are so very dilute, it isn't clear how the vaccines could even be expected to work. One expert in the field assures me that the effect is something like a homoeopathic cure. It doesn't depend on the chemical molecules in the fluid, but rather on the 'energy fields' that are left behind when all the active molecules have been removed. Needless to say, doctors who have been brought up with more traditional ideas of medicine find these notions hard to believe or to understand. And the absence of any clinical trials to back up the claims does nothing to reduce their scepticism.

Of course, it may not matter what orthodox doctors think. Many patients receiving environmental treatment have been to not one, but many, regular doctors first. They couldn't find anything wrong. Patients often feel so desperate, even suicidal, that finding the ecological specialist who is prepared to take their problem seriously comes as an enormous relief. For such patients, orthodox medicine has failed them, and they are quite prepared to turn their back on whatever it has to say about the treatment that they are currently receiving.

Living with *Candida*

Perhaps the clearest rejection of conventional medicine is the widespread belief that a great deal of illness is due to our weakened immunity leading to overgrowth of the yeast *Candida albicans*.[18] We all carry this organism in our body. But the suggestion from clinical ecologists is that if we are exposed to antibiotics, cortisone, oral contraceptives or other drugs; if we consume too much carbohydrate or are exposed to pollutants like petrochemicals, perfumes or tobacco, then our immunity is compromised. As a result, *Candida* grows all over the body, giving rise to a huge number of different possible symptoms, from lethargy to hyperactivity and from itching to diarrhoea.

It has to be said that such symptoms are so wide-ranging that they could describe almost any sick person at some time in their illness. That's to say, there is nothing very specific about the so-called candidal syndrome. Then again, there is no proof that *Candida* is actually involved (ecologists say that laboratory tests don't help very much). Nor does there seem to be any published proof that anti-candidal treatments (either conventional ones using drugs or even desensitization by vaccines) actually makes patients better. On the other hand, there is reason to believe that long-term anti-candidal treatment might possibly create resistant strains.

Try it yourself

So what is the life-affirmer, the person who wants to look after her body, to make of these various claims from environmental medicine? In practical terms, should she be doing anything about them? Surprisingly perhaps the answer is yes, but she doesn't have to go to elaborate lengths, or take the whole ecological story on board.

Even 'ordinary' doctors recognize that some people are sensitive to different foods, possibly because they lack the enzymes to break them down. For example, people with coeliac disease can't eat the gluten in wheat without damaging their intestinal tract. Fortunately, serious complaints like these are rare. But many of us have noticed that certain foodstuffs make us feel slow, or heavy, or out of sorts.

And it is worth trying to identify any that might have such an effect on you, without having to believe that they disturb your immunity. Among the most common foods that people are believed to react to are wheat and dairy products – milk, cheese and eggs. Some people also react badly to coffee or chocolate. Often we have been taking them for so long that we have come to regard our present level of activity as 'normal'. So it's worth planning an 'exclusion diet', a period of say two to four weeks when we leave these things out altogether and substitute something else.

You will need some ingenuity to design your new menus. But, for example, you can substitute oats for wheat, soya milk and cheese for the dairy variety and herb teas for coffee (though the purists suggest that you drink only spring water).

Give it a try and see if you feel better. And if you're not sure, then after a few weeks reintroduce the original foods one by one and see if you feel worse. Many people who don't buy into the whole clinical ecology business have nonetheless improved the quality of their lives by eliminating very common parts of their diet that were actually making them feel underpowered. I am one of them.

You can do the same for potential toxins in your environment as well. To see how you react to say petrol or bleach or insecticides, some ecology specialists recommend that you put five drops of the particular substance under a cottonwool pad at the bottom of a sealed jam jar. Leave it with its lid on for four days to saturate the atmosphere, then open it and sniff it briefly, holding the jar about a foot from your nose.

The original suggestion is that you should take your pulse before you open the jar, then immediately afterwards and then again after taking two more sniffs, five and ten minutes later. A rise in pulse rate will (they say) tell you that you are sensitive. In addition you should record any mental or physical symptoms that you feel. Since you just might be particularly sensitive to one of these materials, sniff them only briefly at these three time points, and experiment with only one substance a day.

And what if you do react? Then you have good reason to believe that the material in question is one for you to avoid, whenever you can.

There are also far more sophisticated tests available, like measuring the levels of particular suspect food products or chemicals in your blood. However, this rough and ready approach (involving the do-it-yourself exclusion diets and the cautious self-exposure to possible sources of trouble in your environment) should go a long way to reducing your contact with anything you may react to, without the need for more professional help.

So life-affirmers believe in looking after their bodies. As part of that plan they try to take suitable precautions about not exposing themselves, if they can help it, to foods and chemicals that they would react to.

But the chemical environment is only one feature of the world outside that impinges on us every moment of the day. There is another set of pressures that are less easy to define, and often less easy to avoid. They exact their toll nonetheless, unless we take steps to neutralize them. They are a kaleidoscope of events that impinge on us everyday.

It is one of the hallmarks of the life-affirmer that rather than waiting to see where they will lead, he gets actively involved in shaping the things that are happening in his life.

CHAPTER 10

Eventful Lives

———

How do people deal with the constant stream of changing events that marks out one day from the next? And how far is it true that the events in our lives just happen to us out 'of the blue' and add together to decide whether we stay healthy or not? By now you will have realized that it's not true at all.

The dynamic biography

Many books and magazines simply haven't caught up with the fact. They still invite you to check your 'stress-rating' – to assess your chance of falling ill – on the basis of what had been happening in your life over the previous weeks or months.

The study of life changes has a long pedigree. It goes back to the 1940s. It originated with the American psychologist Adolf Meyer, one of the founders of a study then called *psychobiology*. Meyer seems to have been the first to create a 'life chart' for his patients, organizing an individual's medical history into the form of a 'dynamic biography'. Major change in that person's life, say shifts in location or job, births and deaths in the family, successes and failures, were charted in sequence, alongside the changes observed in his health. By looking at the chart it seemed clear that life events and periods of illness were somehow related.

This work continued through the 1950s and 1960s. The studies were led by Thomas Holmes (whose later work on sick and rarely sick people we have already seen) and Richard Rahe, a researcher with the US Navy.

When Holmes and Rahe asked patients in a sanatorium with tuberculosis what had happened to them in the years leading up to their illness, they found a cluster of stressful events in the two years or so before the patients fell ill. It was as though these events had started to overwhelm them, and their illness had been the result. The same clustering of events was found in patients with tuberculosis living outside the sanatorium. And it was not confined to people with respiratory diseases. Patients with coronary disease, skin complaints or even inguinal hernias all reported a similar concentration of life events in the one to two years before their illness started.

By the late 1960s Holmes and Rahe had collected life-event data on over 5,000 people. The events fell into two categories – those resulting from the person's own lifestyle and those that seemed to occur from outside. Some were clearly undesirable, like losing your job or being separated from your spouse. But others were the sort of thing you would want to happen, like being promoted. They were 'socially desirable and consonant with the American values of achievement, success, materialism, practicality, efficiency, future orientation, conformism and self-reliance'.

Even so, good or bad, all these life events appeared to exact their toll. It seemed to be the amount of disruption that they caused in the person's life and the amount of effort it took to readjust – to get back on an even keel – that was more important than the emotions that it produced.

But what Holmes and Rahe needed was a scale to compare the impact of different events and the individual's needs to readjust afterwards.

So they created one.

The life-change meter

They took a list of life events and asked a volunteer panel to rate them in terms of how much readjustment would be needed to get their lives back in order after experiencing each one. They were told that marriage scored 500 and the other events should be rated in relation to that.[1]

The forty-three events were then ranked in order (the scores being divided by ten to make the arithmetic simpler) and thus was born the Social Readjustment Rating Scale, perhaps the best known of all psychological questionnaires. The events on the scale range in severity from death of a spouse, rating a score of 100 and divorce at 73, through being fired from work at 47, to a child leaving home at 29 and even living through Christmas has a score of 12.

Your total score is found simply by adding up the individual scores for each event that has occurred to you in your recent life (see Box 13). This total is your number of life change units of LCUs over that period. The whole questionnaire takes perhaps fifteen minutes to complete and the LCU score gives an exact-looking estimate of how disturbed your life may have been and how likely you are to become ill as a result. Little wonder that it has been used in over a thousand different scientific studies. Little wonder too that it became so popular with the public. Just add up the numbers and see whether you are at risk.

In the early days some researchers concluded that if you report an LCU score of less than 150 in any given year, your chances of staying healthy during the following year are excellent.[2] People scoring between 150 and 300 have a 50 per cent chance of falling ill and for scores over 300 the odds of later illness were estimated at 70 per cent. Life events were said to predict not only minor ailments but also a wide range of other, more serious diseases including heart attacks (fatal and otherwise), accidents, athletic injuries, leukaemia, multiple sclerosis and psychological problems.

Disillusion sets in

We have seen how life events are linked to mental health. Some of George Brown's predictions of who gets depressed were fairly close. But for physical health, it's quite a different story.

So what went wrong? Why is it that ten years ago many scientists were optimistic about the link between life events and bodily illness, whilst today many of them have become disillusioned?

Firstly, the best predictor of how healthy someone will be in the future is how healthy she is *right now*. Adding information about the events that she has experienced over the last six months rarely makes the prediction of physical health much stronger.

Next is the fact that many of the earlier life-event studies con-

Rank	Life event	Mean value
1	Death of a spouse	100
2	Divorce	73
3	Marital separation	65
4	Jail term	63
5	Death of a family member	63
6	Personal injury or illness	53
7	Marriage	50
8	Fired at work	47
9	Marital reconciliation	45
10	Retirement	45
11	Change of health of family member	44
12	Pregnancy	40
13	Sex difficulties	39
14	Gain of new family member	39
15	Business readjustment	39
16	Change in financial state	38
17	Death of a close friend	37
18	Change to different line of work	36
19	Change in number of arguments with spouse	35
20	Mortgage over $10,000	31
21	Foreclosure of mortgage or loan	30
22	Change in responsibilities at work	29
23	Son or daughter leaving home	29
24	Trouble with in-laws	29
25	Outstanding personal achievement	28
26	Wife begin or stop work	26.
27	Begin or end school	26
28	Change in living conditions	25
29	Revision of personal habits	24
30	Trouble with boss	23
31	Change in work hours or conditions	20
32	Change in residence	20
33	Change in schools	20
34	Change in recreation	19
35	Change in church activities	19
36	Change in social activities	18
37	Mortgage or loan less than $10,000	17
38	Change in sleeping habits	16
39	Change in number of family get-togethers	15
40	Change in eating habits	15
41	Vacation	13
42	Christmas	12
43	Minor violations of the law	11

Box 13.   *The Social Readjustment Rating Scale.*
Perhaps the most famous of all questionnaires used in 'pop' psychology, this scale, devised by Thomas Holmes and Richard Rahe, is still used to 'check your stress rating'. What it misses is that the impact of any life event depends on the vulnerabilities and resources of the person who is going through it, at least as much as the event itself.

tained a basic mistake – a 'retrospective bias' – in the way they were designed. They involved locating people, say perhaps hospital patients, after a heart attack, and asking them to recall whether they had any stressful events in the period before they got the crushing pain in the chest. For patients who hadn't survived, it was common to ask their relatives if they had been under any special stress in the months before the attack.

But as we have seen, questions like this will always get the answer 'yes'. Victims or their relatives will search their memories and inevitably find some event in the past to account for the illness. All of us want explanations for why we feel bad and, given the chance, all of us will find them.

Finally, the use of the Schedule of Recent Life Events (as it came to be known) has usually been based on a wrong assumption. Holmes and Rahe were careful to distinguish between factors linked to the person's lifestyle and those arising from outside. Many later researchers ignored this distinction. They simply assumed that the scale somehow measures 'Acts of God', events which come out of the blue and which strike you down without warning. A minority of life events do represent factors 'in the world' over which we have no control. But many others result directly from the sort of person you are and the life that you lead.

In other words we manufacture many of our life events for ourselves. Indeed Holmes and his colleague Minori Masuda said as much in 1978 when they suggested that 'life events that happen to people, as well as how they are perceived, are a reflection of their life-style and culture'.[3]

They found that medical students and professional football players (two groups particularly concerned about their health, because their livelihoods depend on it) on average clocked up only five life events a year. In contrast, 'average' people, responding to an invitation on TV to have their stresses measured, scored twice as high, at the same rate as a group of patients in hospital with fractures. In contrast again, alcoholics had three times and heroin addicts five times as many annual life events as the medical students did.

Young people record more events, often many times more, than the elderly. Single people experience more events than those who are married. And whilst people in lower social groups may not necessarily suffer more events overall, they do appear to experience more 'high-impact' events of an undesirable kind.

But time and again we come back to the realization that for

most of us, most of the time, it is not just the pressure of real events out there in the world that crushes down on us. Whether we fall ill or not also depends on how we see the world, and on the pattern of responses that our personal 'world picture' generates inside us.

Each of us has our own vulnerabilities. Most of us also possess a set of resources that help us deal with stressful events and reduce the impact that they have on us. Money is one, and education is another. It is no coincidence that people with both income and know-how are generally healthier than those without. And the best-known factor (after having money) is having friends – the resource that specialists refer to as 'social support'.

Is marriage good for your health ?

Isolation and loneliness are risk factors for a wide range of diseases. Conversely, people committed to some sort of social network are frequently protected. Married people (especially men) are healthier than those who are single, widowed or divorced, although staying in an unhappy marriage may be more hazardous than getting out of it.

The single major investigation that did most to put social support on the map was the nine-year follow-up of adults in Alameda County. It started in the mid-1960s, and over 4,000 households were visited by interviewers who asked a wide range of questions about health-related factors in people's lives. Over the next nine years, records were kept on those who died. By the end of the Study in 1974 over 95 per cent of the original volunteers, alive or dead, had been accounted for. So the Alameda Study stands out as a truly 'prospective' investigation with an extremely detailed follow-up.[4]

Four kinds of support

It confirmed that unmarried men were two to three times more likely to die than those who were married, depending on their age – the younger unmarrieds having the highest risk. For women the difference wasn't so great. Unmarried women only had a 40 per cent higher chance of mortality. In terms of health, men get more out of marriage than women do.

The study also looked at other forms of social contact. People who said that they had few friends or relatives, or that they didn't see them very often, were at greater risk than people who experienced extensive social contact. And here the effect of sex was reversed. Women without friends or relatives were two to three times more likely to die. Contact with family or friends seems to be more important for women.

Even belonging to a church or temple is good for your health. Regular churchgoers had lower risks than those who didn't go. But a church or other group wasn't as protective as having friends or relatives.

When the researchers put all these sources of support into a single figure they came up with some striking findings. The most disconnected men were more than twice as likely to die than the best connected, and for women the risk from isolation was raised nearly threefold. Not taking care of yourself as well as being isolated made the problem even worse.

There was no particular pattern of disease involved. All causes of death, including heart disease, cancer and strokes, were more frequent in people with poor social ties.

People can make a trade-off between these various types of support. Unmarried people with many friends had the same risks as married people with few friends. By combining various forms of support more than half the sample managed to maintain a low mortality risk. It was only for those who had few links of any type that mortality levels started to rise sharply.

How does support keep you healthy?

Just how does social support protect against premature death? One possibility is that lonely people simply don't look after themselves. We've seen how the researchers explored people's health practices, like drinking and smoking, and found a roughly twofold difference between those who followed a set of simple rules (taking exercise, eating breakfast, not getting overweight) and those who didn't. But the effects of social support could not be explained away. It wasn't *simply* that disconnected people let themselves go.

When we are exposed to some powerful virulent infection, then our body's resources may be totally overwhelmed. Any amount of support won't help much. But in more marginal situations, where the pathogens are not so powerful, it may be precisely factors like social support that swing the balance in our favour.

The right kind of support

Of course, social interaction involves costs as well as rewards. Frequent interactions with friends or neighbours may lead to disputes, embarrassment or the invasion of privacy. And negative experiences may have a greater impact than positive ones.

To test this possibility Karen Rook of the University of California at Irvine[5] interviewed a group of elderly widows. She asked them about their social ties, and not solely the beneficial ones. She also asked about how often they had their privacy invaded, and about those people who they felt took advantage of them or consistently broke their promises. Before trying to relate social ties to well-being, she controlled for the effect of age, health and socioeconomic status, which are themselves well known to influence psychological well-being among old people.

Negative social interactions were found to have more effect on well-being than positive ones. But a third of those who caused the problems were friends, and another third were relatives. So we can't assume that any group of people is going to be supportive all the time. It is often better, even for older adults, to try to deal with their problems by themselves than to enter into new relationships in the hope of solving them. And certainly Rook's data gave no support for the popular notion that old people are always eager for *any* form of social contact.

Younger women too may gain little benefit from the wrong sort of social contact. Remember how Janice Kiecold-Glaser found that women who had recently separated from their husbands had poorer immune responses than those who were still married. But remember too that, among the married group, those whose marriages were unhappy were more depressed and also showed signs of weakened immunity.

In control of your life?

So connected people are more tolerant of negative life changes. They are better able to handle the challenge that it creates. But that is only part of the story. There are other features protecting us as well. One of the most important is the extent to which each of us feels that we are in control of our lives.

In the mid-1960s psychologists discovered a now famous distinction between 'externals', those people who feel that events are largely dictated by forces outside their control, and 'internals', who see themselves as having influence over events. A special rating scale was devised to measure the place where people think the control in their lives is located. It is called the Locus of Control or LOC scale. Recall how a belief in being able to control one's life is one of the basic features that people in our survey believed to be life-affirming. It's those of us who experience high levels of change but feel that they don't have much control over them who are most vulnerable.

Attempts were made to see whether LOC also protects our physical health against the ravages of change, or at least whether it affects the way that people *report* their bodily symptoms.

Moderates do best

The National Longitudinal Survey of Middle-aged Men measured levels of distress in 2,000 fifty-year-olds. It asked them whether they suffered from a series of health-related items.[6] They included tiring easily and having no energy; suffering from aches, swellings and feelings of sickness; having fainting spells and suffering from shortness of breath. The amount of stress they were under (and middle-aged men are often in a high-stress group, particularly because of economic difficulties and problems with status) was measured with a short questionnaire. For example, they were asked whether they had lost their jobs or suffered financial losses during the last few years; whether they were discriminated against because of their age; whether the job put them under greater pressure or if they were finding the pace more difficult.

Finally, they answered a series of questions about their sense of control, for example whether getting what they wanted depended on luck, whether what happened to them was largely their own doing and whether, when they made plans, they were fairly certain of being able to make them work.

Those men with an external locus of control generally had higher levels of distress occurring in response to stressful events. Internals did better. However, it was not the extreme internals, but rather the moderate internals who enjoyed the greatest stress-buffering effects.

These results are in line with common sense. Internals are able to handle success and failure in a more realistic manner than externals do. Put another way, they practise better mastery and coping skills.

But only up to a point. The extreme internal, believing that he is responsible for *everything* that happens to him, may simply become paralysed when things go wrong. The paralysis results from an overwhelming sense of guilt that he allowed all of this to happen in the first place. Moderate internals are more fortunate. They can step back and react in a more appropriate way when things do go wrong. They have the flexibility to put them right again.

So we are back to coping. It seems that wherever we start with our life-affirming features they all point in the same direction. They are all health-enhancing because in some way they allow us to deal with reality in the most effective manner.

But notice that locus of control by itself doesn't always reduce the effects of stress. It may only do so when it interacts with social support as well. Internals may be disposed towards depression on the one hand, but be capable of considerable resilience on the other. What tips the balance between the two may be their access to a support network. 'Social support ... may be the very balm that serves to protect the more solitary adventurers who regard themselves as the agents of their own experiences.'[7] Certainly it seems to be of more value to those who use it sparingly.

Illness is not a rare event

All of the ideas I have been describing so far fit into the same 'model' of stress and illness. It's the model that researchers have been using for thirty years. It suggests that events happen that disturb the balance of our health or well-being. But the resources that we have either reduce the disturbance itself or at least reduce the impact that it has on us. All that is perfectly true. Where it goes haywire is in its implication that stress is an abnormal feature in our lives. It is quite undesirable and something we want to neutralize as quickly as possible, so that we can get back to our normal equilibrium.

But there is a different view emerging, an alternative model, one that turns this idea of 'health is normal, illness is not' completely on its head.

Aaron Antonovsky is a medical sociologist at the University of the Negev in Israel. He worked for many years in the United States, particularly studying the problems of under-privileged groups, like poor blacks. His earlier work also concentrated on Jewish survivors of the Nazi holocaust. As a result of such studies, the question which he posed in his book *Health Stress and Coping*[8] is not why people fall ill, but rather how it is that the majority of us manage to stay well.

The question partly came out of his studies on the emotional health of a group of middle-aged Israeli women, many of whom had been prisoners in concentration camps.[9] He found that about a third of such camp survivors were still in good emotional health. By contrast, among women who had not been in the camps, about half could be described as emotionally healthy.

Faced with these results, most researchers would try to explain just how and why the survivors' emotional well-being had suffered. But for Antonovsky the more striking finding was that so many of those women who had gone through dreadful war-time conditions, followed by years living as displaced persons before finally settling in Israel, a country which was to be involved in three different wars with its neighbours, could be emotionally healthy at all.

His reading of the medical literature also led him to believe that at any one time perhaps a third of the whole population in Western nations is suffering from some form of illness. Sickness, it seems, is not a rare event. Nor indeed is stress. In Antonovsky's view, we are all constantly buffered and bombarded by stresses. It is simply not possible to insulate ourselves from them. So we have to look at the whole subject from quite a different viewpoint.

Salutogenic thinking

Antonovsky suggests that, rather than adopting a 'pathological perspective', we should come to develop a more 'health-centred' or, to use his word, *salutogenic* focus.

Instead of simply dividing 'sick' people from those who are somehow defined as being 'well', he believes that all of us exist on a continuum between what he calls 'health-ease' and 'dis-ease'. Some people move towards and perhaps even manage to stay at the health-ease end. But they don't do so by insulating themselves from stresses that bear down on them. We simply can't avoid them. All of us constantly have to confront the problems in our lives. And doing so creates tensions within us. It is how we manage those tensions that determines whether we fall ill or not. 'The study of factors determining tension management, then, becomes the key to health sciences.'

The people who handle their stresses best, and hence are more likely to stay healthy, are those who have a number of 'resistance resources'. We have seen some of them already – money, self-esteem, social support. But Antonovsky, as a sociologist, also includes more wide-ranging factors like cultural stability. People in stable environments are less likely to fall ill, partly because they have fewer problems to contend with.

He searched for some single feature that all of these resistance resources have in common. Eventually he concluded that they all help us to make *sense* out of the constant stream of stimuli that bombard us. Over time people with resistance resources come to see their world as being predictable. We may not like many of the events that we predict will happen, but we have the confidence to know they will unfold in some roughly ordered way. We are not simply the victims of a chaotic universe.

This realization led to an underlying principle that Antonovsky calls a 'sense of coherence'. People who possess it are more able to resist breaking down. As he put it, 'Coherence is the extent to which we have a pervasive, enduring though dynamic feeling of confidence that our internal and external environments are predictable, and that there is a high probability that things will work out as well as can reasonably be expected.'

Three components of coherence

Antonovsky has refined his original ideas about coherence. He now sees it as consisting of three separate but interacting components. The first is *comprehensibility*. This is the ability to see the events that confront us as ordered, structured and clear, rather than chaotic and unpredictable. That doesn't necessarily mean that the world is the way that we would like it: only that we can understand it.

Secondly comes the idea of *manageability*, the sense that we have at our disposal adequate resources to meet the demands that are placed upon us. This is not quite the same as having an internal locus of control, where we are confident of doing things for ourselves. The resources that go with manageability may include a sense that we can depend on friends, or on our countrymen, or on God in our times of trouble. The key result is that we feel able to cope, because of the total network that we can call on.

The third part of coherence is a sense of *meaningfulness*, the feeling that the events in our lives are worth engaging in, putting our energy and commitment into. This echoes what H. M. Lefcourt, one of the pioneers of the LOC concept, said about vitality. For him vitality is the capacity to grapple with the important concerns in our lives, rather than simply walking away from them. The person with a strong sense of coherence sees life events as challenges to be welcomed rather than problems to escape from.

But how does coherence originate?

Obviously, it develops as a result of our life experiences. Indeed, Antonovsky believes that by the age of thirty our sense of coherence about the world is more or less fixed. Because it results from our long-term exposure to so many different features of life, he doubts whether it can be significantly changed in adults (for example as the result of counselling), at least not without a great deal of effort. In that respect, I don't agree.

Three types of experience are important in deciding whether a particular person will end up high or low on the continuum of coherence. The first is the feeling that the events in his life have been consistent with one another. A life full of unpredictable surprises obviously makes for low coherence. The extent to which we are under- or over-loaded by the demands placed on us from birth also has an important effect. People high on coherence generally find themselves able to respond effectively to their level of demands. But carrying a slight overload may be healthy, to develop energies and talents that we may not have previously realized we had.

Finally people high on coherence will feel that they have been properly consulted and allowed to participate in making the decisions that have influenced their lives. Only if we approve of and agree with what we are being asked to do will we give it our best effort.

What do coherent people say?

If all this seems a bit abstract, we can flesh it out from interviews that Antonovsky conducted with people high and low on coherence when he was originally trying to put some shape into the concept.[10]

For example, a woman whose son was killed in action said, 'I decided you just have to go on, I won't let myself be broken'. A woman with polio that left her partially disabled said, 'I always had a strong will, never felt that there was something wrong with me. . . . you have to know how to use your life.' And another Israeli housewife whose only son was also a war victim said, 'It all hurts terribly, but I have to live in the real world. I can still share the joys of others. . . . you swallow your tears and go on.'

All of these people obviously share a high sense of coherence, despite the problems that have befallen them. Compare that with complaints like 'Nothing can be done in a case like mine', or 'there's no pity, only exploitation',or 'all of life is a constant battle. . . . I just have to keep on dragging this burden.' Such remarks are typical of people at the other end of the continuum.

Individuals with a well-developed sense of coherence remind us of those old people with high levels of stamina studied by Elizabeth Colerick. They too constantly found new ways to use their energy and to avoid the feelings of helplessness and hopelessness that lead to passiveness, withdrawal and giving up.

Coherence and health

Antonovsky developed the idea of coherence in an attempt to explain how some people stay healthy, despite being under pressure. And he proposed three different ways in which it might work. They are encouragingly similar to many ideas that we're familiar with by now.

Firstly, those with a strongly coherent sense are less likely to expose themselves to unhealthy situations. They consider it worth their while to stop smoking, drink moderately and take exercise. Those without this sense lack the motivation to do so. Here he draws a parallel with the notion of *self-efficacy*. This idea was developed by Albert Bandura at Stanford University. It measured our inner feelings about our chance of succeeding at a particular task. Our feelings of self-efficacy strongly influence just what we are prepared to try out, how much effort we will put into it and how long we will persist in our attempts to succeed.

People with a strong sense of coherence are also less likely to regard a problem in their lives as something to run away from. They won't be paralysed into inactivity when they have to make a decision about what to do next, or even where to start. Instead, they are likely to see many problems as potential challenges that are worth investing energy in because they give the chance of producing rewards.

Finally, and in a sense the crux of the whole idea, people high on coherence will think through the list of the coping resources that are available to them. They will employ some creativity in using the ones that are most likely to produce a solution. The key is not to use any one strategy all the time but to develop a flexible set of coping styles.

Those low on coherence lack this flexibility. When things start to get difficult they are more likely to decide that (as one of them actually said in an interview) 'It's all hopeless; nothing can help me now.' With this attitude, they are far more likely to give up prematurely.

That then is the theory of how coherence might influence health. But does it work? What reason does Antonovsky have to suggest that 'When one searches for effective adaptation of the organism, one can look to imagination, love, play, meaning, will and ... to theories of successful coping'?[11]

Testing out coherence

When I first read *Health Stress and Coping* I wrote to Antonovsky, more in sorrow than in anger, to say that I had found the experience profoundly disappointing. I explained that the book itself had been full of intriguing, innovative ideas that had sparked my imagination. The disappointment came from the almost total lack of any real data to support them.

His reply was courteous. He explained that he saw the book as a 'way station' and that a number of studies were now being started to see how well the notion of coherence predicted physical and mental health.

The first stage was to produce a measuring instrument, a scale to establish where different people stand in terms of coherence.

This was accomplished with a twenty-nine item Orientation to Life Questionnaire. This asks respondents to say, on a scale of 1 to 7, how far a number of different statements apply to them. They include, for example, 'When you think about your life, you very often feel how good it is to be alive (or, at the other extreme, ask yourself why you exist at all)' and 'Most of the things you do in the future will probably be completely fascinating (rather than deadly boring).'

The scale seems to measure what it is supposed to. A group of Israeli army officers came out higher on coherence than health professionals in either Israel or Canada, who in turn scored higher than a group of American students.

However, using the scale for the prediction of health is still at an early stage and Antonovsky himself in his latest book agrees that any judgement of the track record of the coherence scale must be 'held in abeyance'.[12] Believers in the mind–body connection, myself included, hope that it will produce more concrete results. Because such an approach, if it were justified, 'not only opens the way for the formulation and advance of a theory of coping but compels us to devote our energies to it'.

Whether that happens or not, there is still another 'theory of coping' which looks like coherence but which is far better known. Its greater popularity reflects the fact that it is equally elegant in the way that it is put together. But it also has more facts to back it up. It is the notion of the *hardy personality*.

CHAPTER 11

How Are You Coping ?

The importance of being hardy

Suzanne Ouellette Kobasa is petite, elegant and enormously energetic. Recently she has been working at the Graduate School of the City University of New York. However, the research for which she is best known, and which she continued in New York, was begun in collaboration with Salvatore ('Sal') Maddi at the University of Chicago. It revolves around one very simple question (simple to ask, that is). Like Antonovsky, she is primarily interested in why some people manage to remain healthy even though their lives are going through a series of upheavals. In short, she wants to know why some people are hardier than others.

Having followed her work for several years, I became intrigued to know how her interest in this problem of health and illness got started and just how the idea of hardiness took shape. Fortunately, I got the opportunity to ask her.[1]

She said that she sees her work as partly reactive. In the early 1970s when she came to look at the subject, she found the emphasis among stress researchers was almost entirely on the negative – on why people fell ill. She felt unhappy with this pathological emphasis. To her, an equally important question was what positive consequences might come out of life events. In part, the question came from her own training in existential philosophy, a way of thinking that is very much concerned with how people find their purpose in life and how they relate to the world and other people in it.

As a psychologist, she took this rather theory-laden set of existential ideas, and together with Maddi and other collaborators turned them into something concrete – something you could use to predict health and illness. From the outset her main interest was in physical health. As she told me, 'The idea of correlating hardiness with positive mood was not very exciting. But the idea of showing a relationship between hardiness and an absence of, say, coronary symptoms or migraine headaches, seemed to me the chance to make a much more powerful statement.'

The three Cs

Kobasa felt from the outset that people who stayed healthy must have more than simply one thing going for them. Not for her the tendency found among so many psychologists and writers on health to isolate some single feature, like *Candida* or social support, and say *this* is what makes the difference.

Firstly, it seemed to Kobasa that healthy people had some feeling of being able to *control* their environment. They didn't feel entirely at the mercy of their surroundings. Secondly, they seemed to be prepared to get involved and engaged in what they were doing; to feel some sense of *commitment* in their lives. And lastly, she was struck by existential ideas about those people who are always creating situations for themselves, always looking for something new. They are the ones who are flexible enough in their ways of thinking to live with situations even when the outcome isn't clear. This ability to tolerate ambiguity and paradox and to accept change she identified as *challenge*.

A lot has been written about these three Cs. We have already seen them emerging (though not so closely linked together) in our own set of life-affirming characteristics – things that people see as important in 'saying yes to life'.

Those people with some sense of control will want to know *why* events are happening to them. They will see many stressful events as being predictable, and even as being largely the result of their own actions. Consequently, they should be able to change them.

To be committed means believing in the importance of who you are and what you are doing. Being committed to *yourself* provides the essential sense of purpose in life. It is a form of self-identity, but it is different from self-esteem or personal competence, because it involves other people as well. Hardy individuals are committed to their jobs, their families and their relationships. They feel that they can turn to others in difficult times, but they are also the ones whom others depend on for strength when everyone is under pressure.

People with a sense of challenge believe that change, rather than stability, is the normal state of the world. So they accept the possibilities that change brings, rather than worrying about the threats that it might pose to their security. They may even be on the look-out for new and interesting experiences. But they have a built-in protection. They know how best to marshal their resources.

In one of her papers Suzanne Kobasa puts the whole idea into one sentence: 'Persons high in hardiness easily commit themselves to what they are doing (rather than feeling alienated), generally believe that they can at least partially control events (rather than feeling powerless) and regard change to be a normal challenge or impetus to development (rather than a threat).' As a result, hardy people 'find opportunities for the exercise of decision making, the confirmation of life's priorities, the setting of new goals. ... they are capable of evaluating any given event in the context of an overall life plan'.[2]

People always ask Suzanne Kobasa about the connection between hardiness and Antonovsky's sense of coherence. As sometimes happens in science, the two ideas grew up at much the same time but quite independently of each other. The two researchers have compared notes and found that there is a strong correlation between coherence and the commitment aspect of hardiness, as one might expect. There is some overlap with control as well, but none at all with challenge.

And here is the basic difference between the two concepts. Antonovsky believes that people who seek out new situations and look for change are actually putting themselves at risk of stress-related disorders. Kobasa looks out of her window on to 42nd Street in New York. Simply to live and work there, she has to be able to appreciate new and changing circumstances. Without this ability, she feels, she couldn't be hardy at all.

Measuring the hardy

So much for the background. But how can we measure hardiness and how do we know that it actually does protect those who possess it from falling ill?

The way it is measured has gone through several changes. When the idea was being developed there seemed little point in producing new scales to capture it when there were already existing questionnaires that seemed to assess its three components. For example, a person's sense of commitment could be tapped by a questionnaire that measured its opposite – his sense of alienation. Typical items on this Alienation Scale included 'Life is empty and has no meaning for me' and 'I find it hard to believe that people actually feel that the work they perform is of value to society.' People with a high sense of commitment will obviously reject these statements. But they are endorsed by those who feel alienated from themselves and from the work that they see themselves as being forced to do.

Commitment was originally measured using the Locus of Control Scale plus another part of the Alienation Scale. It involved statements like 'People's misfortunes result from the mistakes they make' and 'It doesn't matter if people work hard at their jobs; only a few bosses profit.' Obviously someone with a sense of commitment will agree with the first but not the second.

Finally, challenge was also assessed from two pre-existing questionnaires with items like 'Governments should guarantee jobs for all' and 'New laws should not be passed if they damage one's income.' People high on challenge would disagree with both.

Unfortunately, there proved to be problems with measuring hardiness in this way. Many of the statements were set up to measure alienation, so hardy people had to respond negatively. In addition, there were about ninety questions to answer. Maddi and Kobasa produced a shortened form with thirty-six items, but even that had some difficulties in the way that people answered.

Finally they came up with a fifty-item questionnaire containing statements like 'I like a lot of variety in my work,' 'Planning ahead can help avoid most future problems' and 'It's exciting for me to learn something about myself.' This questionnaire, which people endorse on a scale of 0 to 3, they call the Personal Views Survey. It will be used in all their future research. The results published to date, however, use the earlier versions. Despite their problems they have produced some very exciting results.

The break-up of Illinois Bell

To test the value of hardiness in predicting who would stay well, Maddi and Kobasa needed to find a large group of people living in chronically stressful conditions. They found just such a situation at Illinois Bell, part of the giant Bell Telephone Company which after years as a conglomerate was forced to break up as a result of US Government legislation in the mid-1970s.

This period of 'divestiture' was traumatic for all concerned. No one was sure what shape the new, smaller organizations would take, what products and services they would offer and how successful they would be. No one knew whether his job was safe either. This period of indecision was punctuated at all levels by vague, sometimes conflicting instructions being handed down from corporate headquarters and filtering through the management system. Ambiguity and lack of firm directives were everywhere.

It was in this environment that the research team began their work. Their investigations took over seven years to complete and they examined a wide range of different factors that might influence the workers' health. The full story has been told several times, both in scientific papers and in their book called *The Hardy Executive: Health Under Stress*,[3] so I will only summarize their major findings.

First of all Maddi and Kobasa wanted to know whether stressful events did actually have any effect on illness in this group of industrial workers. Secondly, they wanted to go beyond any simple finding that illness *now* might be related to life events *in the past*. Recall how much bias can occur when we try to remember what happened to us six or twelve months ago. What they wanted was a *prospective* study to see whether such events were linked to the appearance of illness in the future. And finally, they were interested in the sort of illness that would be reported to a doctor, rather than vague subjective feelings of emotional distress.

Accordingly, the Chicago team selected a group of the middle- and upper-level managers at Illinois Bell and sent them a questionnaire, a modified version of the Holmes and Rahe *Schedule of Life Events*. Some extra items were added that particularly related to the lives of these white-collar, middle-aged male executives. They were asked to record their life events over the previous three and a half years.

Included in the package was a questionnaire about their symptoms of illness. A separate study had shown that self-reports using this scale correlated well with the symptoms that people report to their physicians. So they gave a fairly 'objective' picture of illness.

The men were also asked to complete the six different questionnaires to measure their ratings on control, commitment and challenge.

Taken together these data allowed the investigators to see whether life events did have any effect on illness, and whether being high on hardiness reduces any harmful effects. But only in retrospect. To make predictions about *future* illness they mailed out the same schedules again one year later, and again one year after that, in each case asking the respondents to report what changes had happened to them in the previous twelve months.

Kobasa and her colleagues got complete replies for all three years from about 250 of the original sample. They found that stress did indeed correlate with illness measured in retrospect. Life events accounted for less than 10 per cent of the change in illness patterns. Even so, hardiness acted as a buffer between events and symptoms.

To assess its effects more exactly they divided their executives into four groups – those who had experienced only few events as opposed to those with many, and those who were high on hardiness compared to those who were low. Looking at the figures they found that low-hardy men with high levels of stress suffered about twice the rate of illness as high-hardy individuals with the same stress levels. When stresses were low, there was not much difference. So it seemed that 'to remain healthy, it is especially important to be hardy if one is experiencing intensely stressful life events'.

And what about prediction? They found that life events were only weak predictors of illness one or two years later. However, after controlling for the men's original state of health they found that even the small association that did exist between life events and subsequent illness was also reduced in the hardy men. So it seems that, looking both backwards and forwards, hardiness protects the physical health of business executives against high levels of stress on the job.

A question of interaction

I said that Suzanne Kobasa rejected the idea that any one factor could account for the difference between vulnerability and resistance to stress-related disease. And she is well aware that even hardiness itself is not the whole story. She actually proved the fact by taking a group of Illinois Bell executives who had above-average life event scores and asking them both about their current levels of social support and about how much exercise they were taking.[4] One year later their illness symptoms were recorded. This gave the opportunity to see how these three resistance resources – hardiness, support and exercise – would predict the onset of illness over the subsequent year.

Kobasa and her colleagues again divided the men into four groups – this time identifying those high on all three resistance resources, or two or one or none. She then looked at their illness ratings, both in the year that their resources were measured and in the year following.

And the findings were striking. Among these highly stressed subjects, the highest levels of illness occurred in those men with the lowest levels of all three resources. Conversely, those with the highest resource levels showed the lowest illness ratings at both time points. And those with one or two resistance resources came in between.

The figures actually showed that men with all three resources had only a 10 per cent chance of being ill at the time the measures were taken compared to those men with no resources. And when resources were used to predict subsequent illness, those high on all three had only a quarter of the risk.

But the analysis they used allowed them to go further. Among these various resources, which was the most important? The answer, you will not be surprised to hear, was hardiness. It was by far the major buffer, being more powerful either than social support or exercise.

The reason is because of the fundamental change that hardiness makes in people's lives.

Social support is a mixed blessing. Its effects on health depend on who receives it and who gives it. For executives with low levels of stress, support from any source has little effect – obviously there is little for it to buffer. For those with high levels of stress, support from the boss at work reduces the impact of work-related events on illness. But for low-hardy executives with high levels of stress, support from their families actually increases their illness level.

Why? Because during periods of great work stress, low-hardy men may be inclined to stay at home and simply let their families look after them. In the short term this relieves their distress. In the longer term, however, it does nothing to start solving the problems that led to the distress in the first place. Indeed, it leaves the employee even more alienated from his work and even less likely to come to grips with his problem.

Exercise is not likely to have this type of adverse effect. But the results that it does have are only of short-term value. Being fit may allow your body not to overreact in a highly charged situation. It may help you to break down your adrenaline more quickly. But it does nothing to stop that situation from recurring in the future.

Hardiness does something quite different. It alters the situation itself.

How hardiness works

Hardiness alters the way you see the world. The three Cs give you the ability to engage and be involved in your surroundings and the people in them. Hardiness alters the way that you cope with your problems. It helps you to say yes to life.

There are two contrasting ways for all of us to respond to any stressful situations. The first is simply to try to forget the whole thing, to spend our time day-dreaming and imagining that things are better than they really are. We might also pray for a miracle to get us off the hook. We all have a tendency to act in this way some of the time. Specialists call it 'regressive coping'. It is sometimes valuable for getting through short-term crises. But it does nothing to alter the problem. We still have to deal with that at some stage.

Hardy people do so by transforming it into something less stressful. For example, they examine the problem from several different perspectives, so as to come up with a solution. And when they have found one that looks as though it might work they increase their efforts to try to get on top of it.

Two ways of coping

We know that hardy people engage more in 'transformational' coping because the Chicago team asked them. Men from Illinois Bell were asked to describe the most stressful event that they had lived through in the last six months. Then they filled in a long questionnaire about how they had dealt with it. Their replies showed a high proportion of 'transformational' responses – active, decisive actions aimed at changing the situation into something they could more readily deal with. As Maddi has put it, 'persons high in hardiness remain relatively healthy despite the encounter with stressful events ... through coping with them transformationally'.

You may have the sense that you've been here before, that the attitudes I'm describing have appeared elsewhere. And of course they have. Regressive coping results from looking at the situation in a pessimistic way. If you expect the worst it isn't surprising that you will do your best to duck out of it. You may seek solace from your family; you may find it in a bottle. You may compensate yourself for the problems weighing you down by eating more, sleeping more or smoking more.

By contrast, transformational coping is based on an optimistic assessment of the problem. The solution may not be clear, but you hold to the belief that there must be *something* you can do to influence it. I know of no work that has tried directly to compare Maddi and Kobasa's notion of hardiness with Carver and Scheier's measure of optimism or Seligman's explanatory style. It would be intriguing to know how much they describe the same thing. My guess is that people coming out high on hardiness would score high on optimism as well.

Back to E and N

Apart from optimism, the other obvious link with hardiness relates to our personality, to our levels of extraversion and neuroticism. From what I have said about how hardy people combine a flexible, optimistic outlook with a search for challenge and an active approach to life I am sure you would expect them to be both outgoing and emotionally stable.

Some recent research from Oxford shows this is true.[5] When the Personal Views Survey and the Eysenck Personality Questionnaire were both given to a group of young women, there was a considerable overlap between the replies on each scale. Those low on hardiness were found to be low on extraversion but high on neuroticism. So it seems that the low-hardy person is an emotionally unstable introvert, just the sort whom you might expect to withdraw when the going gets rough because facing up to it gives her such distress.

But the fact that hardiness fits so neatly into the high-E–low-N quadrant doesn't make hardiness scores less important. It may be that their hardiness level tells us more than their E and N scores about how someone will react under stress. For example, the control dimension is not well captured simply by measuring E and N, though we know that people with high N levels have a sense that their lives are controlled by outside forces.

Lawyers and officers are different

The Chicago team had no problem in showing that life events predicted illness among the Illinois Bell executives. But when they looked at a group of some 150 Canadian lawyers they got a different result. Although the lawyers had experienced quite major events in the previous year, their event scores didn't relate to their illness levels. Lawyers have an image of thriving under pressure and simply not getting ill, and these findings seemed to bear it out.

However, the investigators also looked for evidence of 'strain' – signs like heartburn, trouble sleeping and shortness of breath – which might be expected to precede the appearance of any actual illness. These strains were found to be related to life events, and the association between them was reduced by having a sense of commitment. The stress–strain link was also lower among lawyers who avoided forms of regressive coping like getting angry and taking time off.

But for this group of lawyers social support actually made their problems a little worse. Among these emotionally tough, independently minded people, feeling the need to talk the problem over with someone else may even be equivalent to avoiding it.

Army officers represent a different case again. Kobasa examined seventy-five US army captains and majors. She found a very strong relationship between life events and subsequent illness.

And hardiness didn't buffer it. Though commitment and control had some modulating effects, a strongly developed sense of challenge among these men made the appearance of illness more, not less likely. Most of them were ex-Vietnam officers who were now commanding a desk. They were forced to develop a new role for themselves shuffling pieces of paper. Their sense of risk-taking and adventure had fitted them well as field officers. But as cogs in the bureaucratic machine, a sense of challenge actually interfered with the job that they were being asked to do.

Again, Suzanne Kobasa interviewed a group of actors. For them, control over getting a part in a soap opera didn't simply result from hard work. Luck was also hugely important. Their concept of control included getting yourself to the right party at the right time in the hope of meeting a casting director.

Hardiness for all – or only for some?

It is clear then that the way that each person's individual package of hardiness is put together depends on many factors. Among them is the nature of our job, or indeed whether we have a job at all. Kobasa's work is now being extended to other groups, like bus drivers and manual workers. Hardiness seems to emerge in these groups as well. It appears to be independent of sex, colour or social class, but there is still a long way to go before we can claim that it is a feature that we all share.

Obviously, Kobasa is working with that belief. I asked her what she hoped the future would show. She told me that if a sense of purpose, engagement and control and an expectation of being able to deal with change could be found in a wide range of people, irrespective of the jobs that they were doing, then 'we would have increased our confidence that hardiness is a fundamental personality variable'.

Time will show if it is.

In the meantime, fundamental questions remain. The first is how hardiness develops in those people who have it. The second is whether those people who don't can develop it.

Maddi and Kobasa deal with the first question in their book. Obviously, hardiness develops during childhood. They believe that parents who are hostile and disapproving will give their children the feeling that both they and the world are empty and worthless. Parents who expect their children to do things that are too difficult for them will undermine the growth of any feeling of control, and parents who are themselves afraid of change will prevent their children from developing any sense of challenge.

In contrast, hardiness is likely to develop in an atmosphere where children's efforts are approved of, where they are given moderately difficult tasks to do and where the environment changes frequently. Hardiness will emerge when 'parents are warm and enthusiastic enough towards their children that the interactions are usually pleasant, rewarding, and supportive of the child's individuality'.

Fine, but how many of us were brought up in that background? Not many, I suspect. So the problem then becomes one of taking people with less fortunate upbringings and showing them how to be more hardy in adulthood.

Can it be done?

As yet their studies are at an early stage, but even from the early findings it seems that it can. The key is to teach transformational coping – ways of changing stressful encounters into something less stressful. But that isn't always possible. So a second strategy is to teach people how to accept certain inevitable features that they may have to live with, but at the same time find value and meaning in some of the other, more rewarding, things that they can do.

The next two chapters will show how we go about modifying people's attitudes and behaviours. We will look there in some detail at hardiness training, together with other methods for helping people to come to terms with reality.

But is facing up to reality always the most appropriate course of action? I have already suggested that the answer is no. There are times when it is in our best interests to maintain a distorted view of the world. To understand that properly we need to know a little more about the way that we appraise the world around us.

If it changes it must be a process

Richard Lazarus is a psychologist who combines an eye for the detail in his work with an almost tangible enthusiasm for its importance. Over more than a decade he and his colleagues at the University of California in Berkeley have put together the most intricate account of how people cope with their lives.

The essence of Lazarus' view is the idea of a transaction. People are constantly reacting and responding to the conditions they find themselves in. And doing so changes the situation itself. They then react to this changed situation, and so on. In other words, there is a constant dynamic interplay between ourselves and our surroundings. The way we cope with events depends on a continual interaction between ourselves and our world. Lazarus has developed what he calls a 'process model' of coping. As he says in the title to one of his papers 'If it changes it must be a process'.[6]

But what exactly is coping? To him and his team it is a series of efforts that we make, both in our actions and in our thinking. We make them to overcome (or to make more tolerable) the often conflicting demands that are constantly being placed on us. The most obvious demands come from outside, from the things that we have to do. But many conflicts are internal. They arise from what we *think* we have to do. So coping is a twofold process. On one hand we seek to manage our stressful environment. On the other we seek to control the distressing emotions it creates in us. In other words, we constantly practise both *problem-focused* and *emotion-focused* coping.

Also central to the Lazarus view of coping with stress is the idea of *appraisal*. All the time we are scanning the events in our environment, to decide whether they are relevant to our well-being. If, like an earthquake in a distant part of the world, they affect other people whom we don't know, then we don't respond to them at all. However, if they are likely to affect us or our loved ones, then we do react. We try to decide whether the event represents a case of harm, or of loss, of damage already done. Or is it rather a threat to our well-being or our self-esteem, a harm or loss that hasn't happened yet but that could? Or alternatively does the situation actually present us with a challenge, an opportunity for us to gain something positive?

In a much shorter time than it takes to read that last paragraph, we appraise what is at stake for us and rapidly start to sort through our repertoire of coping resources – experience, skills, social support, material possessions – to see how best to deal both with the situation and with our emotional reaction to it.

We cope at two levels simultaneously. People nearly always try to change the situation (problem-focused) and change how they feel about it (emotion-focused) at the same time. We try to regulate our emotional distress, not just because it makes us feel better. It also makes us act more effectively. The less we are disturbed by emotions like fear and panic the more attention we can devote to dealing with the problem in hand.

So the main lesson to come from the work at Berkeley is that the essence of coping is change. Emotional responses and our coping patterns constantly shift as the transactions we are making with our world develop and unfold.

How are you coping?

Think of a stressful event that has occurred to you within the last week. Then think why it was stressful. What was at stake? Did it threaten to lose the affection of someone close to you, or to make you lose your self-respect? In other words, did the stakes have something to do with your self-esteem? Alternatively, did it pose a threat to the health or the safety or physical well-being of someone close to you?

Then consider the options that were open to you in dealing with it. Could you change the situation, or at least do something about it, or did you just have to accept it?

What did you actually do about it? Some possibilities are found in Box 14.

Finally, was the event resolved, unchanged or made worse as a result of what you did?

What I have asked you to do is to be a subject in one of Lazarus' experiments where he wanted to see how people differ in the way they coped, from one stressful situation to the next. Questions about what was at stake and whether the situation could be changed represent your appraisal of the situation. The coping procedures that you could have used come from a list of fifty-six different possibilities which the Berkeley team gathered together and called the Ways of Coping.

Exactly the same questions were put to a group of eighty-five married couples in California. They were interviewed every month for six months about the most stressful event that they had experienced in the previous week. They reported on how they had appraised and coped with it and what the outcome had been.

Putting their replies together showed that when the event was important, so that the stakes were high, people tended to seek more social support. They also favoured forms of coping that involved self-control (e.g. 'I tried to keep my feelings from inter-

Distancing tactics
  Went on as if nothing had happened.
  Tried to forget the whole thing.

Self-controlling approaches
  Tried to keep my feeling to myself.
  Tried not to act too hastily or follow my first hunch.

Attempts at escape—avoidance
  Hoped that a miracle would happen.
  Slept more than usual.

Planful problem-solving
  Made a plan of action and followed it.
  Changed something so that things would turn out all
    right.

Positive reappraisal
  Changed something about myself.
  Rediscovered what is important in life.

Box 14.   *The last time you reacted to a stressful situation, did you use any of these ways of coping?*

fering with other things too much') as well as escape or avoidance (e.g. 'I refused to believe that it had happened').

When they saw the situation as changeable, people used more confrontive coping ('I tried to get the person responsible to change his mind') and planful problem-solving ('I just concentrated on what I had to do next'). In situations which simply had to be accepted they used more distancing ('I didn't let it get to me; I refused to think about it too much') and escape-avoidance ('I wished the situation would go away or somehow be over with').

The bottom line, of course, is whether these different patterns of appraisal and coping actually made any difference to what happened. The answer is that they did. Successful outcomes were more often related to problem-solving strategies ('I made a plan of action and followed it') and positive reappraisal ('I was inspired to do something creative'). By contrast, unsatisfactory outcomes were more likely to be associated with confrontive coping (e.g. 'I expressed anger to the person who caused the problem') and distancing ('I made light of the situation; refused to get too serious about it').

The Berkeley team are the first to admit that these associations are only weak. The way we assess the situation and cope with it is only *at best* a partial predictor of whether it turns out right or not. It is clear that people use more problem-focused coping when they think the situation is changeable; more emotion-focused coping when it appears not to be. But almost invariably the two go together. In over a thousand coping episodes that the Berkeley team analysed, less than one in fifty showed only one type of coping.

Are good copers healthier?

But what about health? Is there any evidence from this sort of work that the way we cope with situations actually affects our susceptibility to illness?

The answer is yes, but given the huge variety of factors that decide our health and illness, the predictive value of coping is small.

For example, good copers are less prone to depression. In a much quoted study from Stanford University,[7] several hundred depressed patients, men and women, were asked about the stresses in their lives over the past twelve months. Had they or their families been physically ill; had they been experiencing problems at home or at work? They were then invited to select one particular stressful event and say how they had coped with it.

Predictably enough, avoiding the problem was linked with more severe depression. By contrast, patients who tried to approach and solve their problems, and those who tried to control their emotional responses, were less severely depressed. These findings fit well with the now familiar idea that people using higher levels of active coping, who can also call on a certain amount of social support, usually experience fewer negative life events.

It helps to go easy

Other researchers in California also set out to test the idea that people who don't run away from their problems are physically healthier, especially if they are also easygoing. They interviewed 300 families and got very detailed information about their mental and physical health. They asked them how they rated themselves in terms of self-confidence (ambitious, energetic, successful) and also where they saw themselves in terms of being easygoing, calm and happy.

Finally, they presented their subjects with a list of life events and asked them if they had experienced any of them, and if so what they had done to cope. Had they, for example, tried to sit back and see the problem more rationally (approach-coping) or had they perhaps taken it out on other people (avoidance-coping)?

To work out their results, they divided their more stressed subjects, as Suzanne Kobasa had done, into two groups. First were those experiencing both high levels of stress and high levels of emotional distress, leading to physical symptoms like acid stomach, headache and insomnia. These were called the *distressed group*. In contrast were those individuals who had equally high levels of stress but who showed little emotional or physical disturbance – the *stress-resistant group*.

What distinguished the two? The stress-resistant people were more easygoing, and less inclined to use avoidance-coping, like keeping their feelings bottled up or being aggressive in their relations with other people. Stress-resistant men were also more self-confident, energetic and ambitious, whilst stress-resistant women felt that they enjoyed more family support.

Obviously these results fit well with the idea of hardiness and the edge that it gives in active coping. Interestingly enough though, it was not the actual amount of approach-coping that distinguished the two groups. Most people in their lives already use more approach than avoidance (two to five times more according to the figures in this study). But healthier individuals seem to keep their avoidance to a minimum. Less healthy ones indulge in it more often. So it seems that avoidance-coping is a risk factor for stress-linked illness in its own right, rather than simply reducing the time available for more positive coping efforts.

Again in this study, the differences were small – we are dealing with only marginal effects. But it is a margin we can do something about. In a world where stress is inescapable, the researchers suggest that 'programs emphasizing adaptive patterns of coping with stress might focus especially on helping stressed individuals to reduce their reliance on avoidance-coping strategies'.[8]

In part this simply comes down to teaching people how to manage their daily routine more effectively. Teaching the basic skills of getting yourself organized is a primary target for any programme of stress-management. George Vaillant would no doubt approve.

Situations are important too

But surely the way you respond depends on what's happening to you as well? Robert McCrae was curious to know just how far patterns of coping depend on the actual situation that people were coping with.[9] He asked several hundred volunteers in Baltimore to remember a particularly stressful event and to say how they had coped with it. To list them he used the Ways of Coping. But McCrae also added fifty extra items of his own to produce a huge checklist of 118 different possible ways of dealing with the problem, grouped into no less than twenty-seven coping strategies, like self-blame, restraint or seeking help.

He found some similarity in coping patterns as a consequence of people facing similar situations. For example, those feeling losses tended to use faith ('put my faith in God or other people') and to express their feelings. Those undergoing a threat showed relatively frequent use of fatalism ('accepted it as unavoidable') and wishful thinking ('I hoped for a miracle'). Among people faced with a challenge there was more use of rational action ('found out more about it') and positive thinking ('looked for the bright side').

So coping depends to some degree on the situation which we are in. No surprises there. And challenges call forth more 'mature', non-neurotic responses. That's not surprising either. It is simply easier to deal with a challenge than with a threat or a loss. Even so, the fit is rather poor. The type of stressor accounts for less than 20 per cent of the range of responses. To make the prediction better another factor is needed – information about personality.

Neurotic or mature?

So McCrae and Costa mounted a more comprehensive study of the same group of volunteers. This time they also measured their personalities and aspects of their well-being.[10] They reasoned that the purpose of coping is to try to buffer stress and minimize its adverse effects – to maintain one's sense of well-being. So actually measuring their psychological well-being should provide an obvious index of how successfully these people were coping.

They asked their subjects how they coped with a particular incident in the recent past. Having determined their levels of extraversion and neuroticism, McCrae and Costa also made several measures of their psychological well-being at the end of the period in which the stressful event had occurred.

The correlations were very interesting. Neuroticism was associated with coping that involved hostile reactions, escapist fantasy, self-blame, sedation, withdrawal, wishful thinking, passivity and indecisiveness. In contrast, extraversion was associated with rational action, positive thinking, substitution (e.g. 'found satisfaction somewhere else in life') and restraint. Many features in the first group have been described in the past as *immature* or *neurotic* forms of coping, and here they were clearly linked to neuroticism. Those in the second category, generally described as *mature* coping strategies, are linked, by contrast, to extraversion.

Mature approaches like rational action and seeking help are more effective in solving the problem and reducing the distress. In contrast, self-blame, wishful thinking and passivity are among the least effective. So even within this population of normal people, who were emotionally quite stable, those highest in neuroticism were more prone to use coping mechanisms that had the least value.

For well-being too, it pays to use a mature approach. Neurotic coping predicted low scores on the Bradburn Scale and on other measures of psychological well-being. Predictably again, extraversion was associated with a more positive affect balance.

Is it worth teaching ways to cope?

Should we conclude from these results that more effective coping will boost our psychological well-being?

Perhaps, but there is another explanation. Our personality may be influencing *both* our coping patterns and our sense of well-being at the same time. It is certainly possible that people high in neuroticism are unhappy because they cope poorly; and that extraverts are happy because they use more vigorous and effective coping. But think for a moment about the possibility that coping itself may have no real effect on the link between stress and illness. Perhaps well-adjusted people use certain coping styles *and at the same time* are happy with their lives. Perhaps maladjusted people use ineffective coping but are unhappy simply because of their neuroticism. Certainly, when the effects of personality are allowed for, the link between coping style and well-being gets smaller.

This possibility raises practical questions. Because of the influence of E and N, and because the effect of coping on well-being is only weak, is there really any point in trying to teach people to cope better? Wouldn't it be more sensible to try to change their underlying personality, which accounts for much of their coping choice, and influences their level of well-being into the bargain?

Fortunately it isn't really a question of either/or. The two approaches go hand in hand. Teaching coping skills alters the way that people think about themselves. Changing their personality (that's to say, altering their patterns of thinking, feeling and behaviour) makes them more flexible in the way they approach their problems. We don't need to decide which is the more important. The two are intertwined, two faces of the same coin. Learning to say yes to life involves them both.

CHAPTER 12

Changing Our Ways

―――

One therapist's week

Imagine a week in the life of a clinical psychologist with a private practice in London. Let's call him Peter Black. He works from a rented consulting room at a clinic within walking distance of Harley Street.

But it wasn't always so. After finishing his psychology degree at a northern university he stayed on to do some research. His interest at the time was in the different capacities of the right and left hemispheres of the brain. This work, written up in a rather uninspired but scientifically respectable thesis, got him a PhD (most psychologists are 'PhD doctors', unlike psychiatrists, who are what most people think of as 'real doctors', with an MB, ChB).

But two years' more research on bilingual children convinced him that he might be more interested in patients in the clinic than subjects in the laboratory. So he applied to get on the Clinical Psychology Course of a London teaching centre. Competition was stiff (forty applicants for five places), but he presented himself well at the interview. Three years and a lot of lectures and supervisions later, he qualified and worked for a while as a basic-grade clinical psychologist in an antiquated mental hospital in Yorkshire.

Peter wasn't happy there. Even a promotion further south couldn't hide the fact that he had little time for himself. Should he get out? The problem was solved for him. When his contract came to an end he was turned down for seven jobs in succession.

So he decided, at the age of thirty-four, to take the plunge and go private. Now he charges a basic £20–25 an hour (more for clients who can afford it) for helping them with a wide range of problems. Though he might not recognize it, he's teaching them to affirm their lives.

Some of them come to him because GPs have heard of him – he is starting to get a reputation. Others come because their friends have been and recommended him. But most simply phone him after looking up 'psychotherapists' in the Yellow Pages. It comes between 'provision merchants' and 'public-address systems'.

What sort of clients come to see Peter Black? A very similar group to those who visit his American colleague (let's call him Paul White) at his office in the East 60s in New York.

On Monday he sees George, a young singer hoping to make a name for himself. George's problem is fatal for an aspiring performer. Although he sings his heart out with an audience screaming back at him, when it comes to trying to make a demonstration tape he goes to pieces. He knows that he has to get it right – a lot hangs on it. But knowing that doesn't improve his performance. Instead, his fear of getting it wrong – with the prospects of never landing a contract – freeze him with horror and stop him from singing at all.

Later on Monday Peter sees Gill, a single parent living in a flat that her mother left her. Last week she put her foot through a rotten floorboard in the bathroom. This week all the lights fused. She couldn't stop the cold tap from dripping and only this morning her daughter was sent home from school for fighting. 'I don't know how I'm going to carry on,' she tells him. 'I can't manage the flat, and I'm a lousy mother.' She seems to be heading for a major depression.

On Tuesday he sees two clients, one who avoids people, the other who chases after them. Edward believes that people are devious, and that they will screw you if they can. His solution is simple. He keeps away from them. The prospects of joining any sort of organization, even a health club, fills him with disgust. But he has to mix with people at work, and he constantly finds himself angry about it. 'I feel so trapped,' he tells Peter. 'I'm sure I'm going to blow a fuse and hit someone.'

Tony, on the other hand, loves people. His problem, as he perceives it, is that they don't love him back. Good-looking and talented, he wants people to tell him so. He puts himself out to give them the chance, but he rarely gets any takers. As a result, his self-esteem drags on the ground. Not only that, but he thinks that it's only a matter of time before someone realizes that he isn't talented at all. A creative consultant in an advertising agency with a string of successful campaigns behind him, he wakes up every day expecting the next client finally to see through the façade and reject his work with the contempt that he secretly *knows* it deserves.

Wednesday is interesting as well. In walks Steve, whose wife left him for another woman. He doesn't know whether that triggered the glandular fever, but being off work for three months certainly helped to make him redundant. 'Things just keep slipping away from me', he explains. 'I can't make anything happen any more. I'm so helpless. I'm terrified about what's going to go wrong next.'

Sally, by contrast, hasn't lost control. She's just lost interest. Straight from Oxford into the City she had instant success as a financial analyst in her early twenties. Now, unmarried and in her mid-thirties, money doesn't interest her. Neither does anything else. 'There's nothing worth doing', she complains. 'Nothing I've ever done is worth anything and I don't know where else to go. I just wish I could get involved in something worthwhile.'

Thursday sees two more problem clients. Henry is concerned because his firm is moving. They want him to move as well, and the shift means moving up the ladder – more money, more responsibility. Though his wife is keen, Henry lies awake at night thinking about it. 'What if we can't find a house we can afford or a decent school?' But the problem is really deeper. Secretly he is thinking, 'What if I can't handle being an area manager? I'm fully stretched just doing my job here already. I'm forty-eight and I don't know if I can learn a new territory. And how am I going to manage all those ambitious young bastards after my job?'

At the end of his week (Peter is having Friday off to go to a conference) he meets Eric, a married man in his sixties who just sits at home in front of the TV. He used to be Secretary of the Bowls Club and Treasurer of the Horticultural Society. These days he doesn't even want to take the dog for a walk. Nothing gives him pleasure any more, so he doesn't do anything.

At the conference Peter meets Paul White, his friend from New York. They talk about Eric, and how his capacity for pleasure has broken down. Paul compares Eric with his own patient Howard, an investment broker with a five-million-dollar house in Connecticut. He has his own helicopter to get him to his office in Manhattan. Nothing gives Howard pleasure either.

'Surely you're pleased about making twenty million dollars on the market last year?' Paul asks him. 'Why?' says Howard. 'Everybody does that.' 'Well, something in your life must give you a boost. What about your new helicopter?' 'Don't talk to me about it,' says Howard. 'The damn thing's so noisy.'

Therapy and life-affirmers

Do these psychologists and their clients really exist? The answer is yes – and no. Peter and Paul aren't real therapists, but they typify many of those whom I have known over the years. Nor are the clients' cases taken from any particular psychologist's files. But people with problems like these go to therapists for advice all the time.

Glancing down the list we find that what all of them have in common is a lack of at least one of our life-affirming characteristics. George and Gill both have emotional problems – anxiety for George, depression for Gill. A personality questionnaire would probably find both of them scoring high on emotional instability. Edward's problem isn't neuroticism. It's hostility, caused by a basic cynicism about his fellow men. Tony can't get enough of people, but unfortunately they don't boost his self-esteem as he wants them to. Incapable of boosting it for himself, his estimate of his own self-worth stays perilously low. He thinks of himself as an 'imposter', playing a role that he really isn't capable of, and waiting everyday to be found out.

Steve simply can't control his life or, it seems, any part of it. Having mononucleosis may have been the crucial factor that weakened him and started to let it slip away. Sally has lost her commitment. Nothing is really worth engaging in, getting involved with. Henry has lost the sense of optimistic challenge that, when he was younger, would make him welcome any new opportunity to see what he could make of it. Eric too has lost his motivation because he simply doesn't enjoy anything any more.

Running through this list of life-denying characteristics it is clear that some of the problems overlap. George and Henry both have a keynote of anxiety in their lives. Gill and Steve are both depressed. Sally and Eric can't motivate themselves to do anything. Peter Black sees these similarities. And they are reflected in what he tries to do for them.

Part of the repertoire

Treating anxiety and depression are standard parts of the repertoire of any clinical psychologist or counsellor offering therapy – what they learn in their training years. Helping people towards goals that are worth pursuing, towards activities that give clients a sense of pleasure or fulfilment are also part of what they train for. Helping them to become less hostile and more sociable is not so easy. But it is possible, once the therapist discovers what it is that makes them angry. And when it comes to control, commitment and challenge, a whole programme is currently underway designed to make people more hardy.

So our clinician has at least some of the tools that help people become more life-affirming. So too do his clients. At least, if they don't have them now, they can learn them. All the procedures that our psychologist may use are designed to be learned and then applied by people to themselves. Indeed to achieve any success, they *have* to be taken on board and administered by the clients themselves. The problem is that at the time they feel the need for professional help clients are so far gone that they have lost much of the ability to grapple with their difficulties. They don't have the perspective. They can't detach themselves. They are just too overwhelmed. That's why they need someone else, to get them over the hump. But in any therapy based on changing thinking and behaviour, the client helps himself.

So what I am going to describe in this and the following chapter isn't a course of 'do-it-yourself psychotherapy'. That's about as practical as trying 'do-it-yourself brain surgery'. Rather, I'm going to consider a package of measures that anyone can eventually apply to themselves. But initially you may need to learn them from a professional, until you are able to help yourself. Eventually they should help to prevent the problem situations in your life from becoming serious enough to need professional help at all.

Some therapists will tell you that you *always* need someone else to help with your problems; that it is simply not possible to deal with them on your own. Psychoanalysts take this view.

And Salvatore Maddi tells us quite clearly that 'There is no way in which merely reading accounts . . . concerning hardiness training will render someone, however experienced, capable of doing what is required in an adequate fashion'.[1] Sometimes one suspects that therapists may have a vested interest in saying so. For example, Maddi goes on, 'There is a rigorous program available through the Hardiness Institute [in Chicago] to develop trainers, and one should not present him or herself as a hardiness trainer without having gone through it'.

But it is not my aim to produce trainers. I simply want to give you some sense of the sort of techniques that are currently available; to let you see what they feel like. If any of them seem to have promise, or if you feel that you would like to take them further, then it may be the time to consult the professionals. But if you are so overwhelmed that you can't even see the direction to go in, then the best route is straight to a specialist – initially to your GP or to a psychotherapist direct.

And what if you try some of these methods but they don't seem to work? The worst that can happen is that you might lose a little faith in your power to change your life. You really might need professional help to get you started. The best that can happen is that you discover that you can help yourself to affirm your life, and gain a measure of self-direction that you may have doubted was possible.

Doing it yourself?

Of course, of the hundreds of different procedures that psychotherapy has devised some are virtually impossible to use without assistance.

For example, there are several different approaches to the treatment of phobias, those irrational but deep-seated fears that some people have, say of snakes, or heights, or of open spaces.

In one form of therapy called *desensitization*, the client produces a list of fearful situations, arranged in order of how frightening they would be if she had to experience them. For example, for a snake phobic the list might start with the image in her mind's eye of seeing a snake locked firmly in a cage at the other side of the room. Increasingly more frightening images would involve approaching the cage, standing beside it, opening it and eventually picking the snake up. Using the form of phobic treatment called 'desensitization' the client first of all learns how to relax (of which more later) then she plays through each of these scenes in her mind. As she looks at each scene in turn, she deliberately relaxes, until that particular scene becomes tolerable enough for her to think about. When it is, she then goes on to the next. Having been through all of them (including handling the snake) in her mind she may find that her fear is much reduced.

The next phase is more difficult. It involves her doing the same thing in real life, one stage at a time, guided by the reassuring presence of someone who isn't scared of snakes. Once she can bring herself to go through them all then she has an excellent chance of being cured. But unfortunately the process of desensitization is time-consuming, and may take many sessions before the object is achieved.

An alternative and much more rapid treatment for phobias is called *implosion* or *flooding*. It involves exposing yourself to the situation that you most fear and staying there for as long as possible. Your anxiety mounts, almost to breaking point. But there are very clear findings which show that if you can stay in the situation for up to a couple of hours, the fear recedes, sometimes completely in a single session.[2]

Real-life exposure is the most rapid of all treatment for people with phobic symptoms. Spider phobics will spend hours searching the house to assure themselves that there are no spiders hiding anywhere. Yet a single flooding session will sometimes cure them. Agoraphobics are scared of being in open spaces or in crowds. They may have such a fear of fainting or having a heart attack on the bus or in the supermarket that they spend months or even years without leaving home. Yet a few sessions of real-life exposure may mean that they can go where they please.

Some psychotherapists are so convinced of the value of exposure that they recommend it as a do-it-yourself procedure.[3] But it is very difficult to expose yourself to something that you have deliberately been trying to avoid for years. Without a therapist's help many clients simply lose their courage. And, of course, each time they allow themselves to escape from the situation makes it more difficult to approach it the next time. This is what every jockey and racing cyclist knows well. If they come off, their first action is to climb back on immediately, to avoid losing their nerve.

So flooding is a powerful method of changing behaviour. But it's not really one that most life-affirmers could manage for themselves without a therapist, or at least a sympathetic 'baby-sitter' who is there to see that they don't cheat and try to escape.

None of the other methods I am going to describe is like that. If you need a therapist to make them work it isn't because they are frightening. It's because she knows more about them than you do, and you simply need her guidance to get started.

Proof of efficacy?

But before we spend our money, we need to be sure that we are not just wasting our time. We are entitled to ask, 'Is there really any evidence that this whole battery of methods used by counsellors and therapists actually do anyone any good?' The question may seem extraordinary when thousands of people spend tens of thousands of hours every year in Britain alone receiving psychotherapy. They must believe that such time is well spent. But is it?

In 1952 Hans Eysenck examined the results of published studies that had been obtained from treating several thousand neurotic patients. Neuroses like severe anxiety and depression are not very common among young people. They generally start to appear in the twenties, become increasingly more common in the thirties and forties and fall off quite sharply in later life. But he delivered a bombshell with his claim that two out of three neurotic patients recover on their own within two years, even without receiving any treatment.[4] The sort of therapy he was describing was 'orthodox' psychotherapy, originated by Sigmund Freud but also including all other forms of 'talking treatment'. At that time, and even when he made a similar claim in the 1960s, such psychotherapy was the standard form of treatment. Behaviour-based therapies didn't take off until the early 1960s (partly under the influence of Eysenck himself) and cognitive therapy came to Britain later still.

Not surprisingly, Eysenck's claim that 'roughly two-thirds of a group of neurotic patients will recover or improve to a marked extent within about two years of the onset of their illness, whether they are treated by means of psychotherapy or not' stung therapists into attempts to prove him wrong.

The debate is still continuing. Being left exposed and vulnerable for a number of years, psychotherapists have put an immense amount of effort into examining their results. And fortunately for them, several detailed analyses of their findings do suggest that what they have been doing for the last fifty years or so is a real help to at least some of their clients.

So, for example, one of the standard works on the subject could assure its readers in 1986 that the effects of psychotherapy are both clearly demonstrated and clinically useful in getting people better. Psychotherapy, say its authors, speeds up the natural healing process and provides the patients with additional coping strategies, at the same time providing the means for dealing with future problems.[5] Such effects, they say, tend to be lasting and give better results than can be achieved simply by making social contact with the therapist without any particular treatment plan.

But the fact that such a debate could drag on for so long (and it is not yet over) must mean that the benefits of the more 'traditional' kinds of therapy are not clear-cut.

We might at least expect to find that some approaches are better than others for particular sorts of problems. But even here the situation isn't clear. The same textbook tells us that 'differences in outcome between various forms of therapy are not as pronounced as might have been expected'. However, it does seem that behavioural and cognitive methods are generally superior to 'traditional verbal therapies'. This is because cognitive and behavioural approaches expose the client, for example, to the source of his anxiety, and actively encourage him to gain some sense of mastery over his difficulties. They encourage people to take charge of their own lives and eventually leave the therapist behind.

A question of meaning

But what can all of these dozens of treatments possibly have in common that gets people well again? The question has been elegantly answered by Jerome Frank, now Emeritus Professor of Psychiatry at Johns Hopkins University in Baltimore.[6]

Frank points to the widely differing sets of assumptions that different therapists make about the origin of their patient's illness. Those of the existentialist–humanist school try to help their clients to achieve self-realization and to deal with their fears of death, to which, they believe, all of their symptoms are ultimately related. Psychoanalytic practitioners, by contrast, believe that such symptoms result from unsuccessful attempts to resolve unconscious conflicts. They see their role as bringing such conflicts to the surface.

For behaviour therapists, symptoms result from a pattern of maladaptive behaviours that clients have learned over the course of their lives. Therapy consists of laying down new, more appropriate behaviour patterns. Cognitive therapists, as we have seen, regard the client's problem as resulting from his faulty thinking about himself, his world and his future, and set out to correct his misguided thinking patterns.

What do all of these approaches have in common? The answer, says Frank, is simple. All forms of therapy depend on the fact that the way we think, feel and behave is not really a response to outside events themselves. Instead it is a response to the *meanings* that we attach to them. Epictetus said something similar two thousand years before. 'We are guided', Frank suggests, 'by our assumptions about reality,' and our distress results from the way that we *think* about our experiences. The aim of all forms of psychotherapy is simply to enable patients to 'transform the meaning of their experiences in such a way as to enable them to feel better and function more effectively'.

When the client seeks help, it is not just for his specific symptoms – say George's fear of singing when it actually matters, or Henry's anxiety about becoming an area manager. Underlying these specific problems there is often a more general feeling, an overall sense of becoming demoralized. This produces a state of confusion, an inability to make any sense out of the problem and certainly a failure to control it.

In a nutshell, says Frank:

> All psychotherapists provide new concepts and information that enable their patients to make meaningful connections between symptoms and experiences that have been mysterious, thereby replacing confusion with clarity. All psychotherapeutic schools seek to help patients transform the meaning of their symptoms and problems so as to replace despair with hope, feelings of incompetence with self-efficacy and isolation with rewarding personal relationships.

He concludes:

> even when psychotherapy has little specific effect on symptoms, by transforming their meanings it can enable the patient to tolerate them better and can strengthen . . . morale

in the face of persistent distress by enabling the patient to transform suffering into, for example, an opportunity for cultivating self-discipline or a spiritually redemptive experience.

For this to happen the psychotherapist collaborates with the patient in 'formulating a plausible story that makes the meaning of the symptoms more benign and provides procedures for combating them, thereby enabling the patient to regain his morale. As a result, he feels better and functions more effectively, leading to progressive improvement.'

What's on the menu?

So much for the background.

But what does all of this mean for the would be life-affirmer, the person who isn't ill but who wants to get better; the individual who may not feel that he needs a therapist, but does want to try some 'therapeutic' approaches for himself?

It means, firstly, that he has recognized his own 'symptoms', his own areas of weakness which he would like to improve. It means as well that he will have sensed the demoralization that goes with them, the beginning of the slide into helplessness. It also means that he will be looking for some credible explanation of why he has got to the point he has, and for some tools to use in pulling himself back to function properly. The more techniques that he looks at the more likely he is to find one (or several) to suit him, and the greater the chance he has of pulling himself around.

So I am going to describe a range of different methods – behavioural and cognitive – that clients have found helpful in improving their insights and altering their lives, a cafeteria menu of approaches that people use to enhance their mental well-being – to say yes to life.

Up to now we have carefully distinguished ways of changing how people act from ways of changing what they think. But when it comes to real-life treatment we will find that this distinction between the cognitive and the behavioural approaches often ceases to exist. Virtually all psychotherapies alter both, whether they set out to or not. So today the new buzz-word among many specialists is *cognitive–behavioural therapy*, with the accent on the hyphen.

Relaxation is a skill

At the basis of nearly all the different approaches to what I would call life-enhancing therapy, you will always find the same technique – relaxation. Recall, for example, how desensitization depends on you imagining a series of anxiety-producing scenes but only after you have become relaxed. The rationale is that anxiety and relaxation cannot exist together in your head at the same time. Being relaxed stops the feelings of anxiety from arising, or at least from becoming uncomfortable. Actually, relaxation is not unique in this respect. In theory we could use any emotional reaction that simply crowded out the anxious response. Anger or sexual arousal might be just as good, though we might wonder about the results of any programme that taught you how to get sexually excited every time some anxiety-provoking stimulus swam into sight.

Valuable as it was in the beginnings of behaviour therapy in the 1950s, desensitization isn't used much any more. Procedures like direct exposure (with a therapist) seem far more effective. But relaxation itself is still used on a massive scale. Programmes of stress-management emphasize it as one of the most powerful means of dealing with distress and many magazines in the health field advertise books and relaxation tapes to teach you how to do it.

And the point is that you do need to learn. Relaxation seems such a natural process that we may think that we are relaxed when we are sitting reading the paper or watching the television. Most of us are simply not trained to tune into our muscles and monitor the levels of tension inside them. If we were, we would realize that, far from being relaxed, as we slump in the living-room at the end of the day, most of the muscles in our body are still tight from the way we have wound ourselves up. And as we get out of bed in the morning, the anticipation of what we have to do during the day starts to tighten them before our feet touch the floor.

So if we are going to take relaxation seriously, we have to forget the idea that it is something we know how to do already. Instead, we have to assume that it's something that we have never done properly, a new skill to be learned like riding a motor-bike. In time it comes naturally, almost without thinking, but when we start, we have to think about every movement.

Because most people can't gauge how much tension they have in their muscles, the original form of relaxation training gets you, paradoxically enough, to tighten your muscles first and to sense what the tension feels like. Then, and only then, can you know what it is like when your muscles really do relax.

This widely used procedure was first developed fifty years ago by Edmund Jacobson at the University of Chicago. In its original form it took many hours of practice with a trainer to get it right. However, it has been simplified over the years. I will give just an outline here, taken from a manual on relaxation training that was put together in 1973.[7] In my view it hasn't been improved on since then. The programme that it outlines involves eight forty-five minute sessions and, as you read it, you will see that it concentrates initially on no less than sixteen separate muscle groups. As time goes by the sixteen are combined, and eventually the tensing part is left out altogether.

Some relaxation teachers suggest that you lie on the floor, others that you sit in a chair, without tie or shoes. Imagine you are there, in your first relaxation session, sitting comfortably in a quiet room where you won't be disturbed.

The trainer proceeds as follows: 'The purpose of this first session is to help you learn to become deeply relaxed, perhaps more relaxed than you've ever been before, and we can begin this session by going over the muscle groups that we are going to deal with in relaxation training. There are sixteen muscle groups to be dealt with, sixteen groups which are tensed and relaxed. As your skill develops, this number will be reduced.

'We will begin training with the hand and forearm. I'll ask you to tense the muscles in the right hand and right lower arm by making a tight fist. Now you should be able to feel tension in the hand, over the knuckles, and up the lower arm. Can you feel that tension? Now just let it go.

'After we have relaxed that group of muscles we will then move to the muscles of the right biceps, and I'll ask you to tense these muscles by pushing your elbow down against the arm of the chair. You should be able to get a feeling of tension in the biceps without involving the muscles in the lower arm and hand. Can you feel the tension there now? Then simply let it go.

'Now after we have completed the relaxation of the right hand

and lower arm and right biceps, we move over to the muscles of the left hand and left lower arm and tense and relax them in the same way as we did on the right side.

'After we have relaxed the arms and the hands, we relax the muscles of the face. We are going to divide them into three groups: first the muscles in the forehead area, then the muscles in the central part of the face and finally the lower part of the face (the jaws and the lower part of the cheeks). We'll begin with the muscles in the upper part of the face and I'll ask you to tense them by lifting your eyebrows as high as you can and getting tension in the forehead and up into the scalp region. Can you feel that tension now? Then let it go.

'Now we'll move down to the muscles of the central part of the face and to tense these muscles I'll ask you to squeeze your eyes up very tightly and at the same time wrinkle up your nose. Can you feel the tension there in the upper part of the cheeks and through the eyes now? Then let it go. Next, we'll tense the muscles in the lower part of the face, so I'll ask you to bite your teeth together and pull the corners of your mouth back. You should feel tension all through the lower part of your face and jaw. Can you feel the tension in this area now? Now let it go.

'After we have completed the facial muscles we'll move on to relax the muscles of the neck. To do this I am going to ask you to pull your chin downwards towards your chest and at the same time try to prevent it from actually touching your chest. So I want you to counterpoise the muscles of the front part of the neck against those of the back of the neck. You might feel a little bit of shaking or trembling in those muscles as you tense them.

'We'll then move to the muscles of the chest, the shoulders and the upper back. We're going to combine several muscles here, and I'll ask you to tense them by taking a deep breath, holding it, and at the same time pulling the shoulder blades together. Pull the shoulders back and try to make the shoulder blades touch. You should feel tension in your neck, shoulders and upper back. Can you feel this tension now? Then let go.

'Now we'll move on to the muscles of the abdomen. To tense them I'm going to ask you to make your stomach hard. Just tense it up as though you were going to hit yourself there. Can you feel that tension? Hold it, then simply let it go.

'After relaxing the muscles in the stomach area we'll move to the legs and feet. We'll begin with the right upper leg, the right thigh, and I'll ask you to tense the muscles there by counterpoising the one large muscle on the top of the leg with the two smaller ones underneath. You should be able to feel that large muscle on the top get quite hard, can you feel that now? Let go.

'Then we'll move to the right calf, the right lower leg, and I'll ask you to tense the muscles here by pulling the toes upwards towards your head. You should be able to feel tension all through the calf area. Can you feel that tension now? Let go. Then we'll move on to tense the muscles of the right foot by pointing the toe, turning the foot inward and at the same time curling your toes. Don't tense these muscles very hard, just enough to feel the tightness under the arch and in the ball of the foot. Can you feel that tension now? Let it go.

'Then we'll move to the muscles of the left upper leg and tense and relax them just as we did on the right side, then the muscles of the left lower leg the same as we did on the right side, and finally the left foot, tensing it and relaxing it just as we did on the other side.

'A very important point to remember is to release the tension that you build up in these muscle groups immediately on cue. Don't let it dissipate gradually. For example, when you've been tensing the muscles in your right hand and right lower arm and when I ask you to relax I'd like you to completely and immediately release all the tension that is present there. Don't gradually open the hand; let all the tension go at the same time.'

Despite the initial feelings of self-consciousness most people do manage to tense and relax most of their muscle groups, if not the first or second time then certainly after a few more tries.

Eventually we get to the stage of relaxing our tensions directly, without having to go through the tensing procedure. The therapist's only job then is to focus the client's attention on any tension remaining in any of the muscle groups, and to help him recall the feelings that go with the release of that tension. The instructions go like this:

'I would like you to focus all your attention on the muscles of your arms and hands and very carefully identify any feeling of tightness or tension that might be there now. Notice where the tension is and what it feels like.

'Just recall what it was like when you release these muscles, just letting them go and allowing them to become more and more deeply relaxed.'

After about half a minute, the therapist asks the client to signal if that particular muscle group feels completely relaxed. If so, he continues to the next one. If not, the client focuses again on where the residual tension is, and again tries to relax it. The eventual aim of the sessions is to have the trainee learn how to monitor his own muscles for any tension and then learn how to let it go completely.

Procedures differ widely, depending on the therapist you are working with or the book or tape that you are using. Some approaches are much briefer than this. But all trainers will emphasize the importance of practising at home. Some of them will lend (or sell) you a tape to practise with, and there are many commercial tapes that you can buy in book stores or health shops.

There is some doubt about whether listening to a tape is as good as having a trainer in the room with you. But some research does suggest that patients can do just as well with a tape as with a live therapist. Perhaps the ideal is to have a therapist get you started. Her role may simply be to introduce you to the procedure. By helping you to believe that it is going to work, she also provides the credibility that Jerome Frank stresses as being so important for you to make progress.

Ideally, you should practise at home twice a day. Recognizing the difficulties that many people have in getting an uninterrupted half-hour to themselves, many therapists agree that once-daily training might be enough. But once having mastered the technique, many people find it so gratifying that they actually want to practise it frequently. They make remarks like 'How did I ever manage without it? Why did I spend all those years wound up?'

The ultimate aim of relaxation training is to use the events that normally create anxiety, like the phone ringing or suddenly realizing that you have forgotten to do something important, not to get you uptight, but as *cues* to switch on your relaxation sequence.

But before we get into switching on the relaxation response when you need it, it is worth looking briefly at some of the direct effects that relaxation has on physical health – for example on blood pressure.

Getting your blood pressure down

Learning to relax is now a well-established way of bringing raised blood pressure (hypertension) back into the normal range. It is also a way of reducing the need for anti-hypertensive drugs.

This has now been found by medical groups in various parts of the world. For example, Bernard Engel and his team at the Baltimore City Hospital found that practising relaxation by a group of hypertensive patients produced a significant fall in blood pressure which was sustained over a follow-up period of eighteen months.[8] And a number of those patients who had been on diuretic drugs to keep their pressures down were able to give up the medication and still remain normal. So impressed were they by these results that Engel's team recommended that all patients with only mildly raised blood pressure should be taught relaxation first, before any drugs were used at all. Only if it failed did they then recommend a drug regime.

One interesting feature is the fact that blood pressures started to go down just as soon as the patients were taught how to measure it for themselves and how to record it at home every day. The simple act of 'self-monitoring' had a beneficial effect, before the relaxation or other approaches were even begun.

On reflection, we shouldn't be surprised. There are many factors that can put your blood pressure up. Most of the mechanisms inside the body that lead to hypertension are not well understood. But for some people at least, being exposed to constant hassles has the effect of shooting it up many times a day. Whether this long-term exposure to demanding or unpleasant events puts it up permanently isn't certain. But it seems reasonable to imagine that, for some people who are particularly responsive, daily hassles may reset their blood pressures at a higher level.

One solution is to help them notice the times that it goes up – the sort of situations that produce this sudden rise. Amazingly enough, until it is pointed out, many of them simply haven't noticed. But self-monitoring concentrates the mind. It focuses our attention, perhaps for the first time in our lives, on our blood pressure and on the things that disturb it. A phase of self-monitoring or self-awareness forms the basis of many different programmes of self-management for mental as well as for physical health. You can't start altering the problem until you know something about what causes it.

A team in Heidelberg took this idea further.[9] They taught Jacobsonian relaxation to a group of about fifty hypertensives. From the start they emphasized that it was not some sort of 'medical' procedure to be used only in the therapist's office. Instead, it was a basic coping skill, something that clients could switch on for themselves whenever they found themselves in difficult situations. They were encouraged to list the sort of situations that led to trouble and to record their reactions to them. Then they were taught to take a deep breath and relax each time, rather than just responding automatically as they had done in the past. They also learned how to listen to the constant monologue going on inside their heads ('I'm not going to be able to do this'; 'I can't afford to make a mistake') and to notice how their levels of tension could be brought down by substituting a different set of phrases ('I'm not going to get upset'; 'I've managed to handle more difficult situations in the past').

Self-monitoring showed many patients the sort of problems that put their pressures up. Some were related to work, like not having enough time to do things, being interrupted, having to accept responsibility and that constant feeling of having to be competitive or self-assertive. Others related to home life, to disputes with the family and neighbours. For some patients the stress was related to some specific life events. Others seemed to have many, long lasting life problems.

But both groups could be helped, the former from counselling about their particular problem, the latter through being taught a more general set of problem-solving skills. In both cases the ability to switch on the relaxation response proved to be of great value. The results showed a blood pressure fall which was still maintained up to a year after the original treatment.

Relaxation or meditation?

There are other ways to relax apart from clenching and loosening your muscles. For example, the early work in Britain on reducing blood pressure was carried out by Chandra Patel, then a general practitioner in Croydon, using a biofeedback system, among other methods.

She invited a group of seventeen hypertensive patients at her practice to take part in a relaxation treatment. They lay on reclining chairs and were asked to breath in and out slowly and rhythmically. They were to feel the air filling their lungs, starting at the diaphragm and going right to the top of the chest. Then the breath was let out again. They made no effort to force their breathing or to slow it down. All they had to do was to make it gentle and even.

Once they had learned this breathing technique, they were

taught how to direct their attention to each part of their body in sequence and to make mental contact with it. So, for example, they might start with the right foot, leg and hip, and simply by thinking about them, let all the tension go. As they did so, they were to become aware of every muscle and nerve as the whole side, from toes to hip joint, became completely relaxed. Then they were to do the same on the left side, followed by the right hand, arm and shoulder and then the left.

Their attention was next directed to the base of the spine and moved up, one vertebrae at a time, until the whole back felt completely relaxed, as though it was sinking into the chair below. Then came the head and face, and finally the chest and shoulders. This whole relaxation process (letting go of the tension *already there* rather than creating it to begin with) only took about ten minutes. Once completely relaxed the subjects could then spend perhaps twice as long just concentrating on the flow of their breath in and out.

They were also hooked up to a biofeedback machine which measured either the electrical resistance of their skin or their levels of muscle tension, say over the forehead. As people become more relaxed, their skin resistance increases, but their forehead tension goes down. Both of these changes can be translated by the machine into a sound tone which is played back through headphones. As patients become more relaxed the tone gets lower, and the change in the sound shows them how well they are doing.

In the 1970s there was great hope for biofeedback as a way of allowing us to bring about bodily changes that we didn't normally do consciously, for example increasing blood flow to the brain to try and relieve migraine headaches. The machine would measure some feature related to blood flow (like the temperature of your skin). All you had to do, hooked up to it, was to make the feedback tone change in pitch. People found they could do so even though they didn't know just how they were doing it.

Today biofeedback is not so popular. Its results have been disappointing – much less than was expected in the heady days of the 1970s, when some researchers believed that almost any part of our unconscious, autonomic nervous system could be brought under conscious control. And although it is helpful, it certainly isn't essential to achieve the relaxation effect.

Whatever the essential component may be in this mixture of breathing, relaxation and feedback, Patel's results were remarkable. Blood pressures fell dramatically (by 26/15 blood-pressure units, known technically as mmHg) in the treated group. This was far more than occurred in a similar group of 'controls' (8/4 mmHg) who had simply been asked to relax on the reclining chairs but without being given any instructions on how to do so, and without being connected to the feedback machine. But when this control group were themselves invited to take part in a similar twelve-session programme, in which they too learned to relax properly, they showed similar blood-pressure falls.

This work is important, apart from being the first in the field, because Chandra Patel and her colleagues then took it out of general practice and into industry. In 1981 they reported the results of a similar relaxation programme applied to a group of nearly 100 works employees, all of whom had an increased risk of coronary disease, partly because of raised blood pressure. They attended eight one-hourly relaxation sessions where they learned the breathing and relaxation exercises from a cassette tape (so much for the idea that the therapist has to be there all the time). They were also lent the tape to practise at home. Blood pressures were measured eight weeks and eight months after the end of the trial. In both cases they were lower than in the control group who had not had any special instructions.

Even more interesting is the fact that some of the same individuals were examined again four years later. In this 1985 follow-up,[10] the reduction in blood pressure was maintained, and other evidence of heart disease was also reduced in the relaxation group. Indeed, the researchers calculated that this simple procedure resulted in a 20 per cent reduction of coronary risk straight after it had been learned, falling to a still important 10 per cent reduction in risk some four years later. Any manufacturer producing a drug to reduce coronary events would be delighted to achieve falls of this size.

Do you need to meditate?

One extra component in Chandra Patel's package consists of a type of meditation. Patients are invited to imagine a peaceful scene and to experience it fully in their minds. Then, feeling warm and relaxed, they choose a word that makes them continue to feel good, and start to repeat it effortlessly, the word forming the centre of their attention.

This concentration on a word is a form of 'mantra' meditation. It resembles transcendental meditation or TM. Great claims were made at one time about TM producing a 'fourth state of consciousness', and creating a 'hypometabolic' state in which the meditator's physical activities, like breathing, oxygen-consumption and heart rate, are brought to a very low level.

The question is whether meditation with its quasi-religious overtones is actually necessary to achieve this state of deep physical rest. And the answer appears to be no. A collaborative study between workers at Yale and the University of Washington could find no difference between progressive relaxation ('tense and relax') and TM as far as bodily responses were concerned, except that people practising the Jacobsonian relaxation daily for five years or more achieved deeper levels of bodily relaxation than those who had been meditating for three years.[11]

Meditation is primarily concerned with fixing one's mental attention. And there is some evidence that meditators can achieve mental gains over relaxers. But as far as bodily changes are concerned, relaxation is as good as meditation or better. This is fortunate for those people who want to start taking an active role in directing their lives but who are unwilling to buy into any form of Eastern religion, even TM, the highly Westernized version that has been promoted in Europe and North America since the early 1970s.

Managing anxiety

So relaxation improves physical health. But its main use will always be for emotional problems. We have seen how it is used in desensitization, but it is also valuable in other approaches to the treatment of anxiety.

To feel anxious about really dangerous or threatening events is both natural and healthy. It is a response that alerts us to the fact that we need to take action (if only avoiding action) to prevent ourselves or those close to us from being harmed. It is one of the things that has kept us alive as a species.

But the majority of anxious feelings that most people experience today don't relate to real threats to our physical well-being. Instead they are triggered by symbolic threats to our self-image or our self-esteem. Often they have to do with whether we will be able to perform well enough – at our job, in competition with others, even in bed.

But though the threat may be largely imagined, its effects are real enough. Anxieties about being able to perform simply ensure that we will perform worse at whatever we have to do. Far from sharpening our responses, excessive anxiety reduces them still further. That was George's problem when he came to see Peter Black. To allow yourself to indulge in such 'inappropriate' anxiety is a prime feature of life-negating people. It is one of the most obvious qualities that go with a high level of neuroticism.

We become aware of our anxiety in at least three different ways. The first is a subjective feeling, a sense of apprehension and dread, that accompanies the arousal of our sympathetic nervous system. The second is the way that it disrupts our ability to think about anything else. And finally, there are the effects that it has on our behaviour – a general falling off in our ability to do things and a strong wish to get away from whatever is causing the problem.

The feeling of emotional tension and the heightened arousal that goes with it can make us more likely to suffer from headaches, sleeplessness, exhaustion and even some skin complaints. The cognitive disturbances mean that it is difficult to concentrate and to remember anything. Highly anxious people lose their flexibility for solving problems. They tend to approach them all in the same stereotyped way. They also spend a long time obsessively worrying about what has happened and, even worse, what might happen in the future.

But perhaps the most insidious feature of anxiety, and the one that makes it persist, is the fact that, given the opportunity, anxious people will slide out of the situation rather than facing it squarely.

Indeed, one view of how anxiety arises is that we had some unpleasant experience in the past that was sufficiently noxious for us to want to avoid it in the future. And it is the process of avoidance itself that sets up the anxiety. It is the fear that we may have to face it again that puts us constantly on the alert. But the more the situation is avoided the more anxious we become about having to face it eventually, and so on in a vicious cycle.

With so many aspects of anxiety to choose from, it may seem difficult for the therapist to know where to start, when it comes to treatment. Obviously, she needs to look at the causes. If the problem originates, say, from some tension within the family, then it makes more sense to try to remedy the problem rather than simply trying to treat the feelings that it produces. If the anxiety stems from not having particular skills or knowledge, then we can make an effort towards gaining them – for example, learning how to write a job application or how to behave on some important occasion.

But at some stage it becomes essential to treat the anxiety itself – the dread and foreboding, the confusion and irritation, the loss of concentration and all the other life-denying features that go with it. There are many ways of going about it. One involves the use of drugs – anxiolytics – that alter the biochemical pathways of anxiety in the brain. Many doctors still believe that they have a valuable place, at least for treating short-term problems. But when the difficulty is embedded in the patient's whole lifestyle, then short-term solutions just aren't enough. A clinical psychologist will try to treat the disturbance that the anxiety brings about in such a way that they *stay* treated. We'll look at just two non-drug approaches. One concentrates on correcting the feelings and the behaviour that the anxiety generates. The other goes for the distorted thinking behind it.

Relax on cue

Anxiety-management training (AMT) was developed in the early 1970s largely to overcome the failings of desensitization. Desensitizing anxiety, you will remember, is a lengthy process and unfortunately it only works for those fears that you set out to cure, say a fear of spiders. Desensitizing a spider phobic does nothing for his fear of heights. You have to start again and go through a whole new process, using images of going to higher and higher places and relaxing away the fear at each stage.

AMT works differently. It uses the sensation of anxiety itself as a cue to start relaxing and disarming the anxious feelings. So it decreases the impact of the anxiety whatever its cause. You don't even need to have a clear idea of what the cause is. AMT lets you live with your anxious thoughts, without them destroying your life.

In the first stage of training, the client is taught to relax.[12] This may take the first three sessions. Next, in his mind, he imagines (one at a time) a series of situations that arouse his anxiety. They usually aren't difficult to recall. They don't have to be related to each other, and he doesn't even have to understand why he finds them so unpleasant.

Instead, he simply lets each one build up in his imagination. He tries to experience it fully, how it feels and what it does to him, before the therapist tells him to stop. But how does he stop? He does so, when he hears the instruction, simply by switching to his relaxation exercises, and by changing the anxious mental picture and instead thinking about a peaceful, relaxing scene. Eventually he finds that the therapist isn't needed any more. The client becomes bold enough *on his own* to imagine the things that make him feel uncomfortable. He lets himself fully experience what they do to his body, making his muscles tight, his breathing race or his stomach churn. In other words, he comes to discover his own 'stress profile' – the physical responses that anxiety creates in him. He then turns them off, again *on his own*, by switching to his physical feeling of relaxation and his mental sense of calm.

Once he is able to do this in his mind, he takes his newly acquired skill out into the world. When some unpleasant event occurs and his anxiety starts to build, he notices the cues (the tensing, the breathlessness) this time far more quickly than he did in the past. Then he actually uses these cues to trigger his relaxation, and his well-practised inner sense of calm. What could have been a full-blown anxiety attack is defused. He makes a note of the event that caused it. He doesn't any longer try to block it out of his mind. But he does end up with a sense of controlled, low-level arousal instead of the physical and mental upheaval that it might have caused him in the past.

The key to AMT is the ability to relax when you want to and use the early feeling of anxiety as the trigger for doing so. What it actually teaches is how to control both the feelings and bodily reactions that are generated by a sudden surge in our autonomic nervous system. The unpleasant feelings themselves trigger the relaxation response – which in its turn stops them from escalating.

AMT has produced many 'spin-off' therapies, all slightly different, all with their own particular emphasis. But all of them revolve around using your anxious feelings, as soon as you become aware of them, to trigger the response that stops them from building up.

But what about the thinking that lies behind these feelings of anxiety – the thoughts about the anxiety-provoking event that create the apprehension in the first place? Just like depressive thoughts, there are ways of dealing with those as well. And by working on his anxious feelings whilst changing the thoughts that produce them *at the same time* the would-be life-affirmer has an even better chance of keeping his anxiety within manageable limits.

CHAPTER 13

Thinking Makes It So

—————

THE two basic goals of all human beings are to stay alive and to be happy. They are closely linked. The therapist who finds himself trying to stop his client from committing suicide will work overtime to help him to find a reason to live – to help him to be just happy enough to want to stay around. But he may not succeed. People differ so much in what they think is worth living for, what they personally find meaningful or fulfilling. The therapist's job is to get inside the client's head, to discover what his personal world is made up of, and why it has fallen apart.

Once he knows that, he can explore whether the client is acting in a way that helps to achieve his basic goals (whatever they may be) or whether he is actually sabotaging himself from achieving them.

Some therapists would say that if we are living so as to achieve our goals, then we are acting 'rationally'. If not, then our thoughts, emotions and actions are 'irrational'. They are stopping us from getting what we really want out of life. There is a whole school of psychotherapy that deals with the difference between rational and irrational living, defined this way. It was started in the 1950s by Albert Ellis, now an internationally famous psychotherapist in New York. It is called Rational Emotive Therapy or RET.

Into hedonism

The basic philosophy behind RET is that we are all hedonists – we want to stay alive and be happy. The word 'hedonism' usually has overtones of physical or sexual pleasure, and that's okay as well. If sex is your goal in life, then living rationally means going about it in a way that will maximize the amount of sex you get. But if your goal is to help famine victims, or to save the whales, or to write the history of Albania, it is still all important to live in such a way that you maximize your chances of succeeding.

RET teaches us that the ability to achieve our goals depends to some degree on our circumstances. But when we fail, it is usually us and not our environment that's to blame. To a large extent, people hold themselves back from achieving what they want. They do so by not being able to distinguish between short-term and long-term goals. Going all out for pleasure and satisfaction *now* may well jeopardize our greater pleasure and satisfaction in the future. But more than that, we sabotage ourselves by stubbornly holding on to a set of irrational beliefs that keep us anxious, depressed and angry and make us hate or pity ourselves by turns.

Therapists of the RET school (like others concerned with our cognitions) are fond of quoting Epictetus. Remember he said that 'Men are disturbed not by the things which happen, but by their opinions about those things.' This is the cognitive view in a nutshell. Fewer people seem to know that he went on: 'When we are impeded or disturbed or grieved, let us not blame others, but ourselves, that is, our opinions. It is the act of an ill-instructed man to blame others for his own bad conditions; it is the act of one who has begun to be instructed, to lay the blame on himself; and of one whose instruction is completed, neither to blame another nor himself.'

The ABC of RET

According to RET, the source of most of our unhappiness lies in the opinions that we hold about things. Ellis describes it according to a simple formula of ABC. A is the activity, action or agent that comes just before we start to feel disturbed – a confrontation with a shop assistant who couldn't care less, or the news that you have failed your driving test. C is the consequence of that action – the feeling of anger that wells up inside you or the sudden shocking sense of being completely useless.

But the unseen link between A and C is found at B – the beliefs that you have about what *ought* to happen.

The key to all RET teaching is that the feeling that you experience and the way that you subsequently act is not caused directly by the event itself. It only arises because of the set of beliefs that you hold about the way that the world *should* be or *must* be. When we use these beliefs to decide on how to react to what has just happened, the inevitable result is to feel disturbed. Our beliefs prevent us from achieving our goals and purposes because they are *irrational*. The aim of therapy is to extend this ABC model to the D and E. At D the client learns how to dispute these irrational ideas, how to see them for what they are and finally reject them. And at E he feels the benefit of disputing them effectively. His anxiety and depression fall away, his ability to accept himself is boosted.

Ten irrational beliefs

Irrational beliefs lead to our damning either ourselves or the world. In the first case, if the demands that we make on ourselves aren't met then we imagine that we are bad or worthless. In the second, if the demands that we put on the rest of the world aren't fulfilled then we become equally disturbed. These two reactions are the exact opposite of the self-acceptance and tolerance of frustration that mark out someone who is psychologically healthy – someone who is living in a life-affirming way.

But just what are these irrational beliefs that people hold to so strongly that lead to anxiety and blaming yourself on the one hand and to hostility and blaming the world on the other?

There seem to be at least fifty of them, but they reduce to a group of ten. Six lead to anxiety, panic, self-blame and self-doubt. The other four create anger and a low tolerance of frustration.[1]

Probably the most important irrational belief in the whole of RET is one that says, 'It is absolutely essential for me to be loved or respected by almost everyone I come into contact with.' I remember sitting in a conference on cognitive therapy at which this example was mentioned. The audience already recognized it for the irrational belief that it was. But I turned in my confusion to the person next to me and asked, 'What's wrong with that?' My own acceptance of this belief over so many years had become quite unconscious. It was what motivated me in much of my life. And it is what made me so unhappy when, time and again, it led to feelings of disappointment and rejection.

The second irrational belief has more to do with what you think about yourself. It is that 'I should be thoroughly competent, adequate and achieving in everything that I do if I am to be considered worthwhile.'

Then come two that relate to how we see the world beyond ourselves. They are: 'Human unhappiness is caused by outside factors and we have little or no ability to control our sorrows or distress' and 'My past history exerts an all-important and inescapable influence on my present actions.' Finally among the anxiety-generators comes the notion that 'There is invariably a precise and perfect solution to all human problems and it is catastrophic if I can't find it,' followed by the belief that 'If something is dangerous or terrifying I have to keep dwelling on the possibility of it happening to me or happening again.'

The four beliefs that make us angry about the world are that 'Certain people are wicked and should be punished for their crimes,' followed by the notion that 'I ought to become upset over other people's problems.' Add to that the suggestion that 'It is catastrophic when things are not the way that I very much want them to be' and that 'It is easier to avoid a lot of difficulties and responsibilities than to face them,' and you have a formula guaranteed to produce a low level of tolerance to frustration.

The problem with musturbation

According to RET, it's not just the irrational beliefs themselves (so like the 'dysfunctional assumptions' of cognitive therapists like Aaron Beck) that lead to our unhappiness. It's the strong, stubborn, tenacious way that we hold on to them. Beliefs are expressed not in terms of what I would *like* to happen, or what I would *prefer* not to happen, but rather as what 'ought', 'has got to' or 'must' happen, otherwise everything will be terrible, catastrophic, awful beyond words. Ellis referred to this way of holding beliefs as the 'tyranny of the shoulds'. I once heard him remark that one of the sources of human unhappiness was 'not masturbation, which is good for you, but rather "musturbation" – the belief that things either must always or must never happen – which certainly isn't'.

Most disturbed human emotions arise from these irrational ideas. For example, much anxiety springs from the belief that 'such a thing must not happen and it would be terrible if it did'.

The rational alternative to anxiety is concern, where someone is well aware of some threat that hangs over their well-being. However, they say, 'I don't want this to happen, but there is no reason why it mustn't happen. It if does happen, then I will deal with it.'

Similar distortions relate to depression. RET agrees with many other schools of therapy that depression may follow a loss – either the loss of a loved one or of some personal capability, or of some goal that we once valued but now can't achieve. The irrational response is that 'I simply can't bear this loss; it should never have happened; it means that I am simply no good.' The twin dangers are slipping into thinking that there is nothing we can do now to respond to the loss (we feel helpless) or that we will *never* be able to do anything to improve our situation (we feel hopeless). The rational reaction to a loss is 'I didn't want it to happen, but there is no reason why it shouldn't have done. It's bad, but it's not terrible.'

Or finally, take anger. There are at least three types of action or agent at A that are followed by anger at C, in the ABC of RET.[2] We may get angry if the world (or the other people in it) frustrates us from achieving the goals that we find important. Or someone may go against the personal set of rules for human behaviour that we have produced for ourselves (and, by implication, for other people), for example, that people must stand in an orderly queue and not push to get on the bus. Or thirdly, something may happen that threatens our self-esteem and our anger is part of our attempt to defend ourselves.

In each case the irrational belief at B that leads to the angry outburst is something like 'You absolutely must not act in that way and you are beneath contempt if you do.' You may react that way about someone else (your landlord, the taxi driver) or about some institution (the gas board, the city council) or about yourself.

A more rational person would substitute annoyance for anger. They would still see the frustration or the rule-breaking or the threats to self-esteem, but their response to the person involved would go like this: 'I don't like what you are doing and I'd rather you didn't do it. But there is no reason why you mustn't do it. You are not beneath contempt. You are just a fallible human being who I think is acting badly.'

Being able to accept some-one (especially yourself) as fallible is very important in RET. It teaches you not to try to evaluate yourself as good or bad, worthy or unworthy. That sort of global rating doesn't make any sense. Instead, you are encouraged to rate only your *behaviour* as good or bad. And you try to accept that it isn't always good because you, like everyone else, are fallible.

What keeps us irrational ?

Just why people show what Ellis calls these 'deep-seated ... human tendencies towards fallibility, over-generalization, wishful thinking, gullibility and short-range hedonism' isn't clear. He believes that they are somehow part of our biological nature. Windy Dryden of London University, one of the leading figures in RET in Great Britain, agrees. He points out that virtually everyone shows this tendency to irrational thinking. The 'musts' and 'shoulds' are found in many different cultures. And merely giving people insights into their irrational thinking often fails to change the behaviour that goes with it. Irrationality may be somehow built into our constitution, perhaps even into our heredity.

Needless to say, few other schools of psychotherapy would accept that this particular pattern (or indeed any other) is actually passed on with our DNA. But more important is the issue, not of where the beliefs come from, but of how they get fixed so firmly in people's minds and why they become so difficult to shift.

Partly they are reinforced by the very strong desires that we may have to be outstanding or exceptional in at least some respects that will enable us to be loved and admired. Partly too they result from the very strong feeling that if things are not as we want them, then we can't stand the situation and might as well be dead.

People also get themselves into a vicious circle. Having made themselves anxious about some terrible threat that they see in front of them, they then start to become anxious about their anxiety. After becoming depressed about a recent loss they allow themselves to get depressed about their depression.

Then again, beliefs that we would reject if we expressed them in an obvious and blatant form can take a more subtle and seductive quality in our minds. They may even start to seem quite reasonable. For example, 'Because I want to do everything perfectly I simply must do outstandingly well' becomes 'Because I want to do everything perfectly and *because I am a person with outstanding abilities* then I absolutely must do everything well.' And another blatant belief like 'Because I strongly desire to have people's love and approval then I simply must have it, otherwise I am worthless' becomes transformed into 'Because I want the acceptance of other people and *because I try hard to be nice to them* (or *because I feel deprived in other areas of my life*) then I simply must have their approval.'[3]

What's to be done?

So according to RET it is this seductive, all-pervading human tendency to think irrationally that produces emotional distress (poor mental health) with feelings of anxiety, depression, worth-lessness, rage and self-pity, as well as providing at least part of the basis of many phobias, compulsions, addictions and other self-defeating habits.[4]

How can we get rid of it? The simple answer is that it isn't easy. In one of his more pessimistic moments Albert Ellis has suggested that 'even when helped by the most efficient forms of psychotherapy, contemporary humans still find it virtually impossible to consistently achieve and maintain good mental health'.

The basic principles of the treatment are clear enough. Initially they aim to provide the client with a series of insights. The first is the basic idea that psychological disturbances are primarily caused by the absolutistic, irrational beliefs that we hold about the events in our lives. The next is that we *keep* bringing on our problems by reactivating these beliefs all the time instead of neutralizing them. And finally, clients are shown how people keep on distracting themselves by looking for reasons from their past to explain their present problems, instead of trying to tackle them in the here and now.

But RET specialists are the first to admit that thinking, feeling and behaviour are intimately tied together. Each has a profound influence on the other two. So all three become the focus of atten-tion during treatment. Being able to use a simple talking therapy that successfully transforms the client's beliefs and produces a fundamental change in the way that he acts in the future is what Ellis would call the 'elegant' use of RET. However, in its more common, 'inelegant' form RET uses as many different approaches as any other form of psychotherapy.

Running the film

From the outset the counsellor explains that the client has to change those things in his life that he can change – his thoughts, feelings and actions. Counselling will not get him a job or a better place to live or get his wife back, though his new rationality may help him to do these things for himself.

Will the counselling work? Neither the therapist nor his patient can say at the outset. Though RET seems to produce better results with educated, articulate clients, it has also had beneficial effects for more lower-class, deprived people, at least in helping them to choose between alternatives in their lives, none of which was ideal. Some therapists suggest that the client commit himself to a trial period of say only five or six sessions to see whether he finds it helpful. But much has to be achieved in the first hour. Dryden admits that the most common number of sessions is one. Often clients simply don't come back for more.

The RET counsellor spends much of the initial time discussing the client's beliefs and actively disputing them. 'What reason do you have for saying that you must do your job perfectly?' 'Why do you have to have this woman's love?' 'Who says that you can't go on living if you don't get the promotion?' The aim is to help him distinguish the *must, should* and *have to* from the *want to, wish to* and *would like to*.

He also challenges the idea that things would be awful, beyond human endurance, if something happened, by inviting him fully to think through the situation and explore just how bad the 'worst case' would really be. Those who arrive convinced that they couldn't possibly stand something happening are shown that, although they might not like it, they could stand it perfectly well. They play through the whole sequence in their imagination, running the imagery like a film, and feel as graphically as they can what the worst case would really be like.

But the client's problems occur out in the world, not in the therapist's office. And so homework is a most essential part of the treatment. Often the client takes home a form on which he records the appearance of disturbed feelings or self-defeating behaviours, together with the actual events that preceded them. So he records the C and the A. The form also contains a list of irrational beliefs ('I am bad if I get rejected,' 'People must treat me fairly,' 'My life must have a few major hassles'). He tries to identify the irrational belief at B that came between the events at A and C.

But that's only a start. The form has two other columns. In the first he disputes the irrational belief that he has just identified ('Who says that rejection means that I am thoroughly bad?' 'Why does my life have to be easy?'). In the second he writes down the appropriate rational response that would help to make him feel less distressed ('I don't like to be rejected, and maybe it's because of the way I am behaving, but that doesn't mean that I am thoroughly bad').

At the bottom of this Self-Help Form is a statement that the client needs to read repeatedly and to take on board. It says, 'I will work hard to repeat my effective rational beliefs forcefully to myself on many occasions, so that I can make myself less distressed now and act less self-defeatingly in the future.'

This isn't some form of nebulous 'positive thinking' like 'every day and in every way I am getting better and better'. Instead, it is an action plan, a description of *what he is actually going to do on many occasions* to change his thinking and his behaviour.

Start with the behaviour

But RET also starts at the other end, trying to influence the client's behaviour quite directly as well. Windy Dryden has actually admitted that 'behavioural change is often the best way of encouraging clients to change their irrational beliefs'. Unlike some forms of behavioural change such as desensitization, which take place by slow degrees, those involved in RET are meant to be as dramatic and vivid as possible.

One of the best known is the use of *shame-attacking exercises*. The client is encouraged by the therapist to act in a way that is 'shameful' to him – to perform some action that he believes will draw attention to himself and make people think the worst of him. At the same time he says to himself, 'They may think that I'm an idiot, but I choose to accept myself even though I may be acting stupidly.'

It doesn't matter what it is, as long as he believes that it is 'shameful'. For example, he may wear his clothes back to front, or ask for a bar of chocolate in the butchers. There is at least one distinguished professor of psychology (who shall be nameless) who was greatly flattered at a conference by being asked to dance by not one, but two attractive young women. He might have been less flattered had he known that neither could actually stand him. They were dancing with him as a shame-attacking exercise, part of the RET course that they were involved in.

Another attempt at behavioural change is to have the client directly confront some situation that he fears, like riding in a lift. Clients with a fear of lifts are asked to ride in them twenty times a day until their fear recedes. This is obviously a form of 'flooding', like the flooding exercises that are sometimes used for phobics. It suffers from the same problem, in that not all clients can be persuaded to do it. But those who can confront and experience their discomfort at its highest intensity often report a rapid and dramatic improvement.

A third form of behavioural modification involves punishing yourself for engaging in the behaviour that you want to avoid by giving yourself some stiff penalty, like burning a £10 note every time you do it. The punishment has to be so severe that you would rather change the behaviour than pay the price. Again, not all clients will accept this assignment.

One characteristic of RET counsellors is that they are very forceful in the way that they dispute their client's irrational beliefs. Indeed the therapist may deliberately avoid being warm and empathic, to prevent the client from becoming dependent on him or from changing merely to seek his acceptance and approval. And the therapist himself, if he practises what he preaches, doesn't need his client's approval at all.

Does it work?

So RET, despite its 'cognitive' bias, uses all the devices that other forms of 'cognitive-behavioural' therapy employ – homework assignments, desensitization and conditioning together with the teaching of self-control and life skills. What marks it out from other forms of therapy is its attempt to create a profound philosophical change in the client's thinking. It looks towards flexibility and the acceptance of uncertainty; to a willingness to take risks; to commitment to vital interests and to a tolerance of oneself and other people as fallible human beings who will inevitably make mistakes.

But is RET based on firm foundations; and, more importantly, does it work?

There are questionnaires designed to discover just how many irrational beliefs people actually hold. Several studies have shown that those who endorse a lot of them are more likely to believe that they have little control over the world (to be 'externals'), to be unassertive, to have low self-esteem and to be more prone to depression.

The problem is that these studies (and there are dozens) only show that irrational beliefs and depression are linked. They don't show that one causes the other. Irrational beliefs have been linked to anxiety, psychiatric symptoms and even aggressive, coronary-prone Type-A behaviour. But no one has yet proved that the irrational beliefs come first, or that they don't simply relate to a more general state of emotional distress of which proneness to depression plays a part.

More sceptical specialists even doubt whether cognitive procedures are the treatment of choice in altering people's beliefs. They point to evidence that exposure to direct behavioural methods – changing what they do – actually works better for getting people to change what they think.[5]

We've been here before, when we looked at cognitive theories of depression. Are the thoughts causing the depressed state or are they just a consequence of it? This question is of enormous interest to therapists. Fortunately, for patients who are simply interested in improving their mental health, it doesn't matter at all. Changing irrational behaviour certainly makes people feel better. And changing beliefs is one of the 'levers' that can be pushed to get the behaviour to change. What matters more, it seems, is that the clients should *believe* that this is how things work. If the therapy has meaning, at least for him, then it has a good chance of succeeding.

Since cognitive methods make people feel better many therapists are not really concerned that the original cognitive theory may have holes in it.

Enter the automatic thoughts

You will remember that cognitive therapists like Aaron Beck also believe that certain types of thought come between an event and our reactions to it. For Beck however it is not so much the irrational belief – the stable, enduring idea – that does the damage. He is more concerned with the sequence of fleeting 'automatic thoughts', ideas that flash through our minds so fast that we may not be aware of them but that colour our emotional reactions to whatever is happening.[6]

Automatic thoughts are 'self-statements', bits of transient dialogue that we have with ourselves about the things that are going on around us. They may result from our early experience and from the way that our parents treated us. But most cognitive therapists don't concentrate on what shaped us in childhood. They assume that wherever they come from, our 'dysfunctional assumptions' ('unless I am loved I am worthless; unless I am loved I can't be happy') lie dormant in our minds until some particular event triggers a stream of thoughts that makes us disturbed.

For example, someone with assumptions about the need to be loved may get on with his life quite happily until his lover walks out on him. At that point, and without him even realizing it, a whole set of distorted ideas rush through his mind, distorted you will remember by arbitrary inference ('She's gone because I've failed her'), selective abstraction ('No one cares for me now') and over-generalization ('I'll never find anyone to take her place').

These distorted thoughts can lead to depression, with its multitude of symptoms – sadness, guilt and shame; apathy and inertia; indecision and failing concentration; loss of sleep, appetite and interest in sex. In serious cases there is a slowing down of all activities and a withdrawal even from those things that used to give us pleasure.

Before he can start treating such a depression, the cognitive therapist believes that it is essential to capture these automatic thoughts, to look at them and to show the client just how unrealistic they are. So in the early stages of treatment, he spends a lot of time getting clients to identify the events that preceded their current feelings of, say, sadness or anxiety. Then he asks, 'What went through your mind when this happened?' Often they don't know. So the question becomes 'If you don't have any words for it, do you have a mental image of what was going on?'

Getting more active

Cognitive therapy uses other procedures apart from catching and examining the automatic thoughts to help a client, and particularly one suffering from depression, to get back to normal, to see herself

as a 'winner' instead of a 'loser'; to think of herself as being master-
ful rather than helpless.

A lot of the treatment certainly does involve talking, for example examining just why she feels too tired or weak to do anything, or why she thinks that nothing is going to work. She is
invited to think her way into how she would do things if she
could ('cognitive rehearsal') and to identify the particular problems that might arise.

But much of the treatment crucially involves not just talking
about action, but action itself. For example, the therapist schedules a series of activities for her, starting with the simplest, like
walking round the block (or, in the case of the seriously depressed,
even walking around the room) and gradually building up. Beck
refers to this graded type of task assignment as 'success therapy',
because each success, however minor, is the stepping stone to
the next. It takes time and a good therapist to persuade the really
depressed client even to try. The key is in building in rewards
for succeeding. Sometimes the activity is its own reward. On
other occasions the client is rewarded by the therapist or by those
close to him, or he is encouraged to reward himself by doing
something that he still enjoys. Remember how exercise may be
a form of success therapy as well.

With all this emphasis on behaviour, it is clear that today there
is really no such thing as pure cognitive therapy. Indeed there
never really was. What all of these therapists use is a combined
attack on the way their clients are thinking *together* with an
attempt to change their behaviour. They are really using cognitive–behavioural therapy (or CBT). And the most comprehensive package of CBT put together so far has been developed by
Donald Meichenbaum of the University of Waterloo in Canada.

Multi-model therapy

Donny Meichenbaum is a forceful man. His workshops are so
highly charged that he can leave his audience feeling quite tired.
Meichenbaum acknowledges the wide variety of methods that
therapists use to change their client's behaviour. Like Jerome
Frank, he believes that if the treatment is credible to the patient,
then the actual approach is less important. As he says, 'clients
who see therapists of wholly different persuasions go through

similar psychological processes in achieving behavior change. The final common pathway to behavior change is alteration of the internal dialogue in which our clients engage.'

His own work has been particularly involved with stress and what people can do about it. The major problem for seriously stressed clients is that awful feeling of being overwhelmed and simply not knowing how to proceed. To help them Meichenbaum and his co-workers have devised a procedure called *stress-inoculation training* or SIT.

In medicine, an inoculation allows the body to respond to a *small* amount of a killed or weakened virus or bacterium. The immune defences are mobilized without being overcome. Similarly with SIT. The client is taught *progressively* what to do when exposed to stressful situations. Like Aaron Antonovsky, Suzanne Kobasa and many others, Meichenbaum believes that stress cannot be avoided. But we can learn to respond to it without being overwhelmed.

SIT is a truly 'multi-modal' therapy – it contains many different elements. For example, all clients learn to relax, using the methods that we have already looked at. They learn to use relaxation imagery and breathing exercises as well. The aim is to allow the client to identify the physical cues that tell him that he is getting stressed, and then to use them as a signal to switch on his relaxation programme. In other words (as with AMT) he relaxes on cue.

But stress inoculation also involves the use of cognitive strategies. So clients are taught to catch their automatic thoughts like 'The future is just one string of problems,' or 'Life has no meaning' or 'It's such an effort to do anything,' and to test them against reality. But such cognitive interventions are only one entry point into the client's multi-faceted problem. The therapist's attention might equally well be directed to his emotional reactions or his bodily responses, or to his actual behaviour.

A strong emphasis in SIT is in problem-solving. The stressful situation isn't seen as some overwhelming emotional state that will sweep him away. Instead, the stressor itself or his reaction to it is seen as a problem to be solved. He is taught to identify what he really wants to achieve out of the situation and to look at possible ways of doing so. He then rehearses the various possibilities in his mind. Using imagery he tries to play through the whole sequence (behavioural rehearsal) and to decide which of the various possibilities is the one most likely to succeed.

The next stage is actually to do it. He tries out the solution he decided on, not expecting to be completely successful, but rewarding himself for the success that he does achieve. Finally, he looks at the problem again. He puts it through another loop in the light of what he has learned and comes up with an improved strategy.

But of all these stages it is probably the initial one, identifying the problem, that is the most difficult. This is the one which most requires another person (in this case the therapist) to help you to define it clearly.

Guiding your own dialogue

Much of the early contact between the therapist and the client is spent in actually identifying those situations that the client finds stressful. He will be well aware of the more obvious ones – they are what brought him into therapy. But there may be other sources of stress that he is hardly aware of. So he is asked to monitor his thoughts, feelings and behaviour between sessions. He also makes a careful note when he does get stressed of the events that preceded it and what he told himself about them.

The aim of this self-instructional training is, first, to help him to assess the actual details of the situation and prepare for the stressor. Then he needs to know how to control his negative, self-defeating, stress-inducing thinking pattern. One of the key features of SIT is the way that it teaches the client what to say to himself to help him through a stressful situation. Stress will make him aroused but he has to learn how to acknowledge that arousal for what it is – his body preparing to deal with a threat, not a sign that his whole life is falling apart. Even so, the stress may produce an initially uncomfortable emotional experience and he has to learn how to psych himself up to face it, then how to deal with it when it does break all over him.

Finally, the client needs to be able to reflect on how he did, once it's all over, and to reward himself for having attempted to cope in the first place. Self-statements don't make stressful situations comfortable, but they do allow people to tolerate them. They let you talk yourself out of panicking.

SIT divides the stress experience into four sections – preparing for its arrival, handling it when it does arrive, coping with the feeling of being overwhelmed and finally looking back over how you did and rewarding yourself for doing it.

Four stages of SIT

In the first stage, your focus is on what you have to do – the way you are going to plan and prepare. During this phase you are saying things to yourself like 'What exactly do I have to do? It will be difficult but I can work out a plan and handle it. It's natural for me to feel uptight at times like this: maybe it's just that I'm eager to get on and deal with it.'

The coping self-statements in the second phase are to control the stress reactions and remain focused on the task in hand. Self-talk may include ideas like 'Just take it one step at a time. Relax and remember to breathe. I'm in control as long as I keep my cool.'

The worst problem is a feeling of being totally overwhelmed by the whole affair. So during his training the client learns to prepare himself for the possibility of becoming extremely disturbed. He needs to remain in the situation and to stay focused on the present. To do so he will be telling himself things like 'When the stress arrives, just pause. I should expect it to well up occasionally. I can't eliminate it but I can keep it manageable. Now, what is it that I have to do *right now*? My muscles are getting tight, so it's time for me to take a slow, deep breath.'

Eventually the problem passes, but its passage doesn't go unmarked. In the final phase you try to see what was helpful and what wasn't – what would you have done differently or better? At the same time you recognize the small gains that you have made and praise yourself for them. So the self-talk at that time will go like this: 'That wasn't as bad as I expected. I made more of it than it deserved. Bits of the plan didn't work – what can I learn from that? I generally handled it pretty well. Next time I'll do it even better.'

The whole point about these self-statements is that they are tailored to be used during the stressful period itself. They are each linked to different parts of it. So this self-instruction is very different from the sort of 'positive thinking' approach that says 'Every day and in every way I am getting better and better.' That doesn't tell you *why* you are getting better, what you are getting better *at* or even *how* you are actually doing it. Repeating this monologue may make you feel good to start with. But after a while it loses its power because it doesn't tell you either what you should be doing, or how to go about it.

Flexible coping

The reason why clients are taught so many procedures – relaxation, cognitive restructuring, problem-solving and self-instruction – is that none of them is effective in all situations. So it is important to have a repertoire of coping skills to call on. You then allow yourself a more flexible response to the problem in hand.

But all of them together are useless unless they are actually put into practice. So if the first phase of SIT is analysing the problem and the second is learning the skills to deal with it, then the all-important third stage is putting that knowledge into operation.

You do so first by rehearsing the way that you would deal with a stressful situation in your head. You make it as graphic and detailed as possible and imagine yourself making the appropriate coping responses. Rather than running a film through your mind you might use a real film. Some therapists actually do use films of people dealing with difficult situations. The therapist and client look at them together and subsequently talk about what was helpful and what wasn't.

More graphic still is a 'role play' where the trainer and client act out a particular situation and the client discovers how to deal with it. Most instructive for the client is for him to role-play the part of the counsellor, and to teach the 'new client' (actually the therapist) how to deal with the problem. Being involved in teaching these skills to someone else helps the client to produce the set of strategies that he personally finds most convincing.

Eventually the client leaves the therapist's office with a homework assignment that both have agreed on beforehand. A stressful situation has been discussed, together with the way that he will approach it. Then he goes out and deals with it on his own. When he returns they together examine whether the experience has been successfully handled, and if not, why not. The lessons are then applied to the next assignment.

As time goes by the client starts to handle his life increasingly on his own. He meets the therapist less often and the sessions are slowly tailed off until the only contact is a series of follow-up, booster sessions at say three, six and twelve months.

SIT is a very comprehensive approach to stress-management and, I think, because of its many facets, the best one currently on offer. But it won't prevent your stressful problems. Nothing will, and we would be deluding ourselves if we think that anything might. As Meichenbaum himself puts it: 'Because stress is a normal part of life, clients should recognize that they will continue to experience it even after successfully training. The goal of SIT is not to eliminate stress but to learn to respond adaptively in stressful situations and to be resilient in the face of failure.'

Easing the pain

Stress inoculation training may be of particular benefit to prepare patients to undergo surgical operations. For example, a group of children in hospital were shown films of other children coping with their surgery. As a result, they appeared to do better both before the operation and afterwards. Films in which the actors themselves were learning how to cope were better than those where they knew all the answers. Seeing other people learning what to do seems to be the key to reducing anxiety among those who are watching.

In a similar way, adult patients have been taught how to produce calming self-statements that helped them to concentrate on the positive aspects of their surgery. They rehearsed them before the operation. As a result, their post-surgical distress, their need for sedatives and the length of their hospital stay were all reduced.[7]

Similar procedures have been used with the nursing staff themselves to reduce their rate of job burn-out. Individual counselling concentrated on monitoring the events that lead to stress, then to the development of coping skills like relaxation, changing their thinking by changing their self-talk and learning how to manage their time better. These subjects then went through a series of role plays of situations which are known to be particularly difficult for nurses, with the counsellor playing an uncooperative patient or an unsympathetic superior. At the end of the programme many nurses said that their experience of stress on the wards had been reduced.

Sometimes it is impossible to change the situation that you find yourself in. Victims of rape or major accidents, people suffering from bereavement or from incurable illnesses are not able to turn the clock back. But even here some elements of SIT may be valuable if they help the victims to express and re-experience their sense of shock, anger, depression, helplessness or anxiety.

The idea is not just to live through the experience again. In itself that is not likely to be beneficial. Instead, the idea is to let victims reappraise what happened to them in a more positive light and help them regain their sense of self-efficacy and self-esteem. As Meichenbaum himself says, 'SIT cannot remove the pain or loss, but it does help clients come to terms with the view that bad things can and do happen to people but that one can somehow function in spite of such losses.'

SIT helps people redefine their reactions to such events. Remember how Shelley Taylor's work with cancer patients in Los Angeles showed that such people often have a remarkable capacity to see their problems in a positive light. They may compare themselves to someone less fortunate. The fact that these 'less fortunate' people don't really exist doesn't make any difference. Or they might think about an even worse scenario that could have happened to them but didn't. Some people say that they have found benefits to come out of their difficulties, like being more loving and caring to other people. It is not how badly they are victimized but how they appraise their victimization that has the biggest effect on how well they function.

Of course, in extreme cases such appraisals can be a total denial of reality that doesn't help at all to adapt to the situation. The major problem is to decide when seeing things in a positive light is valuable, and when it may be a distortion that removes the patient's motivation and stops him from coping in effective ways. This is something that the client and therapist have to decide together.

Many professionals see their role here as helping clients to say and really understand the prayer that goes 'God grant me the serenity to accept the things I cannot change, courage to change the things that I can and the wisdom to know the difference.' Some things have to be accepted. But the trainer's job is to stop the client dwelling on past misfortunes, and encourage him to see life as a series of problems to be solved, both now and in the future.

Controlling your anger

One final example of the way that SIT has been used successfully is in the treatment of anger. Anger is linked to coronary heart disease. It also disrupts people's family and social lives. So controlling it is desirable for both our physical and our mental health.

We all know the physical feeling that you experience welling up inside you in response to some provocation. Naturally enough, SIT trainers believe that these feelings don't result from the provoking incident itself but rather from how we appraise it. It is what we say to ourselves about the event ('He can't talk to me like that; who the hell does he think he is? I'm going to cut him down to size') that switches on the angry emotional response.

So SIT for anger begins by getting the client to record the events that made him angry over the course of the past week. He brings these events to the treatment session, where there are often a small group of people, say four or five, all with the same problem being helped by the same trainer. They run a particularly strong provoking incident through their minds (like playing back a video) and examine the thoughts and feelings that were occurring during the encounter. They feel themselves getting upset as a result.

The therapy consists of two parts. First, clients are taught how to relax. Their relaxation is to be used on cue when they start to feel the first angry reactions appear (perhaps quickening of the pulse, tensing of the shoulder muscles or a tightening in the pit of the stomach). At the same time, they learn what to say to themselves to diffuse their angry reactions. Raymond Novaco of the University of California at Irvine, one of the pioneers in the treatment of anger, followed the SIT model used for anxiety.[8] So he divided the whole angry incident up into four phases, teaching clients appropriate self-statements for each.

For example, when preparing for the provocation to appear, the client with an anger problem might tell himself, 'This is going to upset me but I know how to deal with it. It's time to take a few deep breaths and relax. Remember to keep your sense of humour.'

When the confrontation arrives he switches to 'Think what you want to get out of this. You don't have to prove yourself; I'm not going to let him get to me.' But even thinking this way his body may still start to get aroused. To diffuse his arousal he says, 'My muscles are starting to feel tight. Time to relax and slow things down. Time to take a deep breath; take it easy. Don't get pushy.'

Eventually the provocation will pass, leaving him time to reflect. If the encounter has been successful then he might think, 'I handled that one pretty well. It wasn't as bad as I thought.' Alternatively, the situation may not have been resolved. Many are not. So what does he do to stop himself stewing about it? Novaco suggests statements like 'Try to shake it off, don't let it interfere with your job; it's probably not so serious. Don't take it personally.'

Notice here that, just like managing anxiety, the provocation is seen as a task to be done, a problem to be solved, not as a threat calling for an attack and certainly not as a wave that will sweep you along and drive you into irrational action. The hope is that with practice you may be able to short-circuit the emotional outburst that made you a victim in the past.

Raymond Novaco taught police officers to manage their anger, often against extreme provocation. This was provided by professional actors especially hired to play the role, say, of a couple having a heated domestic dispute. When he looked at the results Novaco found that both the relaxation and the self-instruction training were valuable in managing anger. Of the two, self-instruction was the more powerful though the combination was better than either alone.

Interestingly enough, however, some more recent findings suggest that relaxation, even without the self-instruction, is also surprisingly effective in managing anger, better than had been previously thought.[9] This suggests that taking time to improve the purely physical aspect of the training might enhance the combined effect even more.

And it also shows that despite more than a decade of experience, cognitive–behavioural therapy has a lot to learn. We still need to know much more about just what works, with which clients and why.

Learned helplessness

Some experts would go further. They suggest that cognitive therapy, say for treating depression, is still a rather hit-and-miss business. One psychologist who has become famous for this view is Marty Seligman of the University of Pennsylvania.[10] To him, the essence of depression is a sense of helplessness, and the most effective treatments are likely to be those that concentrate on that simple fact.

We have already seen how Seligman's name is associated with studies in which he showed that dogs made to undergo electrical shocks from which there is no escape develop a pattern of behaviour called 'learned helplessness'. They simply cower and seem to lose their motivation to do anything. Even when they could later escape by simply moving from one half of the cage to the other, they don't. They have become conditioned to being helpless by their earlier experience of not being able to do anything to avoid the shock. Although at one time this was thought to be an animal version of human depression, it turned out to be far too simple to explain why people get depressed. This is largely because it takes no account of how people *feel* about what is happening to them.

We also saw how, in his revised model, Seligman and his colleagues suggest that those people who get depressed have three different attributions which they make about the world. They expect bad things to happen to them. They believe that there is nothing they can do to stop them. And they believe that this state of affairs arises because of their own actions rather than outside forces. That's to say, they attribute *internal* reasons for whatever befalls them. And they find the cause of their unhappiness or frustration in factors that are also *stable* ('They will always be there') and *global* ('They will affect everything in my life').

Changing our attributions

Now there is a lot of evidence that people who do see the world in these terms really are more likely to get depressed when they experience something going wrong. And we also saw how a pessimistic attribution affects people's physical health as they reach middle age.

So what is to be done to help people whose attributions make them depressed or hasten their mid-life disease? Seligman suggests four kinds of assistance.

The first is to help them change their environment so that not as many bad things will actually happen to them. Eventually they will cease always to expect them to happen. Help in finding a job or providing a baby minder are obvious examples of this type of practical help.

Second is the need to give them some sense of control over their lives. This involves developing many of the skills that we have looked at already – problem-solving and graded task-assignment, as well as assertiveness-training and help in making decisions.

A third and more controversial suggestion is that such people have to reduce the 'badness' of bad outcomes to make them more tolerable. At the same time it becomes necessary to reduce the 'goodness' of good outcomes, especially those that are not likely to happen, so that we don't make ourselves unhappy craving for them. This Seligman calls 'resignation-training'. It consists of creating a more realistic set of goals so as to avoid disappointment. For example, if you can't be top of the class or have the girl of your choice, resignation-training sets out to show you how to be happy in a lower position or with someone else.

Finally, Seligman suggests using treatments that help to change the clients' attributions directly. For example, they should be taught to have a more *external* view of failure ('It's not your fault you can't get the job, it's the competitive system you're in'). Failure should also be seen as *unstable* ('Times are changing, and your time will come') and *specific* rather than *global* ('There are still lots of other things you can do with your life').

He goes on to claim that most of the techniques so far used in both cognitive therapy and RET are actually tailored (almost without realizing it) to doing just that – to retraining the client's attributions and to increasing his capacity for resignation. For example, self-monitoring to identify negative self-statements and put positive ones in their place is an example of changing attributions. So: 'They didn't fail me because I'm stupid, but just to make me work harder' is changing an internal, global, stable attribution of failure to one that is external, specific and unstable. Telling yourself that you don't have to be perfect reduces the attraction of perfection itself. It helps you to find a more realistic set of aspirations and to see that there are alternative actions which (with a little resignation) you can find just as desirable.

In other words, you learn to devalue the importance of having to be successful or accepted or always perfect. Recall how this is also an important way of boosting your happiness.

But if depression is truly the result of a 'faulty' set of attributions, then are there some more fortunate people who have attributions more in line with reality and who cope better with their lives as a result?

It seems that there are. Rather than suffering from learned helplessness, they seem to enjoy a way of looking at the world that Michael Rosenbaum of Haifa University has called 'learned resourcefulness'.[11]

Learning to be resourceful

Time and again we have seen different psychologists asking why people get emotionally upset or depressed or unhappy. Rosenbaum, like Antonovsky and Kobasa, looks at the problem in a different way. For him the question is how some people, beset by a host of problems, nonetheless succeed in not going under. He points to the fact that when patients do get depressed their automatic depressive thoughts increase and they withdraw from the things that they like to do. But he asks why most individuals, who occasionally suffer from depressive moods, don't descend into a full-blown depression.

The answer, it seems, is that most of us have a basic 'behavioural repertoire' that allows us to control our inner responses and to cope effectively with the things that might otherwise lead us to act in a depressive way. The repertoire is a set of skills that allows us to control our emotions, our pain or our disturbing thoughts. These are the inner sensations which, if we responded to them, would disrupt our behaviour. Learned resourcefulness doesn't make us ignore these internal cues altogether. But it does allow us to override them and get on with whatever we have to do.

As yet, the idea is in its infancy. How it works and where it comes from still needs a great deal of study. But Rosenbaum did find, for example, that people high on his measure of resourcefulness were able to endure a painful stimulus for longer than those whose resourcefulness was low, despite the fact that the two groups reported feeling the same amount of pain. And seasick sailors who were high on resourcefulness were able to perform better on a stormy sea than those who were low.

Rosenbaum sees learned resourcefulness as a coping resource, something that helps us to regulate our feelings about a particular situation and so gives us a better chance of dealing with it. It helps us to 'snap out' of low moods and not become depressed, whatever is going on around us. It is the exact opposite of learned helplessness, where the person is convinced that *nothing* he can do is going to alter the situation. However, resourcefulness and helplessness do have one thing in common. They both result from the person's total set of life experiences from the moment that they were born. In one case he learns how to cope; in the other case he doesn't.

Four-part invention

But how do I know just how resourceful I am?

It won't surprise anyone who has followed me this far to learn that there is a questionnaire to measure its different aspects. For example, an obvious feature of resourceful people is their ability to control their emotions and bodily sensations and get on with the job. This is tapped by asking them to consider a statement like 'When I am feeling depressed I try to think about pleasant events.' The more characteristic this statement is of them (on a scale of 1 to 6) the more resourceful they are likely to be.

Is the person also a problem-solver? If so, then he will endorse a statement like 'When I try to get rid of a bad habit, I first try to find out all the factors that maintain this habit.' Does he go for a quick reward or can he delay his pay-off until a more appropriate time? This aspect is tapped by admissions like 'First of all I prefer to finish a job that I have to do and then start doing the things I really like.'

Finally, and in many ways the most crucial feature, the questionnaire taps the person's sense of *self-efficacy*, the belief that he can actually control his own behaviour without help from outside. We have seen how this idea of self-efficacy, originally proposed by Albert Bandura at Stanford University, is probably the single most important factor in deciding what people are prepared to try, how hard they'll try and how long they'll stick at it. With resourcefulness, this aspect is measured by endorsing statements like 'Often by changing my way of thinking I am able to change my feelings about almost everything.' Someone scoring a 5 or

6 here has a high degree of self-efficacy which fuels his resourceful-ness.

When the answers to these questionnaire items were compared with other measures of psychological health it was found (not surprisingly) that people who report using a lot of these resource-ful measures are more likely to have an *internal* locus of control. I say 'not surprisingly' because both factors are measuring the extent to which making things happen is due to our *own* efforts, rather than to chance, or to forces acting outside ourselves.

Interestingly as well, people who use more self-control methods are less likely to hold irrational beliefs about needing to be approved of by others, having to do things perfectly or blaming themselves when things go wrong.

But if resourcefulness is learned by some people from birth, can it be taught to other people whose life circumstances have prevented them from ever acquiring it? It seems that it can. Rosenbaum believes that methods like stress inoculation may pro-vide the basis for understanding what learned resourcefulness consists of. And from there it is a short step to suggesting that with methods like relaxation, problem-solving and the use of the appropriate self-statements, it should be possible to increase the resourcefulness of those people who never learned it as they grew up.

Back to hardiness

All of this has a familiar ring to it. It can't have escaped you that resourcefulness is like coherence or that it has elements of optimism or stamina. All of these concepts point in the same direc-tion – towards the greater affirmation of life.

But we also need to look at one more training programme that is being used to help people get themselves into gear and cope actively with the problems that beset them. This is the training schedule devised to increase three human potentials at once – to augment the sense of control, commitment and challenge that we feel in our lives. In short, it is the programme devised to increase personality hardiness.

Remember that the purpose of hardiness-training, as taught, for example, by Salvatore Maddi to groups of executives at the Bell Telephone Company, is to cope with stressful circumstances by transforming them into something less stressful. The rationale is to help you continue to function at your job despite the pressures that surround you. It embodies the splendidly American ethic that corporate profitability shouldn't be impaired.

As Maddi puts it,[12]

Through the hardiness approach, the person need not shrink from the pressures, disruptions, and changes marking any active life in our complex, urbanized, industrialized world. His personal and company goals can be pursued vigorously through hardiness, so this approach is as much relevant to career development as it is to stress management. In short, hardiness training is preventive through building resiliency and remedial through nullifying stresses.

The training is meant to encourage transformational coping through guided exercises. These exercises are off the main-line of cognitive–behavioural modification as we have considered it up to now. Indeed Sal Maddi seems to pride himself on the fact that 'the resemblance between hardiness training and cognitive–behavioral techniques is quite small and unimportant'.

The course that he describes consists of twelve one-hour sessions occurring once a week, with six or eight trainees meeting with a trainer (originally Maddi himself). We have already noted how he insists that the trainer must be highly skilled, specially qualified by the Hardiness Institute, and how in his view it is simply not possible to learn the process from a book.

Reconstructing the situation

The first technique is called *situational reconstruction*.[13] It works by stretching the imagination to put the stressful circumstance into a broader perspective so as to establish just where the problem actually lies.

It begins by selecting out a recent event that may have been particularly stressful – so bad that some people might have developed an almost obsessional preoccupation with it.

The first step is to consider three ways in which the situation could have been worse. This is sometimes difficult if it already seems so terrible. Then you imagine three ways in which it could have been better. Next you look at what would have had to be different for the worst and best versions to have actually occurred. Then you concentrate specifically on what you might have done (or could still do if the problem is currently going on) to make the better version more likely to happen. Having decided what action would improve the situation (who to talk to, what additional information is needed, what specific action is called for on your part) the bottom line is to *do it*, if you still have the chance. If not, you store up the experience for the next time a similar event happens.

The aim of situational reconstruction is to generate the type of ideas about change that result from the 'vigorous expression of imagination'. It is said to stimulate a sense both of control and of challenge, and to form the basis for living through future events. Most importantly, it creates the 'fine tuning' needed for decisions to be made in the future.

But sometimes a person may get 'stuck' during situational reconstruction. He isn't able to transform the stressful circumstances, probably because of the strong emotions that surround the event. These have to be pushed aside, at least for the time being. The way to do that is through a technique known as *focusing* that was devised by Eugene Gendlin of the University of Chicago, where Maddi and Kobasa both once worked.

Gendlin has written a book about focusing.[14] He claims that it 'will enable you to find and *change* where your life is stuck, cramped, hemmed in, slowed down. To live from a deeper place than just your thoughts and feelings.' However, it is more than just simply 'getting in touch with your feelings' and he urges anyone embarking on it to put aside whatever they might already know about psychotherapy.

Focusing is based on the belief that we know about things with both our mind and our body. Normally we choose only to use the intellect in trying to understand our problems. But Gendlin suggests that we should use our total resources, body as well as mind, to get at what's bothering us. In focusing we aim to achieve a 'felt sense', a visceral feeling, an immediate body perception of what is wrong. Only then do we bring it up to the mental level to be checked out.

In its short form, focusing goes something like this. It starts with a process called 'clearing a space'. We sit comfortably with our eyes closed and ask ourselves, as though the question were coming from some friend, how we are and what is coming between ourselves and feeling fine right now. There is no attempt to answer the question intellectually. The trick is to let your body do the answering.

Let's say that one particular problem becomes apparent, perhaps the fact that we simply don't have time to do all the things we have to get through. What we initially experience is a bodily feeling of being rushed. Then comes another sense, perhaps a feeling of being undervalued, isolated or vulnerable. As each one of these feelings emerge we don't examine it in any detail. Instead, we just acknowledge it and put it on one side, asking ourselves whether there is anything else coming between us and feeling fine.

In the next phase we pick one of the problems that has come to the surface and decide to focus on that. Again, we don't intellectualize. We just try to discover the feeling in our body when we recall the particular difficulty. We try to get at the 'murky discomfort or the unclear body-sense of it'.

We allow this bodily feeling to develop, and as we experience its quality we ask our conscious mind what is the single word, phrase or image that describes it best. What single word will encapsulate the feeling – perhaps 'rushed', or 'stretched', or 'alone', or even 'terrified'?

We then compare the word with the bodily sense. Is it the right word to describe how we feel? If not, what is a better word? We allow ourselves to resonate back and forth between the word or image on the one hand and the 'felt sense' on the other, changing the word and refining it until it seems the right one to describe our bodily feeling.

When we do feel that we have the appropriate match between the word and the feeling we let ourselves experience both of them together for a while. Then we ask our bodies, 'What is it, about this whole problem, that makes me feel so impatient or alone or afraid?'

If things go well, the deep-seated nature of the difficulty, which is perhaps not available to our conscious minds, ought to emerge at the bodily level. It may also help to ask the reverse question, 'What would it feel like if it was all okay?' Again the trick is to let the body provide the answer, to inform the mind, to bring the nature of the problem to our consciousness.

We complete the focusing process by welcoming the insights that came to us but realizing that they represent only one step in appreciating the problem, and probably not the last. However, now that we know more about our particular difficulty we can leave it and come back to it later. The only question is whether this is a good place to stop focusing, or whether you want to go through the same process again with a different problem.

There are whole techniques to use if the focusing itself gets stuck or if it seems to be failing. Using Gendlin's book it is certainly not difficult to try focusing for yourself. However, I can vouch for the fact that going to workshops where it is taught by a competent trainer provides an added dimension, producing a 'shared experience' that can give you a great deal of satisfaction and even joy.

When it does work, focusing is said to increase both our imagination and our judgement, and so to build up a sense of challenge. It is also believed to increase our sense of control. One example that is given by Maddi and Kobasa is being able to transform the general feeling that 'They never give you enough time to do anything at this place' – a phrase that everyone uses – into the more private realization that 'I haven't been able to work because I am afraid of failing.' Achieving this more personal insight may then increase your sense of commitment ('Maybe I can get on with working now that I realize how it's my fear that has been holding me back').

Compensation and paradox

But focusing may not give any new insights into the problem. And this may mean that we are up against a situation that simply can't be changed. So it has to be accepted, but accepted as *serenely* as possible ('God grant me the serenity . . .'), so as not to jeopardize our sense of control, commitment or challenge. The procedure recommended to do so is called *compensatory self-improvement*. It involves accepting that you may not be able to exert much influence over particular areas of your life, but realizing at the same time that there are other areas where you can. Trainees are encouraged to develop their hardiness in these other directions, and to explore the satisfaction to be gained from improving some other aspect of their life.

For example, in their book, Maddi and Kobasa describe a woman who had very low self-esteem because her husband was having an affair with somebody else. There was nothing she could do to prevent it from happening. She had to accept that she had lost him. But one of the things she had always dreamed about doing but had been too scared to try was learning to ski. So her counsellor encouraged her in this direction, though actually getting her started was a major production for both of them.

Eventually she became quite proficient. As a result of her changed self-image she also found enough energy to do other things that she had put off because of feeling so worthless. Her depression receded and she was able to develop a much more positive view of her problem with her husband. Her attempt at self-improvement had spilled over into other areas of her life. At last she started to feel in control and able to direct her own future.

There is one other technique that hardiness trainers include to increase the control people have over their lives. As we have seen, what often holds us back from achieving what we want to are the symptoms of anxiety or depression, like shaking and sweating or being unable to sleep. One way of getting a grip on such difficulties is a SIT approach aimed at diffusing the anxiety or recognizing the automatic thoughts at the basis of the depression. But the technique that hardiness trainers recommend is the complete opposite. Instead of trying to control their anxiety, clients try to exaggerate it, to become as anxious and fearful as they possibly can, to lose control completely. The procedure is called *paradoxical intention*, because it seemingly aims to produce the very opposite of what you actually want to achieve.

The paradox is that sometimes the very act of trying to accentuate and exaggerate the things you are afraid of simply makes them disappear. Hardiness trainers believe that trying to precipitate the symptoms actually re-establishes the client's control over them. This in turn helps to rebuild his self-control and self-confidence.

They cite the case of a young doctor who would always sweat profusely, which was a major embarrassment during ward rounds with a senior physician. The treatment was not to try to bring his sweating under control by 'conventional' means. Rather it was to try to sweat as much as he possibly could, to show everyone just how apprehensive he really was. But when he did try to do so, he found that it simply didn't work. As a result of deliberately trying to sweat he discovered that he couldn't sweat at all.

Paradoxical intention is obviously similar to flooding – throwing the client in at the deep end to experience what he fears in its worst possible form.[15] Perhaps its success is due to the fact that it combines both the 'deconditioning' effects of exposure with an inevitable change in our beliefs about the thing that we fear the most. We come to the sudden realization that the worst fears we could imagine are tolerable after all.

Does hardiness training work?

So hardiness training consists of situational reconstruction, focusing, compensatory self-improvement and paradoxical intention. But let's repeat the question that we have heard so often in this book. Does it work? In particular, do people get hardier through learning it and, more importantly, does their mental or physical health improve as a result?

To the first question the answer is certainly yes. Scores on the hardiness measure definitely go up after training. For the second, we have to reserve our judgement for now, because so far there have been only a limited number of small-scale studies on the effects of hardiness training.

For example, Maddi describes the results of treating a group of seventeen managers at Bell Telephone and comparing them with a second group who were put on the waiting list for training. They then took part in the course the following year.

The results showed that job satisfaction went up as a result of training in both groups, with falls in their total scores on a measure of 'mental stress' – a mixture of anxiety, depression, obsession and so on. Their hardiness scores after training were higher than before, and higher than the control group on the waiting list. Interestingly enough, blood pressure also fell significantly over the training period by values of about 5–10 mmHg. These are respectable falls, though not as great as Chandra Patel achieved with relaxation. But the gains seemed to persist, and to be maintained six months later.

There was no shortage of endorsements from participants about the value of the course. They said things like 'Your hardiness training has made an almost incredible difference in my life' or 'A stress management course that really works – glory be!' No less than 93 per cent of them said that they had 'definitely improved' in managing their stresses and they felt that the improvements would last.

So it all looks very encouraging.

But testimonials are not enough. It needs a lot more throughput of a lot more trainees before we start to celebrate about improvements in mental health. And with the exception of blood pressure, there are no measures of physical health at all.

Suzanne Kobasa once told me that she would greatly welcome someone else making physiological measurements that might make the mechanisms underlying hardiness training more clear. There are currently plans to look at the effects of such training on immunity[16] and even on survival among sufferers from AIDS. But only time will tell how successful they are.

What is the best buy?

We have covered a lot of ground in the last two chapters, from relaxation and anxiety management through cognitive therapy, RET, SIT and now training for hardiness.

Which of these techniques is of most value for increasing our vigour and vitality, for the affirmation of our lives? The answer to that question will reflect the bias of whoever is answering it. All practitioners inevitably have some sort of vested interest that will colour their replies.

And obviously there is no single answer. We need a whole repertoire of approaches, both physical and mental. And we need to mix and match them as the occasion demands, to give us a flexible response to match each problem as we face it. But for my money, someone who has learned how to relax; who has defused the most destructive of his irrational beliefs; who has worked on his problem-solving; and who has the flexibility to restructure situations and to feel his way through them when he gets stuck, is well on the way to saying yes to life.

CHAPTER 14

Learning to Say Yes: A Sort of Conclusion

Those of you who have stuck with me to the end may feel that you've been bombarded along the way by a whole battery of facts – names and dates, numbers and analyses. It's something I warned you about in Chapter One. The reason I did it is not just because I'm a 'data-driven' person myself (though people tell me that I am). It's because I personally don't believe the 'experts' and the conclusions that they try to sell to me until I've seen the facts that they're based on (and sometimes not even then). I wanted to give you the same chance, to decide for yourself whether the things I say seem to be worth believing or not. So we've been through lots of lab experiments, questionnaires and surveys.

And if you can take it, I'm going to end with just one more. It was only published when this book was underway. So it didn't figure in any of my own thinking about health and disease. But when I discovered it later, I found that it gave a boost to some of the ideas that we have been developing here about the affirmation of life.

Feeling well – take two

By British standards the *Health and Lifestyle Survey*[1] is an enormous undertaking, more like the data collections from samples of the whole nation that we are used to seeing from the United

States. It is the result of interviewing some 9,000 adults from all over Britain and asking them about their health and well-being. It contains a wealth of information on many of the topics that we have already described, and not only the obvious ones that you might expect, like eating habits and smoking. It also looks at social support, at extraversion and neuroticism, and at people's perceptions of their locus of control in relation to their health. Specialists will be dissecting the data for years to come.

In a sense, the *Health and Lifestyle Survey* is an extension of the Alameda follow-up and of another American study carried out in the 1970s in which several thousand men and women in the USA were asked whether they felt tired and if so how often.[2] In addition, they were asked if they had any physical health complaints like anaemia or rheumatic problems, and the study also enquired about their mental health status.

It came as no surprise to find that people with problems like anaemia were more often tired than those without. However, the big surprise was to discover that the most powerful predictors of exhaustion were not physical at all. Instead, they were psychological. People who said that they were depressed or anxious were *seven times* more likely to feel tired than those with no emotional problems.

I only have space to deal with two results from the British *Survey*. They extend these American findings and they deal very much with the idea of saying yes to life.

Recall for a moment how in our own small survey we found that most people we asked said that vigour was one of the basic characteristics of life-affirmers. They also placed great importance on having an optimistic outlook. Based on these results, we suggested that 'On the physical side, the life-affirmer can be recognized by his energy, vigour and vitality. And on the other side of life-affirmation is mental health.' In other words, we said that saying yes to life is doing well and feeling well.

The *Health and Lifestyle Survey* asked a slightly different question, one that focuses on the nature of health itself. Instead of thinking about life-enhancement, the researchers invited their respondents to think about someone they knew who was healthy, and then to say what was healthy about them. In other words, whilst we asked how you recognize a life-affirmer, the *Survey* asked how you recognize someone who is healthy.

Nearly half of the young men said that a healthy person is one who is 'fit, strong, energetic and physically active'. Even

older men and women also regarded this as an important characteristic. And all of them thought that physical fitness was a more
important indicator of health than being 'psychologically fit
(relaxed, dynamic, contented, able to cope)'.

But when they were asked what it meant to be healthy *themselves*, they gave quite a different story (Box 15). More than half
of them (both sexes and all age groups) said that psychological
fitness was a major part of their *own* health. Being relaxed and
able to cope got at least twice as many mentions as being physically fit when people thought about themselves, rather than
someone else. And this was true for both men and women, young
and old.

So this huge survey tells us something very significant about
doing well and feeling well. Both are important features of any
healthy person. But when we think about *ourselves* and our *own*
health we place greater importance on being contented and able
to cope than we do on being energetic and physically active. Deep
inside ourselves, we believe that feeling well is more important
even than doing well. When it comes to affirming our own lives,
it's our mental health that we value most. It's not how much
we can do, but how we feel about it that decides if we're going
to be happy or not.

Where's your energy right now?

Throughout the book we have seen how these two features –
health as the capacity to function, and health as the feeling that
goes with it – are closely intertwined. That's why trying to
measure them separately (so as to look at the way they interact)
is difficult to do.

Even so, in Oxford we are currently trying to do just that.
After years of studying the way that distress leads to dysfunction
and then to disease, my current interest is in what makes people
feel vigorous and energetic. But for all the reasons that we have
been through so far, my guess is that the way that all of us perceive
our vigour depends on the way that we think about everything
else in our lives.

So we are looking at people's perceptions of their energy, both
mental and physical. We are measuring how it varies during the
day and over the course of a week. We will then relate these

	Age					
	Men (%)			Women (%)		
	18–39	40–59	60+	18–39	40–59	60+
Healthy features in someone else						
Physically fit (strong, energetic, physically active	46	28	13	30	21	11
Psychologically fit (relaxed, dynamic, controlled, able to cope)	9	9	6	11	8	5
Healthy features in yourself						
Physically fit (strong, energetic, physically active)	25	18	12	36	28	24
Psychologically fit (relaxed, dynamic, controlled, able to cope)	55	60	54	58	62	54

Box 15.   *People think of health as being both physically and psychologically fit. But the balance between them depends on just who we are thinking about. When people are describing someone else, physical activity overshadows mental health. But when we think about our own health it is psychological fitness that counts. Well over 50 per cent of people in the* Health and Lifestyle Survey *stressed the importance of being psychologically fit, more than twice as many as those who linked their health with physical vigour.*

energy measurements to the way that the same people's affect (both positive and negative) shifts over the same time-scale. Eventually we should know more how our mental and physical energy are related to each other, and how both are linked to the balance between our positive and negative emotions (remember Bradburn's Affect Balance Scale in Chapter Five?).

Using Fordyce's Happiness Measures that I described in Chapter Seven we will see how these swings, both in mood and in energy, relate to how happy people feel. And of course we will link all of these changes to their underlying personality, knowing as we do how in general extraversion relates to high levels of energy and vigour, and neuroticism to exhaustion and fatigue. We want to look more closely at how the personality pattern that is so characteristic of each one of us actually influences the way that our energy shifts on a day-to-day basis.

No lack of malaise

The *Health and Lifestyle Survey* gives us another clue to what we may find. It doesn't have much to say about energy, but it did produce some striking findings about fatigue.

Respondents were asked another question about health, this time about mental health, and particularly their own. The *Survey* team wasn't interested in looking for complete mental breakdowns in this group of 'ordinary' people. Fortunately, major mental illness isn't common in people outside hospital. Instead they wanted to examine the low-grade psychological 'malaise' that every one of us suffers from to some extent. So they asked their respondents to think about the last month, and to try to remember whether they had slept well, whether they felt constantly tired, whether they found it difficult to concentrate and if they had worried a lot.

And even allowing for lapses of memory, their results are remarkable (Box 16).

About one man in every five confessed to having some difficulty in sleeping and the same number said that during the last month they had felt constantly tired. For women the figures were even higher. At least a quarter had a sleeping problem and no less than one woman in three said that she had been tired. These are the people who go to their doctors feeling 'tired all the time'. And it is no wonder that GPs see so many tired patients if there are so many of them walking round. This *Survey* and others, like the American study we mentioned earlier, show that fatigue is amazingly common, even among 'normal' people – that's to say you and me.

It's when we're chronically tired that our mood starts to fall – the negative affect starts to creep in. People with long-term fatigue get depressed. I think that this is one of the clearest of all mind–body links, this tendency to feel badly because we're doing badly.

In some cases, the fatigue may have a real, organic basis. There are some people whose exhaustion is due to the after-effects of a viral illness. Indeed, lab tests show that they still carry the virus around in their muscles. The slightest exertion washes them

Symptoms reported during the last month	Age				
	18–24	25–34	35–44	45–54	55–64
Men					
Difficulty sleeping	19	20	18	20	22
Always feeling tired	22	19	19	17	19
Difficulty concentrating	13	10	9	10	10
Worrying over every little thing	14	12	12	14	16
Women					
Difficulty sleeping	23	24	21	38	39
Always feeling tired	34	33	32	29	25
Difficulty concentrating	14	11	14	18	17
Worrying over every little thing	26	24	23	33	30

Box. 16.   *Psychological malaise is remarkably common among ordinary people. The British Health and Lifestyle Survey showed that one man in five had difficulty sleeping and felt consistently tired last month. An even higher proportion of women, up to one in every three, experienced these problems. At least one person in ten also found it hard to concentrate. This survey confirms another well-known fact – that women worry more than men do. Even so, men aren't so tough. Apparently one man in every seven also worries about every little thing.*

out. But for every true case of *post-viral syndrome*, there are dozens of others who tire easily simply because life constantly gets on top of them. They are people with what is called *chronic fatigue syndrome*.[3] It may not be due to a virus but they may be just as depressed about it.

That's why there has been so much debate about ME and whether it is a physical disease at all. People with true 'organic' fatigue may be very difficult to distinguish from those suffering from an emotional disorder. Depression is so common among tired people that it doesn't give any clue to the cause.

But, of course, whatever creates the fatigue and whatever produces the depression, our personality can always make it worse.

The lens of personality

Time and again we have looked at people with the type of personality that amplifies any symptoms that they may be suffering from. Someone scoring high on neuroticism or negative affectivity will genuinely feel his fatigue more severely than someone who is more emotionally stable. His high level of N acts like a lens to magnify his symptoms. And the way he thinks makes matters worse. As his mood falls, he selectively remembers things that put him down even further. So when they feel tired, from any one of a dozen genuine physical causes, from over-exertion to simply being hungry, people like this consistently come up with a pessimistic attribution like 'I'm always going to feel like this; there's nothing I can do about it.' No wonder their depression is maintained.

Let me say again, for the last time, that teaching people to say yes to life means changing this self-defeating personality pattern. It means getting them to change the way that they think and the way that they behave. Because, in the final analysis, that's all personality is – a habitual way of thinking and behaving. Changing the way they feel may seem more difficult. But actually that's the easy part. The feelings fall into line, the mood lifts, the positive bias returns once the behaviour and the thinking have been dealt with.

We have seen some of the ways that therapists try to produce a shift in the way people behave, from activity-scheduling to shame-attacking exercises. Clinical psychologists now know a great deal about behavioural change. Changing the way we think is the province of cognitive therapy and RET. And they have also made great strides.

Treating the cancer-prone

So far programmes of cognitive–behavioural change have been reserved for people who are ill. They were originally created to treat people with psychological difficulties. And more recently they have started to find application for people who are physically ill as well.

For example, Stirling Moorey and Steven Greer are currently working on a programme of what they call Adjuvant Psychological Therapy, to help patients overcome the distress that goes with being a cancer victim, and to try to help them develop a fighting spirit.[4] It aims to help them ventilate their feelings, particularly the anger which many cancer patients have difficulty in expressing. On the behavioural side it helps them to find things that they can still do and that give them some sense of pleasure and mastery. And it works hard at teaching them to discover and check their self-defeating automatic thoughts about being helpless and handicapped.

So this is a programme (still in its early stages) that tries to instil optimism about the future 'within the framework of the reality of the disease'. The preliminary results look hopeful. With some patients, fighting spirit does seem to improve and their sense of helplessness is reduced by a sense of establishing control in areas of their lives other than their cancer.

Moorey and Greer are the first to admit that it is too early to say whether this sort of treatment will lengthen the patient's life. In any event, that's not their primary aim.

Other investigators have been less modest in their claims. Ronald Grossarth-Maticek and his colleagues in Germany took a group of 100 cancer-prone individuals (prone, he claimed, because of their lack of an independent, autonomous attitude to life). He divided them into two groups. Half received a particular package of cognitive–behavioural therapy. The other half didn't. After thirteen years of follow-up, sixteen of this control group had died from cancer, and fifteen from other causes. In the therapy group, however, *none* had died of cancer and only five had died otherwise.

What is this wonderful therapy that so dramatically reduces the risk of cancer deaths (indeed, apparently of all deaths)? Unfortunately, the details don't seem to have been published, beyond saying that 'socially acceptable expressions of emotion were encouraged and the person was taught coping behaviours appropriate to his particular experience of stress–strain. Therapy was individual, and attempted to teach coping behaviours appropriate to the individual's particular situation.'[5]

It's not unfair to say that most specialists concerned with cancer treatment are extremely sceptical about these results, if only because they seem to be far too good, with sixteen cancer deaths without treatment and none at all in the treated group. As I suggested to one of the research team, 'sixteen–nil is a difficult score to believe in, even after extra time.' Until these findings can be repeated, we will have to reserve our judgement.

But however good they prove to be, notice how both of these treatment packages emphasize the importance of coping, and especially of teaching individual people to cope with their individual circumstances. This has been a major theme in all the treatment approaches that we have seen so far.

So positive health is real

It may have struck you as odd when I said some way back that so far all these types of cognitive–behavioural treatment have only been used on people who are ill, either psychologically or physically. Who else, you might ask, would need them?

The answer is simple. People who are well but want to get even better. In short, people who want to become more life-affirming.

In this book we have seen many facets of life-affirmation. We have looked at stamina and hardiness, coherence and learned resourcefulness, optimistic attributions and an internal locus of control.

Practising them produces a person who believes that there is some meaning in her life. She tries to maintain her optimistic emotional bias, to face reality head on, and to make a conscious effort not to be overwhelmed by it. At a physical level she takes active steps to look after her body as well.

Now how would it be if some of the centres that currently offer advice on physical health started to provide a different kind of individual service for their clients, teaching them how to get rid of the worst of their irrational thoughts (the 'musts' and 'shoulds'); showing them how to generate more optimistic appraisals of their problems; and above all giving them a course in coping, both with the situations that they find themselves in and with their emotional reactions to them? What would you call a place like that? I think that for the first time such a clinic could truly call itself a *Positive Health Centre* – the buzz-word that we were chasing in Chapter Two.

And although I ask you 'How would it be?' I do believe that it is actually going to happen. Already dozens of stress-management courses teach relaxation and problem-solving. But they simply don't go far enough. They are only concerned with damage limitation, with reducing the wear and tear. They don't make much of an effort to bring about the fundamental personality change that will stop such situations from occurring in the future, or allow us to deal with them if they do. Still less do they restructure our attitudes to help us to see our world in a more life-affirming way.

Or maybe it won't happen this way. Perhaps the push to positive health won't revolve around clinics or health centres at all. Perhaps it will be something that people do for themselves. Led by the *innovators*, the *health confidents*, the *inner-directed groups*, perhaps we will increasingly see those people who already look after their bodies developing more of an interest in their mental health. Perhaps they will seek out a therapist when they need one, to start working through the musturbation that is keeping them anxious or the low self-esteem that maintains their sense of malaise. But having once had the help to get started, they will go on to practise what they have learned on their own – the ability to relax on cue, to change their self-defeating monologue, to focus on what's really bothering them.

Strive to be happy

Why should I be so hopelessly optimistic that people will start to develop this push towards life-affirmation?

There are two reasons.

The first is that they are already doing it. We saw in Chapter Two how the health movement has taken off because it is perhaps the one area where people think that they can get some control over their lives. The emphasis is still very much on physical health. The need to improve our mental health (for those of us who think of ourselves as 'normal') still needs to be fully realized.

But the more important reason why people will move towards affirming their lives is staring us in the face. It is only by making a conscious effort to develop at least some of the life-affirming characteristics that our survey respondents told us about that we have any chance of ever being happy. It is only by developing an optimistic bias, by breaking our tasks down into a series of manageable sub-goals, by deciding what we can realistically achieve then going after it, by spending time on those problems that keep us in the flow, and by allowing ourselves a moment of satisfaction when we do something well, that we can hope to achieve a sense of subjective well-being – perhaps the only thing that we all agree is worth striving for.

Doing well depends on how we treat our bodies. We have to work at that. Feeling well also needs an active effort, the effort to think and behave in ways that really do serve our interests instead of sabotaging ourselves at every turn.

And I hope by now you are convinced that if we're doing well and if we're also feeling well about how we're doing it, then our chances of staying well are about as good as we can make them.

References

Chapter 1: Crisis and Opportunity: A Sort of Preface

1. Mind–Body-Health Digest, *Advances* (Journal of the Institute for the Advancement of Health) (1987) 4:1–5.
2. H. Oldfield and R. Coghill, *The Dark Side of the Brain*, Shaftesbury, Dorset: Element Books, 1988; R. O. Becker and G. Selden, *The Body Electric: Electromagnetism and the Foundation of Life*, New York: Morrow, 1985.
3. C. Wood, 'The Body Electric in Britain', *Advances* (Journal of the Institute for the Advancement of Health, (1986) 3: 56–61.
4. British Medical Association, *Report of the Board of Science Working Party on Alternative Therapy*, London: BMA, 1986.

Chapter 2: The Well-Oiled Machine

1. P. F. Drucker, 'How to Manage Your Energy', interview with T. George Harris, *American Health* (1987) March: 115–18
2. T. G. Harris, 'The New Individualism', *Fitness in Business* (1987) February: 141–5.
3. Gallup Survey, 'Taking Charge', *American Health* (1987) March: 53–7.
4. C. Greer, 'Notes Towards an Empowering Perspective', *Journal of Traditional Acupuncture* (1985) p.33.
5. W. K. MacNulty, 'UK Social Change Through a Wide-Angle Lens', *Futures* (1985) August: 331–47.
6. F. Barron, quoted by J. Horder (unpublished).
7. C. Herzlich, *Health and Illness: A Social Psychological Analysis*, London: Academic Press, 1973.

Chapter 3: People Who Say Yes to Life

1. A. H. Maslow, 'Towards a Psychology of Health', in *Towards the Psychology of Being*, 2nd edn, New York: Van Nostrand, 1968, 3–8.

2. C. Wood and A. Keen, 'Say Yes to Life: A Pilot Study', *Journal of the Royal Society of Medicine* (1988) 81: 152–4.
3. S. C. O. Kobasa and M. C. Puccetti, 'Personality and Social Resources in Stress Resistance', *Journal of Personality and Social Psychology* (1983) 45: 839–50.
4. P. L. Berkman and S. L. Syme, 'Social Network, Host Resistance and Mortality: A Nine-Year Follow-Up Study in Alameda County', *American Journal of Epidemiology* (1979) 109: 186–204.
5. N. N. Weissman, B. A. Prusoff and G. C. Klerman, 'Personality in the Prediction of Long-Term Outcome of Depression', *American Journal of Psychiatry* (1978) 135: 797–800.
6. P. T. Costa and R. R. McCrae, 'Somatic Complaints in Males as a Function of Age and Neuroticism: A Longitudinal Analysis', *Journal of Behavioral Medicine* (1980) 3: 245–57.
7. C. Bass, 'Type A Behaviour in Patients with Chest Pain: Test–Retest Reliability and Psychometric Correlates of Bortner Scale', *Journal of Psychosomatic Research* (1984) 28: 289–300.
8. D. J. Levinson *et al.*, C. N. Darrow, B. Klein, *The Seasons of a Man's Life*, New York: Alfred A. Knopf, 1978.
9. G. E. Vaillant, 'Natural History of Male Psychologic Health: Effects of Mental Health on Physical Health', *New England Journal of Medicine* (1979) 301: 1249–54.
10. G. E. Vaillant and P. Schnurr, 'What is a Case?', *Archives of General Psychiatry* (1980) 45: 313–19.
11. C. T. Veit and J. E. Ware Jr, 'The Structure of Psychological Distress and Well-Being in General Populations', *Journal of Consulting and Clinical Psychology* (1983) 51: 730–42.
12. P. B. Warr, 'The Concept of Mental Health', in *Work, Unemployment and Mental Health*, Oxford: Clarendon Press, 1987, ch. 2.
13. A. Ellis, 'The Goals of Psychotherapy', in *Humanistic Psychotherapy: A Rational–Emotive Approach*, New York: McGraw-Hill, 1973.

Chapter 4: A Question of Personality

1. D. Watson and L. A. Clark, 'Negative Affectivity: The Disposition to Experience Aversive Emotional States', *Psychological Bulletin* (1984) 96: 465–90.
2. H. J. Eysenck and S. B. G. Eysenck, *Manual of the Eysenck Personality Questionnaire*, London: Hodder & Stoughton, 1976.
3. M. Martin, 'Neuroticism as Predisposition Towards Depression: A Cognitive Mechanism', *Personality and Individual Differences* (1985) 6: 353–65.
4. R. Hogan, 'A Socio-Analytic Theory of Personality', in *Nebraska Symposium on Motivation* 1982: 56–89.
5. R. R. McCrae and P. T. Costa Jr, *Emerging Lives, Enduring Dispositions: Personality in Adulthood*, Boston: Little, Brown, 1984.
6. P. T. Costa Jr and R. R. McCrae, 'Influence of Extraversion and Neuroticism on Subjective Well-Being: Happy and Unhappy People', *Journal of Personality and Social Psychology* (1980) 38: 668–78.
7. R. Tessler and D. Mechanic, 'Psychological Distress and Perceived

Health Status', *Journal of Health and Social Behaviour* (1978) 19: 254–62.

8. P. T. Costa Jr and R. R. McCrae, 'Somatic Complaints in Males as a Function of Age and Neuroticism: A Longitudinal Analysis', *Journal of Behavioral Medicine* (1980) 3: 245–57.

9. C. Bass and C. Wade, 'Chest Pain with Normal Coronary Arteries: A Comparative Study of Psychiatric and Social Morbidity', *Psychosomatic Medicine* (1984) 14: 51–61.

Chapter 5: Accentuate the Positive: Biased Thinking and Feeling

1. N. M. Bradburn, *The Structure of Psychological Well-Being*, Chicago: Aldine, 1969.

2. S. D. Harding, 'Psychological Well-Being in Great Britain: An Evaluation of the Bradburn Affect Balance Scale', *Personality and Individual Differences* (1982) 3: 167–75.

3. M. A. Zevon and A. Tellegen, 'The Structure of Mood Change: An Idiographic/Nomothetic Analysis', *Journal of Personality and Social Psychology* (1982) 43: 111–22.

4. D. Watson and A. Tellegen, 'Towards a Consensual Structure of Mood', *Psychological Bulletin* (1985) 89: 111–22.

5. P. R. Warr, J. Barter and G. Brownbridge, 'On the Independence of Positive and Negative Affect', *Journal of Personality and Social Psychology* (1983) 44: 644–51.

6. M. F. Scheier and C. S. Carver, 'Optimism, Coping and Health: Assessment and Implications of Generalised Outcome Expectancies', *Health Psychology* (1985) 4: 219–47.

7. E. J. Colerick, 'Stamina in Later Life', *Social Science and Medicine* (1985) 21: 997–1006.

8. L. Y. Abramson, M. E. P. Seligman and J. D. Tesdale, 'Learned Helplessness in Humans: Critique and Reformulation', *Journal of Abnormal Psychology* (1978) 87: 49–74.

9. P. D. Sweeney, A. Anderson and S. Bailey, 'Attributional Style in Depression: A Meta-Analytic View', *Journal of Personality and Social Psychology* (1986) 50: 974–91.

10. C. Paterson, 'Explanatory Style as a Risk Factor for Illness', *Cognitive Therapy and Research* (1988) 12: 117–30.

11. C. Peterson, M. E. P. Seligman and G. E. Vaillant, 'Pessimistic Explanatory Style is a Risk Factor for Physical Illness: A Thirty-Five-Year Longitudinal Study', *Journal of Personality and Social Psychology* (1988) 55: 23–7.

Chapter 6: In and Out of Depression

1. A. T. Beck, C. H. Ward, M. Mendleson *et al.*, 'An Inventory for Measuring Depression', *Archives of Psychiatry* (1961) 4: 53–63.

2. K. R. Jamison, R. H. Gerner and C. Hammen *et al.*, 'Clouds and Silver Linings: Positive Experiences Associated with Primary Affective Disorders', *American Journal of Psychiatry* (1980) 132: 198–202.

3. G. Gilbert, *Depression: From Psychology to Brain State*, Hillsdale, New Jersey: Erlbaum, 1984.
4. *Ibid.*
5. E. M. Heiby and A. W. Staats, 'Depression and its Classification', in I. Evans (ed.), *Paradigmatic Behavior Therapy: Critical Perspectives in Applied Social Behaviorism*, New York: Springer.
6. M. R. Eastwood and J. L. Whitton, 'Biometeorology', *Canadian Medical Association Journal* (1985) 133: 94.
7. C. S. Aneshensel, R. R. Frerichs and G. J. Hubea, 'Depression and Physical Illness: A Multiwave, Non-Recursive Causal Model', *Journal of Health and Social Behaviour* (1984) 25: 350–71.
8. B. D. Calder and P. G. Warnock, 'Coxsackie B Infection in a Scottish General Practice', *Journal of the Royal College of General Practitioners* (1984) 34: 15–19.
9. S. E. Straus *et al.*, G. Tosato, G. Armstrong, 'Persisting Illness and Fatigue in Adults with Evidence of Epstein-Barr Virus Infection', *Annals of Internal Medicine* (1985) 102: 7–16.
10. L. J. Horwood and D. M. Fergusson, 'Neuroticism, Depression and Life Events: A Structural Equation Model', *Social Psychiatry* (1986) 21: 63–71.
11. G. W. Brown and T. Harris, *Social Origins of Depression*, London: Tavistock Publications, 1978.
12. D. J. Cooke and D. J. Hole, 'The Aetiological Importance of Stressful Life Events', *British Journal of Psychiatry* (1983) 143: 397–400.
13. G. W. Brown, A. Bifulco and T. O. Harris, 'Life Events, Vulnerability and Onset of Depression: Some Refinements', *British Journal of Psychiatry* (in press).
14. A. Roy, 'Vulnerability Factors and Depression in Men', *British Journal of Psychiatry* (1981) 138: 75–7.
15. C. Wood, 'Who Gets Depressed? An Interview with George W. Brown', *Advances* (Journal of the Institute for the Advancement of Health) (1987) 4: 61–5.
16. D. D. Burns, *Feeling Good: The New Mood Therapy*, New York: New American Library, 1980.
17. A. T. Beck, *Cognitive Therapy and the Emotional Disorders*, New York: New American Library, 1976.
18. M. Martin and D. M. Clark, 'Cognitive Mediation of Depressed Mood and Neuroticism', *IRCS Medical Science* (1985) 13: 352–3.
19. S. D. Cocran and C. L. Hammen, 'Perceptions of Stressful Life Events and Depression: A Test of Attributional Models', *Journal of Personality and Social Psychology* (1985) 48: 1562–71.
20. A. T. Beck, 'Cognitive Models of Depression', *Journal of Cognitive Therapy* (1987) 1: 5–37.
21. J. D. Teasdale, M. J. V. Fennell, G. A. Hibbert *et al.*, 'Cognitive Therapy for Major Depressive Disorder in Primary Care', *British Journal of Psychiatry* (1984) 144: 400–6.
22. I. M. Blackburn and S. Bishop, 'Changes in Cognition with Pharmacotherapy and Cognitive Therapy', *British Journal of Psychiatry* (1983) 143: 609–17.
23. A. Matthews, 'Cognitive Processes in Anxiety and Depression: Dis-

cussion Paper', *Journal of the Royal Society of Medicine* (1986) 79: 158–61.

24. P. M. Lewinsohn, W. Mischell and W. Chaplain *et al.*, 'Social Competence and Depression: The Role of Illusory Self-Perceptions', *Journal of Abnormal Psychology* (1980) 89: 203–12.

25. L. B. Alloy and L. Y. Abramson, 'Judgement of Contingency in Depressed and Non-Depressed Students: Sadder but Wiser?', *Journal of Experimental Psychology* (1979) 108: 441–85.

26. *Ibid.*

27. S. E. Taylor, 'Adjustment to Threatening Events: A Theory of Cognitive Adaptation', *American Psychologist* (1983) November: 1161–73.

Chapter 7: Strive to be Happy

1. E. Diener, 'Subjective Well-Being', *Psychological Bulletin* (1984) 95: 542–75.

2. F. M. Andrews and S. B. Withey, *Social Indicators of Well-Being: America's Perception of Life Quality*, New York: Plenum, 1976; A. Campbell, 'Subjective Measures of Well-Being', *American Psychologist* (1976) February: 117–24; A. Campbell, P. E. Convers and W. L. Rogers, *The Quality of American Life: Perceptions, Evaluations and Satisfactions*, New York: Russell Sage Foundation, 1976.

3. T. S. Palys and B. R. Little, 'Perceived Life Satisfaction and the Organization of Personal Project Systems', *Journal of Personality and Social Psychology* (1983) 44: 1221–30.

4. M. Czikszentmihalyi and F. Massimini, 'On the Psychological Selection of Bio-Cultural Information', *New Ideas in Psychology* (1985) 3: 115–38.

5. Diener, 'Subjective Well-Being'.

6. A. Parducci, 'The Relativism of Absolute Judgements', *Scientific American* (1968) 218: 84–90.

7. J. Freedman, *Happy People: What Happiness Is, Who Has It and Why*, New York: Harcourt Brace Jovanovitch, 1978.

8. M. W. Fordyce, *Psychology of Happiness*, Fort Myers, Florida: Cypress Lake Media, 1978.

9. M. W. Fordyce, 'A Program to Increase Happiness: Further Studies', *Journal of Counselling Psychology* (1983) 30: 483–98.

10. A. Zautra and A. Hempel, 'Subjective Well-Being and Physical Health: Narrative Literature Review with Suggestions for Further Research', *International Journal of Ageing and Human Development* (1984) 19: 95–110.

Chapter 8: Mind–Body-Health: Only Connect

1. N. Cousins, *Anatomy of an Illness as Perceived by the Patient*, New York: Bantam Books, 1979.

2. O. C. Simonton, S. Matthews-Simonton and J. L. Creighton, *Getting Well Again*, New York: Bantam Books, 1978.

3. S. R. Birchfield, T. H. Holmes and R. L. Harrington, 'Personality

Differences between Sick and Rarely Sick Individuals', *Social Science and Medicine* (1981) 15E: 145–8.

4. M. Angell, 'Disease as a Reflection of the Psyche', *New England Journal of Medicine* (1985) 312: 1570–2.

5. S. E. Locke and N. Hornig-Rohan (eds), *Mind and Immunity: Behavioral Immunology: An Annotated Bibliography 1976–1982*, New York: Institute for the Advancement of Health, 1983.

6. N. Cousins, 'Intangibles in Medicine: An Attempt at a Balancing Perspective', *Journal of the American Medical Association* (1988) 260: 1610–12.

7. C. S. Aneshensel, R. R. Frerichs and G. J. Hubea, 'Depression and Physical Illness: Multiwave Non-Recursive Causal Model', *Journal of Health and Social Behavior* (1984) 25: 350–71.

8. A. Canter, 'Changes in Mood during Incubation of Acute Febrile Disease and the Effects of Pre-exposure Psychologic Status', *Psychosomatic Medicine* (1972) 34: 424–30.

9. S. Livnat, S. Y. Felten, S. L. Carlson *et al.*, 'Involvement of Peripheral and Central Catecholamine Systems in Neuro-immune Interactions', *Journal of Neurology and Immunology* (1985) 10: 5–30.

10. J. M. Mossey and E. Shapiro, 'Self-rated Health: A Predictor of Mortality among the Elderly', *American Journal of Public Health* (1982) 72: 800–8.

11. G. A. Kaplan and T. Camacho, 'Perceived Health and Mortality: A 9-Year Follow-Up of the Human Population Laboratory Cohort', *American Journal of Epidemiology* (1983) 117: 292–304.

12. J. C. Barefoot, G. Dahstrom and R. B. Williams, 'Hostility, CHD Incidence and Total Mortality: A 25-Year Follow-Up of 255 Physicians', *Psychosomatic Medicine* (1983) 45: 59–63.

13. K. W. Pettingale, T. Morris, S. Greer *et al.*, 'Mental Attitudes to Cancer: An Additional Prognostic Factor', *Lancet* (1985) 1: 750.

14. R. J. DiClemente and L. Temoshok, 'Psychological Adjustment to Having Cutaneous Malignant Melanoma as a Predictor of Follow-Up Clinical Status', *Psychosomatic Medicine* (1985) 47: 81 (Abstract).

15. A. Canter, L. E. Cluff and J. B. Imboden, 'Hypersensitive Reactions to Immunization Inoculations and Antecedent Psychological Vulnerability', *Journal of Psychosomatic Research* (1972) 16: 99–101.

16. R. Totman, J. Kiff, S. E. Reed *et al.*, 'Predicting Experimental Colds in Volunteers from Different Measures of Recent Life Stress', *Journal of Psychosomatic Research* (1980) 24: 155–63.

17. S. V. Kasl, A. S. Evans and J. C. Niederman, 'Psychosocial Risk Factors in the Development of Infectious Mononucleosis', *Psychosomatic Medicine* (1979) 41: 445–66.

18. A. G. Shaper, S. J. Pocock, A. N. Phillips *et al.*, 'A Scoring System to Identify Men at High Risk of a Heart Attack', *Health Trends* (1987) 19: 37–9.

19. T. Khosla and H. Campbell, 'Mortality of Male Doctors and Reduction in Cigarette Smoking', *British Medical Journal* (1980) 280: 331–5.

20. E. L. Rossi, *The Psychobiology of Mind–Body Healing*, New York: Norton, 1986.

21. R. W. Bartrop, E. Luckhurst and L. Lazarus *et al.*, 'Depressed Lymphocyte Function after Bereavement', *Lancet* (1977) 1: 834–6.
22. Editorial, *British Medical Journal* (1884) 1: 1163.
23. S. J. Schleifer, S. E. Keller and A. Meyerson *et al.*, 'Lymphocyte Function in Major Depressive Disorder', *Archives of General Psychiatry* (1984) 41: 484–6.
24. S. Kennedy, J. K. Kiecolt-Glaser and R. Glaser, 'Immunological Consequences of Acute and Chronic Stresses: Mediating Role of Interpersonal Relationships', *British Journal of Medical Psychology* (1988) 61: 77–85.

Chapter 9: Look to the Body

1. A. G. Shaper, S. J. Pocock and M. Walker *et al.*, 'Risk Factors for Ischemic Heart Disease: The Prospective Phase of the British Regional Heart Study', *Journal of Epidemiology and Community Health* (1985) 39: 197–209.
2. L. F. Berkman and S. L. Syme, 'Social Networks, Host Resistance and Mortality: A Nine-Year Follow-Up Study of Alameda Residents', *American Journal of Epidemiology* (1979) 109: 186–204.
3. D. F. Kripke, R. N. Simons and L. Garfinkel *et al.*, 'Short and Long Sleep and Sleeping Pills: Is Increased Mortality Associated?', *Archives of General Psychiatry* (1979) 36: 103–16.
4. K. Adam, M. Tomeny and I. Oswald, 'Physiological and Psychologial Differences between Good and Poor Sleepers', *Journal of Psychiatric Research* (1986) 20: 301–15.
5. J. Wildmann, A. Kruger and M. Schmole *et al.*, 'Increase in Circulating Beta-Endorphin-Like Immunoreactivity Correlates with the Change in Feeling of Pleasantness after Running', *Life Sciences* (1986) 38: 997–1003.
6. R. A. Marhoff, P. Ryan and T. Young, 'Endorphins and Mood Changes in Long Distance Running', *Medicine and Science in Sports and Exercise* (1982) 14: 11–13.
7. R. S. Paffenbarger, R. T. Hyde and A. L. Wing *et al.*, 'A Natural History of Athleticism and Cardiovascular Health', *Journal of the American Medical Association* (1984) 252: 491–5.
8. R. E. Thayer, 'Energy, Tiredness, and Tension Effects of a Sugar Snack versus Moderate Exercise', *Journal of Personality and Social Psychology* (1987) 52: 119–25.
9. J. H. Griest, H. John and M. H. Kline *et al.*, 'Running through Your Mind', *Journal of Psychosomatic Research* (1978) 22: 259–94.
10. E. W. Martinssen, W. Egil and A. Medhus *et al.*, 'Effects of Aerobic Exercise on Depression: A Controlled Study', *British Medical Journal* (1985) 291: 109.
11. D. L. Roth and D. S. Holmes, 'Influence of Aerobic Exercise Training and Relaxation Training on Physical and Psychologic Health Following Stressful Life Events', *Psychosomatic Medicine* (1987) 49: 355–65.
12. J. M. Rippe, A. Ward, J. P. Porcari *et al.*, 'Walking for Health

and Fitness', *Journal of the American Medical Association* (1988) 259: 2720–4.

13. Lipid Research Clinics Programme, 'The Lipid Research Clinics Coronary Primary Prevential Trial results, II: The Relationship of Reduction in Incidence of Coronary Heart Disease to Cholesterol Lowering', *Journal of the American Medical Association* (1984) 251: 365–74.

14. Committee on Medical Aspects of Food Policy, Department of Health and Social Security, *Diet and Cardiovascular Disease*, London: HMSO 1984 (Report on Health and Social Subjects no. 28)

15. British Cardiac Society, *Report of British Cardiac Society Working Group on Coronary Disease Prevention*, London: British Cardiac Society, 1987.

16. C. Wood (ed.), *Dietary Salt and Hypertension: Implications for Public Health Policies*, Royal Society of Medicine Round Table Series no. 5, London: Royal Society of Medicine, 1986.

17. Executive Committee, American Academy of Allergy and Immunology, 'Position Statement on Clinical Ecology', *Journal of Allergy and Clinical Immunology* (1986) 78: 269–71.

18. Executive Committee, American Academy of Allergy and Immunology, 'Candidiasis Hypersensitivity Syndrome', *Journal of Allergy and Clinical Immunology* (1986) 78: 271–3.

Chapter 10: Eventful Lives

1. T. H. Holmes and R. H. Rahe, 'The Social Readjustment Rating Scale', *Journal of Psychosomatic Research* (1967) 11: 213–18.

2. J. G. Rabkin and E. L. Streuning, 'Life Events, Stress and Illness', *Science* (1974) 194: 1013–20.

3. M. Masuda and T. H. Holmes, 'Life Events, Perceptions and Frequencies', *Psychosomatic Medicine* (1978) 40: 236–61.

4. L. F. Berkman and L. S. Syme, 'Social Networks, Host Resistance and Mortality: A Nine-Year Follow-Up Study of Alameda County Residents', *American Journal of Epidemiology* (1979) 109: 186–204.

5. K. S. Rook, 'The Negative Side of Social Interaction: Impact on Psychological Well-Being', *Journal of Personality and Social Psychology* (1984) 46: 1097–108.

6. N. Krause and S. Stryker, 'Stress and Well-Being: The Buffering Role of Locus of Control Beliefs', *Social Science and Medicine* (1984) 18: 783–90.

7. H. M. Lefcourt, R. A. Martin and W. E. Saleh, 'Locus of Control and Social Support: Interactive Moderators of Stress', *Journal of Personality and Social Psychology* (1984) 47: 378–89.

8. A. Antonovsky, *Health Stress and Coping: New Perspectives on Mental and Physical Well-Being*, San Francisco: Jossey-Bass, 1979.

9. A. Antonovsky, *Health Stress and Coping*. Reference 8.

10. A. Antonovsky, *Unravelling the Mystery of Health: How People Manage Stress and Stay Well*, San Francisco: Jossey-Bass, 1987.

11. A. Antonovsky, 'The Salutogenic Perspective: Towards a New View

of Health and Illness', *Advances* (Journal of the Institute for the Advancement of Health) (1987) 4: 47–55.

12. A. Antonovsky, *Unravelling the Mystery of Health*. Reference 10.

Chapter 11: How Are You Coping?

1. C. Wood, 'Buffer of Hardiness: An Interview with Suzanne C. Oullette Kobasa', *Advances* (Journal of the Institute for the Advancement of Health) (1987) 4: 37–45.

2. S. C. O. Kobasa and N. C. Puccetti, 'Personality and Social Resources in Stress Resistance', *Journal of Personality and Social Psychology* (1983) 45: 839–50.

3. S. R. Maddi and S. C. Kobasa, *The Hardy Executive: Health under Stress*, Homewood, Illinois: Dow Jones–Irwin, 1984.

4. S. C. O. Kobasa, S. R. Maddi, N. C. Puccetti *et al.*, 'Effectiveness of Hardiness, Exercise and Social Support as Resources against Illness', *Journal of Psychosomatic Research* (1985) 29: 525–33.

5. K. R. Parkes and D. Rendall, 'The Hardy Personality and Its Relationship to Extraversion and Neuroticism', *Personality and Individual Differences* (1988) 9: 785–90.

6. S. Folkman and R. S. Lazarus, 'If It Changes It Must Be a Process: Study of Emotion and Coping during Three Stages of a College Examination', *Journal of Personality and Social Psychology* (1985) 48: 150–70.

7. A. G. Billings and R. H. Moos, 'Coping, Stress, and Social Resources among Adults with Unipolar Depression', *Journal of Personality and Social Psychology* (1984) 46: 877–91.

8. C. J. Holahan and R. H. Moos, 'Life Stress and Health: Personality, Coping and Family Support in Stress Resistance', *Journal of Personality and Social Psychology* (1985) 49: 739–47.

9. R. R. McCrae, 'Situational Determinants of Coping Responses: Loss, Threat, and Challenge', *Journal of Personality and Social Psychology* (1984) 46: 919–28.

10. R. R. McCrae and P. T. Costa Jr, 'Personality, Coping and Coping Effectiveness in an Adult Sample', *Journal of Personality* (1986) 54: 385–405.

Chapter 12: Changing Our Ways

1. S. R. Maddi, 'Hardiness Training at Illinois Bell Telephone', unpublished, 1987.

2. D. F. Kline, C. M. Zitrin, M. G. Woerner *et al.*, 'Treatment of Phobias, II: Behaviour Therapy and Supportive Psychotherapy: Are There Any Specific Ingredients?', *Archives of Journal of Psychiatry* (1983) 40: 139–45.

3. I. Marks, *Living with Fear*, New York: McGraw-Hill, 1987.

4. H. J. Eysenck, 'The Effects of Psychotherapy: An Evaluation', *Journal of Consulting Psychology* (1952) 16: 319–24.

5. S. L. Garfield and A. E. Bergin, 'Effectiveness of Psychotherapy', in S. L. Garfield and A. E. Bergin, (eds), *Handbook of Psychotherapy and Behavior Change*, New York: Wiley, 1986.

6. J. D. Frank, 'Psychotherapy – The Transformation of Meaning: Discussion Paper', *Journal of the Royal Society of Medicine* (1986) 79: 341–6.
7. D. A. Bernstein and T. D. Borkovec, *Progressive Relaxation Training: A Manual for the Helping Professions*, Champaign, Illinois: Research Press, 1973.
8. B. T. Engel, M. S. Glasgow and K. R. Gaarder, 'Behavioral Treatment of High Blood Pressure, III: Follow-Up Results and Treatment Recommendations', *Psychosomatic Medicine* (1983) 45: 23–9.
9. D. Kallinke, B. Kulick and P. Heim, 'Behaviour Analysis and Treatment of Essential Hypertensives', *Journal of Psychosomatic Research* (1982) 26: 541–9.
10. C. Patel, M. G. Marmot, D. J. Terry *et al.*, 'Trial of Relaxation in Reducing Coronary Risk: Four-Year Follow-Up', *British Medical Journal* (1985) 290: 1103–6.
11. S. Warrenburg, R. R. Pagano, M. Woods *et al.*, 'A Comparison of Somatic Relaxation and EEG Activity in Classical Progressive Relaxation and Transcendental Meditation', *Journal of Behavioral Medicine* (1980) 3: 73–93.
12. J. L. Deffenbacher and R. M. Suinn, 'The Self-control of Anxiety', in P. Koroly and F. H. Canfer (eds), *Self Management and Behaviour Change*, Oxford: Pergamon, 1982.

Chapter 13: Thinking Makes It So

1. E. Ellis, 'The Goals of Psychotherapy', in *Humanistic Psychotherapy: A Rational Emotive Approach*, New York: McGraw-Hill, 1973.
2. W. Dryden, *Counselling Individuals: The Rational Emotive Approach*, London: Taylor & Francis, 1987.
3. E. Ellis, 'The Impossibility of Achieving Consistently Good Mental Health', *American Psychologist* (1987) 42: 364–75.
4. N. D. Vestry, 'Irrational Beliefs and Self-Reported Depressed Mood', *Journal of Abnormal Psychology* (1984) 93: 239–41.
5. T. W. Smith, 'Irrational Beliefs in the Cause and Treatment of Emotional Distress: A Critical Review of the Rational–Emotive Model', *Clinical Psychology Review* (1982) 2: 205–21.
6. A. T. Beck, *Cognitive Therapy and the Emotional Disorders*, New York: New American Library, 1986.
7. D. Meichenbaum, *Stress Inoculation Training*, Oxford: Pergamon, 1986.
8. R. W. Novaco, 'Anger and Coping with Stress', in J. P. Foreyt and D. R. Rathjen (eds), *Cognitive Behaviour Therapy*, New York: Plenum Press, 1978.
9. S. L. Hazaleus and J. L. Deffenbacher, 'Relaxation and Cognitive Treatments of Anger', *Journal of Consulting and Clinical Psychology* (1986) 54: 222–6.
10. M. E. P. Seligman, 'A Learned Helplessness Point of View', in *Behaviour Therapy for Depression*, New York: Academic Press, 1981, ch. 5.

11. M. Rosenbaum, 'A Schedule for Assessing Self-Control Behaviors: Preliminary Findings', *Behavior Therapy* (1980) 11: 109–21.
12. S. R. Maddi, 'Hardiness Training at Illinois Bell Telephone', unpublished, 1986.
13. S. R. Maddi and S. C. Kobasa, *The Hardy Executive: Health under Stress*, Homewood, Illinois: Dow Jones–Irwin, 1984.
14. E. T. Gendlin, *Focusing*, New York: Bantam Books, 1978.
15. L. Michelson and L. M. Ascher, 'Paradoxical Intention in the Treatment of Agoraphobia and Other Anxiety Disorders', *Journal of Behaviour Therapy and Experimental Psychiatry* (1984) 15: 215–20.
16. C. Wood, 'Buffer of Hardiness: An Interview with Suzanne C. Ouellette Kobasa', *Advances* (Journal of the Institute for the Advancement of Health) (1987) 4: 37–45.

Chapter 14: Learning to Say Yes: A Sort of Conclusion

1. *The Health and Lifestyle Survey*, London: Health Promotion Research Trust, 1987.
2. N. K. Chen, 'The Epidemiology of Self-Perceived Fatigue among Adults', *Preventive Medicine* (1986) 15: 74–81.
3. S. Wessley, 'Myalgic Encephalomyelitis – A Warning: Discussion Paper', *Journal of the Royal Society of Medicine* (1989) 82: 215–17.
4. S. Moorey and S. Greer, 'Adjuvant Psychological Therapy: A Cognitive Behavioural Treatment for Patients with Cancer', *Behavioural Psychotherapy* (1989) 17: 177–90.
5. H. J. Eysenck, 'Personality, Stress and Cancer: Prediction and Prophylaxis', *British Journal of Medical Psychology* (1988) 61: 57–75.

Index

References in italics indicate boxes.